FRANZ SCHUBERT

Music and Belief

FRANZ SCHUBERT

Music and Belief

Leo Black

THE BOYDELL PRESS

First published 2003
The Boydell Press, Woodbridge
Reprinted in paperback 2005

ISBN 1 84383 023 X (hardback)
ISBN 1 84383 135 X (paperback)

The Boydell Press is an imprint of Boydell & Brewer Ltd
PO Box 9, Woodbridge, Suffolk IP12 3DF, UK
and of Boydell & Brewer Inc.
PO Box 41026, Rochester, NY 14604–4126, USA
website: www.boydell.co.uk

A catalogue record for this book is available
from the British Library

Library of Congress Cataloging-in-Publication Data

Black, Leo.
    Franz Schubert : music and belief / Leo Black.
        p. cm.
    Includes bibliographical references (p.   ), discography (p.   ), and
index.
    ISBN 1–84383–023–X (alk. paper)
    1. Schubert, Franz, 1797–1828 – Criticism and interpretation.
    2. Schubert, Franz, 1797–1828 – Religion. I. Title.
    ML410.S3B563 2003
    780'.92 – dc21   2003009856

Typeset by Joshua Associates Ltd, Oxford
Printed in Great Britain by
Athenaeum Press Ltd, Gateshead, Tyne & Wear

Without an *intuition* of the supra-sensual,
man would indeed be an animal; but a *conviction*
about it is possible only for fools, and
necessary only for degenerates.

Franz Grillparzer, *Aphorisms*

One might also conclude that [classical] music deals . . . with
those aspects of human life that still remain to be confronted
when the battles of race, class and gender are won, or simply
those inner moments of anxiety, emptiness or sheer wonder
that are not addressed by the merely political.

Julian Johnson, *Who Needs Classical Music?*

Contents

For Felicity

Preface

Anyone who sees fit to publish his first book slightly after the Biblical span must expect the world to ask of him, 'And where have you been all this time?' The work reflects a half-century's exposure to Schubert and his unique magic, and a process of development and maturing with many stages.

Simple piano pieces were learned, mighty ones overheard, even before my teens; an unforgettable broadcast of *Die schöne Müllerin* by Pears and Britten had a fifteen-year-old walking around in a trance for days; there was the impact of artists such as the elderly Schnabel and the young Irmgard Seefried, close scrutiny of chamber works during student years, and an unforgotten hearing of the Great C Major Symphony in Salzburg under Furtwängler. With academic ambitions abandoned after the odd interview, I tried my hand, for better or worse, in publishing, which at least meant a brief but total immersion in all things Viennese. I then found myself taken by the scruff of the neck to serve within the BBC's Music Division as a member of William Glock's New Model Army.

Popularising the Second Viennese and Manchester Schools and generally dragging the British radio listener screaming into the twentieth century was a less simple matter, musically and ethically, than I had anticipated, and it came as a relief when radical evangelism could take second place to an undimmed passion for the classics of an earlier Viennese School. I was free to explore and offer the listening public the Lied, the string quartet and the great piano repertoire; nor did William, well supplied with young lions and himself a Schubertian who'd learned from Schnabel, seem to mind: composers he loved less, such as Brahms, could safely figure in the 'run-of-the-mill' programmes (some mill, some run!), as could those he positively disliked, such as Richard Strauss. Unless he happened to overhear something he found positively misguided (I recall a note suggesting that next time I put Beethoven's Op. 111 piano sonata into a programme I choose someone to play it who knew how it went), he seldom commented on the day-by-day output; I think that insofar as he was ever aware it was going on he tended to be quietly pleased with it.

One supremely satisfying, profitable thing about those decades of BBC work was its constant involvement with *sound*; passages would imprint themselves on my memory, to spring out as and when required, and this book's frequent cross-references between Schubert and, say, the chamber-music of Mozart and Haydn always stem from a perceived similarity of sound, never from mere perusal of scores.

In the 1960s singers like Janet Baker, Heather Harper, John Shirley-Quirk, Elizabeth Harwood, Thomas Hemsley, Ian Partridge, Jeannette Sinclair, Robert Tear, and in the 1970s and 1980s Sheila Armstrong, Margaret Price, Norma Burrowes, Jill Gomez, Elizabeth Gale and Ann Murray were ever-willing to learn obscure Schubert songs they might (but more likely would not) have occasion to perform again after their Third- or Music-Programme or Radio 3 recital. Major foreign artists – Elisabeth Grümmer, Agnes Giebel, Barry McDaniel, Elly Ameling – came to England, further enriching the store of memorable Schubert accumulated in this 'one small head'. There followed the elemental Doris Soffel, who whether charming the ear in the Grillparzer *Ständchen* or freezing the blood in *Der Zwerg*, brought to Schubert a power and intuitive musicality never acknowledged at their true worth, for all her fame in opera. And from time to time the Amadeus Quartet were available to bring the world up to date on how they sensed the great Schubert chamber works should go.

Down to the time I left there were still intriguing new names and performances, such as a riveting *Grenzen der Menschheit* from a young bass, Alistair Miles, whose cause (fellow audition-panellists having proved deaf to his possibilities) I'd had to fight through committee. Elizabeth Marcus, who played for him, enjoyed the unique distinction of making me cry not just once but the first three times I heard her, and long before that there had been among accompanists the supreme performer Ernest Lush and the supremely sensitive Viola Tunnard. The supreme professional Martin Isepp was often in evidence, and I even recorded a South Bank concert at which Vladimir Ashkenazy played *Schwanengesang* with such delicacy that I was in a seventh heaven of concentration following his nuances while trying also to pay full attention to what John Shirley-Quirk had to offer.

Always it was the *sound* that engaged me, endlessly fascinating though the poetry could be; the scores proved a stimulus, and uniquely memorable moments came seated in a silent reference library experiencing with my inner ear unknown German songs as they might sound when sung by some particular one of the musical young singers who in those days still enjoyed the priceless advantage of time to develop and mature. Casting was all, and at the ensuing recordings I seldom found I'd imagined a mismatch or detected what has become all too familiar listening to Schubert singing of recent years – quick study. I shared many a session in the staff canteen and the pub with the likes of Hans Keller, but never came to regard analysis, for which the Oxford Honours course had in its modest way trained me, as my *forte*; music was sound first, marks on paper second. Any virtue in the pages that follow springs from that lifelong frame of mind.

Instruction came in further ways, as when I played the piano part of the *Arpeggione* Sonata with cellists; that opened up a range of nuance linking it to Schubert's song-accompaniments. The performances came on either side of the next watershed, a decision to leave the BBC some years early: there were things in the air that promised laboured breathing, and I soon had time to pursue aspects of Schubert until then neglected by me. At that point the idea of writing about him, on the back burner since two never-published pieces for a symposium that should have marked the 1978 celebrations, turned into something more tangible, if still insubstantial; finally, after at least one false start, I identified a train of thought to carry me through a medium-sized book.

The world still held surprises. Through the 1990s, too late to influence the output of a once-great institution by then besotted with image, personality presenters, marketing and keeping in line with the multinational record companies, I came under the spell of the Schubert recordings made in the DDR during the 1970s and 1980s by the baritone Siegfried Lorenz. His CDs had to be winkled out of the bottom drawer at post-reunification German record shops as if they were impacted wisdom teeth, but became regular listening; here at last was someone above and beyond the word-dominated, big-ego approach that had for thirty years ruled Lieder-singing with the supremacy of mana-personalities like Fischer-Dieskau and Schwarzkopf. As an antidote (not, alas, that it was I who needed one) to two ever-growing, complementary tendencies – to let the rawest greenhorns loose on the greatest masterpieces, and to cut Schubert down to the stature of an Old Music composer – this was not the least among a lifetime's epiphanies. A nine-year campaign to introduce Lorenz to the Wigmore Hall's connoisseur audience finally ran into the sand, but the recordings remain and set an unsurpassable standard.

And there could just be further epiphanies, for even the worst and most anti-musical times need not prevail against major talent, however much they over-cultivate the minor; the tale is not yet done, though the thought of an 'International Schubert Foundation' instructing singers in what they may and may not do when performing his music[1] is one to send a cold shiver down the spine.

What gently emerged, with infinite slowness and inevitability, was the figure of a musician, Schubert, in touch with a different reality. During a break in a BBC recording of his piano-duet music Paul Hamburger, who commands English words most people have forgotten if they ever knew them, exclaimed: 'Now I know what Leo loves about Schubert: his numinous[2] side.' A biographer I never wanted to be; before the erudition of an Elizabeth Norman McKay I can but bow the head, but Schubert is in the Biblical sense 'known' through the sound of his music – and there special antennae are in place.

Setting out on this journey of exploration, it was no part of my intention to concentrate on Schubert's manifestly religious works; if anything, the opposite

[1] Editorial, 'Die Internationale Schubert Stiftung', *Schubert durch die Brille*, Jan. 1999.
[2] Numinous: of or pertaining to a *numen* [= Divine will, divinity, related to 'nuere' to nod (assent); Deity, divinity; divine or presiding power or spirit], divine, spiritual, revealing or suggesting the presence of a God; inspiring awe and reverence (*Oxford English Dictionary*, 2nd edn, 1989). A great English churchman, William Temple (Archbishop of York, later of Canterbury), said in 1933 that it is the quality in the object of religion *before which we do not reason but bow* (Gifford Lectures at the University of Glasgow, 1931/2 and 1932/3, published in 1934 as *Nature, Man and God*). One's experience of outstandingly great musical performers confirms the importance of such a feeling: the critical faculty is suspended.

was what I had in mind – to show how even without the prompting of the liturgy, what he himself called his 'natural impulses of right and true devotion'[3] made themselves felt. But as I came to know the religious music better it became clear that no such distinction held water: in musical terms works such as the Masses were part and parcel of what had captivated me. Nor did I find them treated with the full perceptive affection they deserved. That made a great difference to the book's final shape, as did the discovery of Rudolf Otto's classic exposition of natural religious experience, its splendours and terrors.

An earlier draft of this book prompted a publisher's reader to comment on its reluctance to refer to 'the latest researches'; that has become something of a mantra in today's newest cottage industry, the writing of books and articles about Schubert. A vast amount has been learned of late about aspects of his life: in 1999, for example, it finally became certain that the 'dratted Doctor' Bernhard, in the iconography since the year dot as having treated his illness during his final years, was in fact a civil servant harbouring literary aspirations, and not a medical man at all;[4] another three years and he had become a doctor again, if not the one accepted by scholars ever since Otto Erich Deutsch as Matthäus von Collin's father-in-law.[5] The assiduous reader of *Schubert durch die Brille* likewise knows more than he is ever likely to be able to digest or use about Baroness Drossdik, alias Beethoven's great friend Therese Malfatti, whom Schubert never even met.[6]

This book is not a biography, and (I hope) never or seldom a contribution to the point-scoring that at times seems to motivate writing in that holiest-of-holies, *Schubert durch die Brille*; but when things found out over the past many years seem apposite they are quoted and acknowledged. Certainly Rita Steblin's very recent discoveries about Therese Grob significantly changed the emphasis of my account of her and all she stood for in Schubert's inner life. And those necessarily anonymous comments from the 'readers' greatly helped me to improve the book; I am grateful to them.

My list of acknowledgments to the men and women whose help, work or example made this book possible is almost endless: all but one of those already cited knowingly or unwittingly played a greater or smaller part. I would also name, in no order save the alphabetical, John Alldis, Celia Arieli, Norbert

---

[3] The German word translated as 'devotion' is 'Andacht', a Thomist definition of which in the 1951 *Lexikon der Kirche und der Theologie* could be translated 'willpower turned towards God, easily and gladly dedicating itself to the service of God'. It occurs in Schubert's letter of 25 July 1825 to his father and stepmother, written during the extended holiday described in this book's chapter 'Harvest'. A precise translation of the sentence in question runs: 'I have never forced devotion in myself, but then [i.e. when it does show itself] it is usually also the right, true [kind of] devotion.' This expression necessarily appears many times in the course of the present book, and like 'Voice Doubling Bass' (see chapter 'Years of Reflection') it could have been abbreviated as, say, RTD – but such feelings are not really matter for acronyms.

[4] Michael Lorenz, 'Schuberts Freund Dr. Bernhard: Eine Neubewertung der Quellen', *Brille*, June 1999.

[5] Michael Lorenz, 'Mehrere Bernhards. Die Lösung des Dr.Bernhard-Rätsels', *Brille*, Jan. 2002.

[6] Michael Lorenz, 'Baronin Drossdik und die "verschneyten Nachtigallen"', *Brille*, Jan. 2001.

Brainin, Maurice J.E. Brown, Pina Carmirelli, Ann Collins, Cheryl Collins, Lamar Crowson, Hugues Cuénod, Gerald English, Caroline Friend, Liza Fuchsova, Jamila Gavin, Christopher Gibbs, Hartmut Höll, Colin Horsley, Crawford Howie, Gundula Janowitz, Rudolf Jansen, Hermann Kant, Natalia Karp, Yvonne Kenny, Patricia Kern, Alfred Kitchin, Alexander Kok, Lili Kraus, Michael Langdon, Maureen Lehane-Wishart, Raymond Leppard, Richard Lewis, Lesley Minchin, Margaret Neville, Brian Newbould, Manoug Parikian, Lucia Popp, Brian Rayner Cook, Father Cormac Rigby, Max Rostal, Ann Schein, Peter Schidlof, Peter Schreier, Mitsuko Shirai, Gordon Stewart. Victoria Sumner, Peter Tanner, Andre Tchaikowsky, Robert Tear, Mary Thomas, Ruud van der Meer, Ilse Wolf and Rosemarie Wright. For a start.

One name stands out: that of the late Peter Gould, who as my immediate BBC 'line manager' unreservedly gave my programme-making propensities their head. What a toy-cupboard for an ever-young mind ever more in love with Schubert, what a laboratory and auditorium in which to have the sound of countless new and revelatory pieces dinned into me by artists of high calibre whom I myself had selected! I go on about this since it was the priceless opportunity to hear 'new' Schubert performed with true understanding that confirmed me in my sound-orientated approach to 'Schubert scholarship'. By the time an unfamiliar piece had been recorded and edited, it was familiar.

In recent years the German conductor and scholar Peter Gülke, with his major and illuminating volume on Schubert, pointed my mind in various profitable directions, while finally leaving me convinced that his was not an approach I was qualified to pursue: I hope there will some day be a worthy English translation of his *Franz Schubert und seine Zeit*.[7] Antony Bye, editor of the *Musical Times*, encouraged me in the bicentenary year 1997 by accepting for a periodical devoted in principle to recent music no fewer than five contributions on Schubert, also following up my suggestion of a personal view from Siegfried Lorenz; I am most grateful for such support at a critical stage, likewise to Tom Glasow, editor of *Opera Quarterly*, and Ernst Hilmar, editor of *Schubert durch die Brille*.

But, above all, I very much doubt whether without the passionate interventions of my wife, the master-cellist and lifelong Schubert-lover Felicity Vincent, any of it would ever have amounted to more than the odd article.

If this study of Schubert's religious, passive, wondering side prompts others to look at the subject in more detail, one of its main purposes will have been achieved. It does not try to identify his sense of the numinous in every major work, though that could certainly be attempted, I suspect with some success. And if some of his music is heard with new ears after the book is absorbed, that will be the other main purpose attained. 'Through Schubert we all became friends': such times are gone, but something timeless remains. May the pages that follow offer a hint of it.

---

[7] Laaber, 1991.

Author's Note

Sound says more than words ever can, and this book would most profitably be read within reach of a sound-system on which appropriate music by Schubert could be sampled. I therefore open each chapter with a note of works considered in it, hoping that the reader may be in a position to convert himself into a listener.

At times I refer to five articles on Schubert that I contributed to the *Musical Times* in the bicentenary year 1997. After the first mention of each I do not repeat my name if the article is quoted again; the final one was entitled *Schubert, the Complete Voice*, which could have been confusing since this book's final chapter has a very similar title. In references the article is named complete, as above, the chapter without the composer's name.

Two Schubert songs called *Der Wanderer* are mentioned at various points: that to a poem by Friedrich Schlegel (D. 649), of interest for its evidence of Schubert's submissive streak, musically expressed by his doubling of the voice part with the piano's left hand, and that to a poem by Schmidt von Lübeck (D. 489) equally important for its relationship to the later Wanderer Fantasy for piano, and as a beautiful example of a song where Schubert chose a text that speaks of an unattainable better world. Unless Schlegel is given as text author the title *Der Wanderer* refers to the Schmidt setting.

I am more than happy to acknowledge the invaluable help of Valerie Langfield in preparing the music examples, of Hugh Wood, for valuable comments on the text and a timely suggestion of a title, and of Dr. Josef Angerer, Heimatmuseum Bad Gastein, who located and provided the jacket illustration.

The abbreviations most frequently used are:

Brille   *Schubert durch die Brille*, bi-annual journal, published from Tutzing, Bavaria, of the Internationales Institut für Schubertforschung (International Institute for Schubert Research), which is based in Vienna.

DDR   The Deutsche Demokratische Republik (German Democratic Republic), formed from the post-Second World War Russian-occupied zone, became between 1949 and 1989 the world's fourteenth-largest industrial economy, but the doctrinaire, immovable ways of its successive rulers and a commitment to deliveries of goods to its masters in the Soviet Union led to major economic difficulties and chronic shortages. Along with its human rights record, that caused its population, once given the chance, to vote in 1990 for a right-wing government, which soon agreed to merge the country, formerly a one-party socialist state, with the capitalist German Federal Republic on terms dictated by the latter's Chancellor Helmut Kohl and his minister Wolfgang Schäuble. Much of Germany's great musical tradition lived on in the DDR, freer of commercialism than the corresponding culture in the West, and producing musicians of the calibre of the conductors Klaus Tennstedt, Kurt Sanderling and Kurt Masur, the singers Peter Schreier and Siegfried Lorenz, and at least one exceptional chamber-music pianist/accompanist, Walter Olbertz

DOE   *Dialekt Ohne Erde* (proceedings of 1997 Graz symposium, published in Vienna and Graz, 1998)
McKay   Elizabeth Norman McKay, *Franz Schubert, A Biography*, Oxford, 1996
SandSy   Brian Newbould *Schubert and the Symphony*, Aldershot, 1992
SMM   Brian Newbould, *Schubert, The Man and his Music*, London, 1997
SSF   *Schubert und seine Freunde* (proceedings of 1997 Vienna symposium, published in Vienna, Cologne and Weimar, 1999)

Keys are generally indicated by a capital letter, notes by a small one, but where the context makes it clear that a number of keys, major and minor, are under discussion I adhere to the convention that major is shown by a capital, minor by a small letter. A and B are also used a few times as markers for the contrasting sections in ternary form.

Introduction

Schubert has the right blend of the ideal and the real: for him,
the world is beautiful.

Eduard Bauernfeld, diary, 3 March 1826

We have no business seeking a great man elsewhere than in his
work.

Hugo von Hofmannsthal, Schillers Selbstcharakteristik

The story of Schubert's life 'in the world' has been told and retold, sometimes well and lately in ever-more-vivid detail: early years among talented siblings at his father's schoolhouse in a new suburb of Vienna, leaving home to become a boarder at the State Grammar School and sing as a chorister at the Imperial Court Chapel, friendships with solid citizens like Josef von Spaun, eccentric intellectuals like Johann Baptist Mayrhofer and self-indulgent dissolute Bohemians like The Hon. Franz von Schober; and then the disaster of his contracting a sexually transmitted disease in his mid-twenties, with his final few years of balancing sociability against ill-health, guilt and an uncertain life-span until his death a few weeks short of his thirty-second birthday. This book is rather about his life 'in his work'. It follows the unfolding of the personality we are privileged to meet, come to know and love through experience of it as listener or performer. It tries in particular to tease out a strand in his make-up that has been too little appreciated – a certain strain of wonder.

It struck me long ago – and I had not grown up believing such things – that the power of Schubert's music to bring him vividly before me after the passage of two centuries, purely by virtue of vibrating air, could be among the stronger arguments for a belief in personal survival in some shape or form. No possible disrespect, then, to his omniscient and tireless biographers, but the music is unchanged since November 1828. Were it not there, who would interest himself in an obscure personality, however remarkable, alive in central Europe for a mere handful of years two centuries ago? To all but the most specialist scholars the composer by now amounts to the man, and details of his life should be superfluous where there is a receptive ear. It has been put to me that knowing the biography 'somehow makes him more human'. An exemplary performance of Bach's Goldberg Variations lately left me thinking that such music makes him incomparably more 'human' than anything garnered from reading about his life, but so be it.

The difficulty in talking about a composer's inner life is that the written word is easiest to interpret, misinterpret. Even leaving aside his friends' questionable reminiscences long afterwards, there is enough on record that Schubert himself said and wrote, under this or that passing influence, to let one mould whatever graven image one pleases. As an obvious example, his 1824 poem 'Klage an das Volk' (Complaint to the People) played a major role in the hagiology of Marxist commentators (see chapter 'Partial Understanding'), who ignored its conclusion that art alone ('heil'ge Kunst', not the march of history/triumph of the proletariat) remains as a measure of consolation and a reminder of what is possible. Changes in the perception of Schubert since the late nineteenth century are well summarised in Ilja Dürhammer's 'Der Wandel des Schubert-bildes im 20. Jahrhundert'.[1]

Exegesis of actual music is possible, but demands musical sensitivity and is likely, unless confined to the most dry-as-dust analysis, to be contentiously subjective. That, however, is what a book such as this has to do: trace the inmost person through the sound.

Something similar lies behind the almost universal reaction when those open to music but unlettered in it come into contact with Schubert. A survey of Vox Populi would yield any number of mostly banal characterisations, and yet there would be a grain of truth in them. Time after time the layman, if asked, comes out with words like 'warmth' and 'love'; 'unrequited love' was what a painter declared she sensed in his music. The discipline known as hermeneutics[2] could be relevant in any attempt to put this on a firmer footing, but the relationship between music and life is as contentious as that between music and either biography or aesthetics; scholars, aestheticians and philosophers have argued about it since the time of the ancient Greeks. The Austrian musical scholar Erwin Ratz had wise things to say on the subject:

> If we ask ourselves why so many people seek a closer acquaintance with the works of the great masters . . . we can probably reject from the outset any notion that a general aesthetic pleasure in the meaning or interest of musical forms *per se* is the sole reason. It is surely beyond question that the majority of these people experience an enrichment of the personality, insofar as a work of art releases emotions and transmits experiences which enable them to arrive at new insights into their own natures and their relation to the world.[3]

Music took on a near-sacred significance with the Romantic movement, after having been undervalued by the Enlightenment's emphasis on 'reason'. At the highest philosophical level, Immanuel Kant's *Critique of Pure Reason* (1781) questioned the rational intellect's power to penetrate ultimate reality – the

---

[1] In *DOE*.

[2] Hermeneutics: The art or science of interpretation, especially of Scripture. Commonly distinguished from *exegesis* or practical exposition (*Oxford English Dictionary*, 2nd edn, 1989): in the case of a musical work, correlation of events or moods/emotions from the extra-musical world with ideas in the sound of the music. The German theorist Hermann Kretzschmar summed it up as 'the verbal elucidation of musical meaning'.

[3] 'Analysis and Hermeneutics and their significance for the Interpretation of Beethoven', *Music Analysis*, 3/3, 1984 (original German in 1970). Translation by Mary Whittall.

'Ding an sich' (*noumen*) or Thing in Itself. Arthur Schopenhauer extended that line of thought in *The World as Will and Idea* (1816 and 1844), posing the question:

> What manner of perception can observe that one and only essential quality of the world, which is outside and independent of any relationship, the true content of its phenomena, subject to no process of change and therefore perceived for all time with equal truth – in a word, the ideas that make up the direct and adequate objectivity of the Thing in Itself?

His answer was brief and to the point:

> Art, the work of genius.[4]

Such views of man's insight into ultimate reality were to influence artistic attitudes for a century and more, culminating in phenomena such as Mahler's sense of carrying out a 'fearful office', with his music 'as if dictated to him', or Stefan George's act of the priest-poet. With few exceptions (see chapter 'Years of Reflection') Schubert lived out his philosophy rather than expounding it, nor is there evidence of any such 'creative agony' as Brahms' while he composed: what was undoubtedly there was the supreme concentration recorded by his painter friend Schwind:

> If you go to see him during the day, he says 'Hullo, how are you? – Good!' and goes on writing, whereupon you depart.[5]

Deep concentration of that kind is a creator's road to the secrets of his inner world. It stands at least on a par with the 'meditation' so many human beings employ to make contact with something beyond themselves, and could even be taken as the equivalent of that missing link in any discussion of Schubert's spirituality, prayer.[6] (It is missing for the very good reason that nothing is known of his practice in the matter.)

On a lower level, heroes of German novels from the 1790s 'experienced things at concerts whose rightful place would have been in church, and music now stood at the head of the hierarchy. It made tangible what lay hidden behind the other arts' objectivity'.[7] The more 'enthusiastic' Catholic writers of Schubert's

---

[4] *Die Welt als Wille und Vorstellung*, Book 3, 36.

[5] Letter to Schober, 24 Feb. 1824. Cf. '. . . the scene always missing from Ken Russell films about composers – or indeed, from any romantic novel about them . . . the silent (or noisy) hours of solitude, stretching from the first strong coffee very early in the morning, until about lunch-time: the hours of a composer's most active consciousness, into which a commentator, even more so a psychologist, intrudes at his peril.' Hugh Wood, 'A Photograph of Brahms', *The Cambridge Companion to Brahms*, Cambridge, 1999. The Victorian moralist and apostle of 'self-help', Samuel Smiles, cited Schubert as 'a model of youthful industry' (*Life and Labour*, 1888).

[6] A fourth-century spiritual figure, Evagrius of Pontus, wrote: 'If you pray in truth, you are a theologian.'

[7] Helga de la Motte Haber, *Musik und bildende Kunst*, 1990, part II, *Die Musikalisierung der Malerei*. De la Motte lists novels such as W.H. Wackenroder's *Joseph Berglinger* (1797), whose hero underwent the experiences mentioned above, Karl Philipp Moritz's *Andreas Hartknopf* (1786) and J.J.W. Heinse's *Hildegard von Hohenthal* (1795).

day virtually equated the experience of music with experience of the numinous; even the more cautious, theologically sophisticated Schleiermacher[8] noted a tendency to let the one pave the way to the other. Something of the kind persisted into the twentieth century; in the 1930s Hermann Broch wrote that a great musical work 'architecturises the very threat to life, namely time, which leads us onward towards death';[9] and more recently still the French theologian Fr Marie-Dominique Goutierre has written that while each of the arts in its different way opens the door to philosophy's wisdom and sense of completeness, 'awakening man's sense of something Absolute, and thus lending a profound meaning to his own major experiences', music is the art, not only of sound, but of *time* and of *becoming* ('le Devenir').[10]

None of which would mean much to those who did not already sense, however inarticulately, the power and mystery of something greater by far than themselves. 'Becoming' involves a past and present as well as a future; it could be interesting to examine great men's work and see how far it draws on formative experiences from their earliest years, recast and developed as only they could. For example, the Austrian composer Franz Schmidt (1874–1939) was emphatic in his autobiographical sketch[11] that his strongest musical perceptions in boyhood had been of the sound of the organ in Pressburg Cathedral, which exercised a lasting influence on his inner world of music. Over and above the general atmosphere of great music written by the Viennese masters over the decades leading up to Schubert's birth, and the countless liturgical works he sang while a chorister, he is at times audibly under the spell of certain passages in Haydn's oratorio *The Creation* (see especially 'Harvest'). During his years at the Imperial Court Chapel he also saw the established church at close quarters, and that could have some bearing on the fact that whenever he later set to music the Ordinary of the Mass, he omitted from the *Credo* words expressing belief in one holy Catholic apostolic Church, and, as from his 1815 second Mass onwards, also the expression of belief in the resurrection[12] of the dead. From there it is but a championship-standard long

---

[8] Friedrich Schleiermacher, *Die Religion, Reden an die gebildeteren unter Ihrer Verächtern* (Religion, Speeches addressed to the More Cultivated among her Detractors), 1799.

[9] 'Musik ist Architekturierung des Lebensbedrohenden selbst, nämlich der zum Tode hinführenden Zeit'; Hermann Broch, 'Gedanken zum Problem der Erkenntnis in der Musik', in 1934 *Festschrift* for Schönberg's 60th birthday (reprinted in a revised version, which in fact omits the crucial remark, in volume II of Essays in Broch's *Collected Works*).

[10] 'Art et sagesse', *Aletheia*, École Saint-Jean, 1998, No. 14.

[11] An English translation can be found in Harold Truscott's *The Music of Franz Schmidt*.

[12] One must distinguish between Schubert's views on universal physical resurrection at the Last Judgment, to which the passage in the Creed refers, and his treatment of Lazarus' return to life after the briefest sojourn in the grave. From the eighteenth century onwards, the scientific spirit of the Enlightenment had begun to affect considerations of religion; Schubert's 'Linz circle' friends were in many ways Enlightenment men. Resurrection in any shape or form was bound to come under scrutiny, as seemingly running counter to Nature's laws. Nothing Schubert wrote (and nothing he omitted to set) suggests that he had any trouble with the concept of Christ's resurrection, and his miraculous power to raise Lazarus. In 1825 he wrote home from Hungary teasing brother Ferdinand about his hypochondria: 'if only he could once see these heavenly

jump to the idea (once put to me in all seriousness by a fine musician who had spent his life searching for truth in the performance of the profoundly religious Johann Sebastian Bach) that Schubert was 'an irreligious blighter'. Some salty observations about Hungarian country priests[13] might seem to bear that out, but an hour or two spent listening to music such as the Masses in G, A♭ or E♭ or the second and fifth *Salve Reginas*, gives pause for thought. They point unmistakably to his 'right and true devotion' (see p. xii, footnote 3).

At least one passage in his first Mass, written at seventeen, seems to proclaim an inborn awe and wonder (see the 'Early Masses' section of Chapter 2), and once the seed has had time to germinate it throws out shoots in the most unlikely places. Some such blossoming is what I hope to trace in the Schubert works, great and small, considered in the rest of this book.

Where religion is based on feeling, as well as on dogma and the intellect, contrasting elements mingle inextricably. The sensed presence of the Divine prompts powerful reactions; it is a 'Mysterium tremendum', a mystery inspiring awe and even terror, but it is also the sublime 'Mirum' or 'Mirabile', which leads the spirit through amazement to wonder, encouraged by external elements of fascination and splendour.[14] Such responses of the soul find parallels in Schubert's music.[15] In looking at his development my premise is that since in music sound is paramount, one may argue from similarities of sound to similarities of spiritual and mental state. In that sense, his music offers a covert autobiography, quite specific in some of its correlations with natural religious experience.

What happens in a genius' mind in the white heat of creation? The best thing to go on is the perceived outcome – so, with a composer, the music. Schubert's reputation suffered for a long time from legends not merely about his Bohemian habits but about his 'unselfconsciousness' even as he brought his great music into the world. But if a part of genius is the making of new intuitive connections,[16] then it could be that over and above his sheer knowledge of the art of composition (which has always been underrated), Schubert's mind as he sat at his desk ranged computer-like over a vast bank of available options,

---

mountains and lakes, the very sight of which threatens to crush or engulf us, he would not be so attached to puny human life, nor regard it otherwise than as good fortune to be entrusted to earth's incomprehensible power for new life'. To die was to be reunited with Mother Nature, an impressive, all-consuming figure who had her own ways. There is no way of knowing whether Schubert had already reached that conclusion by 1820, let alone by 1815, when he first omitted the crucial passage from a Mass, the one in G major.

Another omission from four of his six Masses is of 'Jesu Christe' in the section of the *Gloria* beginning 'quoniam Tu solus sanctus'. He invoked the Saviour in only the F and B♭ masses.

[13] Letter to his brothers and stepsister, 9 Oct. 1818.
[14] See the German theologian Rudolf Otto's authoritative account of 'the Non-rational in the Idea of the Divine, and its relation to the Rational', *Das Heilige* (1917). The one religion he found lacking in such experiences was Buddhism.
[15] Specific correlation with phases in mystical experience underlies a series of works by the Swiss composer Klaus Huber (b. 1924).
[16] See Arthur Koestler, *The Act of Creation*, 1964.

some already exercised in previous works, to make his selection, and so the next move, as intuition dictated. Only this view of a great mind at work could explain, for example, the amazing range of references to his own music in the score of his last completed opera, *Fierrabras*.[17]

No other composer shows quite the same creative attachment to his own music, the same 'cathexis', for Bach's endless recasting of music, his own and other composers', shows rather an arranger working at the level of genius; six major Schubert works (the Trout Quintet, Wanderer Fantasy, Octet, A minor and D minor String Quartets, C major Fantasy for violin and piano) refer to a greater or lesser extent to themes from his own vocal music. Other resemblances, such as that between the Trio of the Great C Major Symphony and 'Gratias agimus tibi' in the late Eb Mass, might be dismissed as mere expressions of a similar mood, proving no more than, say, the similarity in Mozart between Cherubino's 'Non sò più' and the opening of the late G minor symphony: but the more one looks at certain connections in Schubert, certain ideas whose recurrence down the years is like Ariadne's red thread guiding the hero through a cave, the more likely it seems that in his case thematic resemblance is rather seldom a matter of mere 'mood', let alone of chance. In *Fierrabras* he came within shooting distance of Wagner's concept of 'Leitmotif', and there he also has things in common with Bach, whose art was underlaid by Baroque concepts of musical motives to match particular 'affects'. The modest measure of analysis needed to show how firmly some of Schubert's major works are built on song-material must be sought elsewhere;[18] what it argues about his view of the world is that his own music was a matter of wonder to him, one among many.

Wonder is the hardest thing to expound: attempts to do so can easily lapse into the vague, the fey. It is easier to understand suffering and feel empathy with the sufferer, and during his short life Schubert went through more than enough to give rise down the years to works of fiction, films and television programmes stressing his isolation and cueing in yet one more performance of *Winterreise* or the String Quintet (immortal works both!). Economics are also in play here: to quote the supreme Schubert singer Siegfried Lorenz,[19] 'too many promoters shy away from the financial risks that just might accrue' from offering their audience anything but the composer's most famous and harrowing song-cycle for the nth time. Nett gain, if one thinks what music by Schubert was performed a century ago – and yet a loss too, an enormous missed opportunity. Hans Keller wrote in the 1970s, 'Our time's simultaneous technical perfection and musical degeneration . . . are, in large measure, due to

---

[17] It was to a commission for the Court Opera, so he had reason to regard it as his great chance. Sadly, he was disappointed, for the failure of Weber's *Euryanthe* at the same theatre meant that *Fierrabras* with its comparable themes of medieval chivalry was never staged, nor was he even paid. See Leo Black, 'Schubert and the Composition of *Fierrabras*', *Opera Quarterly*, Summer 1998.

[18] See Leo Black, 'Oaks and Osmosis', *Musical Times*, June 1997.

[19] 'At One in Solidarity', *Musical Times*, Jan. 1998.

competitive perfection demanding a depopulated, decrepit repertoire, which produces too many performances of too few works'[20] – and even in the handful of years since, 'competitive' has come to mean not only the youth competition circuit but the drive to be 'brand leader' in sales figures for recordings and videos, media appearances and publicity. In this way one side of Schubert is emphasised at the expense of others, and he emerges as a wailer rather than a wonderer.

To be in the world at all is a wonder; music is another, and the individual's gift for adding to the total of great music yet a third. Brahms once wrote, 'I am composing love songs again – not to A–Z, but to music.'[21] The sceptic may object that music offers scant prospect of requited love; the answer to that is 'consider the art before, and then after, a great master had his way with it', for music does not stay unchanged like an unresponsive object of desire. A good recent book on Schubert's life and music[22] was prefaced by two contemporary views of him – Ferdinand Hiller's[23] 'he really did nothing but music – and lived by the way', and Louis Schlösser's[24] 'music was the atmosphere in which he lived and breathed, in which his subjectivity unconsciously attained its highest development, and in which his whole being attained a state of ecstasy'. Such is the language of natural religion, of spiritual searching, where it is essential to obey the command to 'continue the search'. The lifelong commitment is the same, whatever the path – be it art, the love of beauty, prayer or meditation. The medieval Swiss mystic Heinrich Seuse (Suso) wrote:

> From days of childhood on, my spirit sought something with a burning thirst, and what it might be I have yet never fully grasped. Lord, I have now hunted it feverishly many a year and it could never fully become mine, for I know not truly what it may be. And yet it is something that draws my heart and soul to it and without which I can never be transported to a state of perfect peace. Lord, in the first days of my childhood I was all for seeking it in your Creatures, as I saw others do. And the more I sought, the less I found. And the nearer I approached, the farther away I was from that very thing . . . Now my heart rages for it, for I fain would have it. Alas . . . what is it, or how is it constituted, that which plays within me, so utterly concealed from me?[25]

The composer seems at an advantage over the mystic, for he really does know what it is that 'plays within him', namely an art, developed by his great predecessors, with techniques and vocabulary comprehensible, at least in part, by those around him prepared to take the trouble. It is, however, also

---

[20] 'Little-Known Greatness', *Collected Essays*, p. 51.

[21] Letter to Auguste Brandt and Bertha Porubsky, 9 Oct. 1859.

[22] Brian Newbould, *Schubert, The Music and the Man*, henceforth referred to as *SMM*.

[23] German composer, conductor and teacher, 1811–1885.

[24] German violinist, conductor and theatre director, three years younger than Schubert. He studied music in Vienna, and in November 1821 the two of them went to a performance of *Fidelio*. He also visited Schubert at his home in the Rossau district.

[25] *Collected Works*, ed. Denifle, p. 311.

unfathomably deep, so that a whole lifetime is too short to reveal its last secrets: there will always be something more to say. That final, hidden 'something more', like the mystic's unknown 'something', must be unceasingly sought, and in its purest form it may even be unknowable.

All of which could be taken to mean that Schubert was born with a well-nigh religious temperament, and yet fall far short of showing him to have been naturally religious, in the sense of knowing *a priori* the essential experiences – awe, wonder, terror – codified by theology. The only thing that could even begin to do so is the music. To insist too strongly on him as religious figure could moreover be to fall into the trap that awaits the spiritual practitioner when faced by someone with a vocation in this world – the view that such a person's calling, for all their skill and commitment, represents 'the lesser discipline'. But despite that caution, and never forgetting that to Schubert nothing could be as vivid and all-consuming as his art, there are still parallels to be drawn between him and the 'holy man'.

Schubert was only partly able to formulate his sense of wonder in accordance with the religious thinking of his time.[26] In 1825 he wrote home to his family, in the same 'right and true devotion' letter, of 'being entrusted to earth's incomprehensible power for new life' (der unbegreiflichen Kraft der Erde zu neuem Leben anvertraut zu werden). If one takes that literally and thinks its consequences through, then once the body had decayed and been recycled into something new, it could scarcely be brought back in its original form without injustice to someone or something: a daring view, coming from a layman in a Roman Catholic country during the early nineteenth century. Two years later he composed the song *Totengräberweise* (Gravedigger's Song), to a poem by an old friend from his schooldays, Baron Schlechta. It contains the line 'Wird der Leib des Wurmes Raub' (even if the body falls prey to the worm); the song is full of iridescent, exploratory harmonies that make the underlying key seem to fall into decay, and look forward to the work of Bruckner. Schlechta's poem ends with a conventional enough image of the last trumpet sounding and bodies rising transfigured from the dust. Schubert duly set that, most convincingly, and kept his counsel.

The *Salve Regina* hymn was important to Schubert (see the 'Worship and Submission' section of Chapter 2), and much of his other liturgical music has passages of manifest wonder, such as the very brief 'Pleni sunt coeli' in the *Sanctus* of the Mass in A♭, a highpoint in his entire output (strange as it may seem to say so, given the songs of *Winterreise*, the Heine settings or music such as the Trio of the late String Quintet, with its black depths. But that is precisely where this book seeks its justification). And as we shall see, the wonder of that Mass's 'Pleni sunt coeli' is juxtaposed with something at the very opposite point on the naturally religious spectrum.

---

[26] The strophes from Pyrker's *Perlen der Heiligen Vorzeit* set by Schubert in *Die Allmacht* come close.

Wordsworth's heartfelt wish was for his

> days to be
> Bound each to each by natural piety.[27]

As I see them, Schubert's days, fewer in number and beset with the most traumatic fallings-by-the-wayside, all the same make him a fellow-searcher, along with Britain's greatest Romantic poet, after the quiet glory at the heart of creation.

---

[27] Wordsworth, *Referring to the Period of Childhood*.

1

Partial Understanding

I find in every effort to express such thoughts that something is
right, but at the same time that something is lacking!
    Mendelssohn, letter to Marc-André Souchay, 15 Oct. 1842

If Schubert had waited for democracy he would hardly have
written a note.

                                   Alfred Hrdlicka, sculptor

It is only in degree that any improvement in society could
prevent wastage of human powers.
               William Empson, *Some Versions of Pastoral*

Schubertians are at one in their positive reaction to the sound of his music: it
was what first drew them to him, they love it deeply, it brings the man before
them, 'says something unique'. But such is human diversity that each well-
functioning pair of ears finds a different formulation for its loving acceptance.[1]

Until at least the 1928 centenary of his death, Schubert was seen primarily as
an intuitive composer who spent his life as a happy, half-cut Bohemian and
brought wonderful music into the world without quite knowing how. He
provided endless matter for superficial novels and operetta, the legend being
summed up in one of his nicknames, 'Schwammerl' – mushroom. A different
nickname, 'Canevas', has never been in circulation: told of an impending
addition to the circle of his friends, he would ask 'Is he good at anything? –
Kann er was?' Schubert as little mushroom became embodied in countless
works of fiction and pseudo-biography, also in the musical comedy known on
either side of the Atlantic as *Blossom Time* and *Lilac Time*.

After the Second World War cold facts about his background were deployed
to dispel the myth of the carefree minstrel, and a different picture became set in
concrete – that of a man sorely tried, living under a horribly oppressive regime,
afflicted through his own miscalculation with a horrible disease that was bound
to bring an untimely end and make his final years a sojourn in Hell, a man for
that matter blessed with few physical or social advantages – short, short-sighted,
short of money, short of appreciation and opportunity to do what he was

---

[1] See Dürhammer, 'Der Wandel des Schubertbildes im 20. Jahrhundert', and Leon Botstein,
'Reality Transformed – Schubert and Vienna', *Cambridge Companion to Schubert*, Cambridge,
1997.

capable of, and kept above water only by a circle of well-educated but rather stuffy friends who for all their kindness and loyalty never realised the full extent of his achievement.

The editors of *Schubert und seine Freunde* (Eva Badura-Skoda, Walburga Litschauer, Gernot Gruber and Carmen Ottner) stressed in their joint foreword that Schubert's outwardly uneventful life was marked 'above all by musical impressions while he was being educated at the Seminary [Konvikt, though *recte* Akademisches Gymnasium, since the Seminary was where he and his fellow-pupils had their free board and lodging] and by the stimuli he received from friends'; it is curious how much attention is currently paid to the second factor and how little to the first.

With the Cold War at an end, a further, post-Freudian revolution brought altered views of his character and, in particular, new ideas about his sexual orientation. The important question was, 'how did he come to compose music so original and so different from that of the great masters he admired?' Contemporary accounts of him were re-examined, and the darker side of his character emerged, with stress laid on his melancholy, anger and self-destructive hedonism.[2] But politics always seem to take pride of place, along with their twin monster, economics, and that is roughly where the popular image of Schubert put about by film and television has currently settled. Nor does present-day European Schubert research help much in redressing the balance, though discovery of his participation in the 'Nonsense Society' (*Unsinnsgesellschaft*)[3] at least shows him perfectly capable of joining in some quite sophisticated fun.

The post-Second World War European ethos of 'anima naturaliter socialistica' is summed up for many British people by a remark of Harold Macmillan, the country's Conservative Prime Minister from 1957 until 1963: 'We are all Socialists now.' It comes as no surprise that contemporary thinking emphasises the undeniably repressive systems of government throughout most of Europe for a whole century, between the end of the Napoleonic and outbreak of the First World wars. Writers have sought, seek, any sign that Schubert played a part in, or at least held a creditable attitude to, or at the very least had the decency to suffer during, the eventually successful struggle of those forces variously defined as 'democratic' to change the balance of power.

Evidence as to the nature of the regime in Austria in Schubert's time goes as far back as an English book, *Austria As She Is* (published the year he died, 1828) by 'An eye-witness'. That was the pseudonym of an Austrian exile Karl Postl, later known as Charles Sealsfield. Near the end of the preface to his highly

---

[2] Hedonism: doctrine that pleasure is the *chief* [my italics] good or the proper aim (*Concise Oxford Dictionary*). In Schubert's inner world the chief good was music; the emergence of an extreme strain of hedonism in him (drink, tobacco), emphasised by recent biography, looks less like a natural attempt at balance, with the world's good things there to be enjoyed, than a sign of his 'double nature'.

[3] Rita Steblin has brought this voluminous material to light, for example in *Die Unsinnsgesellschaft: Franz Schubert, Leopold Kupelwieser und ihr Freundeskreis*, Vienna, 1998.

partial view, Postl wrote: 'Never, perhaps, has there been exhibited an example of so complete and refined a despotism in any civilised country as in Austria.' A German visitor, Adolph Glassbrenner, put it differently in 1836:[4] the law and its prohibitions were admittedly draconian, but their implementation was somewhere between lackadaisical and benevolent (unless like Schubert's radical friend Senn you made your own bad luck by insulting the police).

As for the seismic shifts that in the twentieth century brought about what the nineteenth's dreaming and striving had suffered for, Marxist theoreticians and biographers understandably led the way, notably a genuine Schubertian from the DDR, Harry Goldschmidt. In *Schubert, ein Lebensbild* he unearthed things arguing for 'Schubert the simple man of the people': no matter that as a son of a God-fearing schoolmaster he spent his life with a circle of bourgeois friends and had only reluctant contact with even the layer of Vienna's population that went to the opera, where Rossini was preferred to him. Nor for that matter did he have much use for the rank-and-file of the musical profession.

Goldschmidt saw Biedermeier Austria as accurately as the next man, as a poison-cocktail of resurgent feudalism, insurgent capitalism, police state, demoralised bourgeoisie and exploited People, all of which Schubert saw with agonising clarity, particularly after his illness ('Pain sharpens the understanding and intensifies the emotions'[5]), hence his occasional explosions. For Goldschmidt,

> Not only does the music of his people provide the musical mother-earth for his entire creative work, but in its affirmation we find the expression of Schubert's commitment to the simple man of the people and his natural, democratic rights in life. In Schubert's life, too, his indissoluble links with the common folk form the true nucleus of his unshakeable humanistic convictions.

(But might it not rather be the other way about?)

Schubert, Man of the People,[6] was a necessary figure by Marxist-Leninist criteria. The idea matches a certain earthiness in his nature, but throws up a problem: whatever folk music may have contributed to his inspiration, what he produced belonged to a different world. One need only compare two melodies to which Wilhelm Müller's poem *Wanderschaft* is nowadays sung. A four-square one with much going up and down the tonic triad is still heard in the 'Volksmusik' that remains a drug in Germany, especially at the eastern end, whereas Schubert's *Das Wandern*, opening song of *Die schöne Müllerin*, immediately uses wide intervals including the difficult diminished fifth, and

---

[4] *Bilder und Träume aus Wien*, 1836, quoted in Hanson, *Musical Life in Biedermeier Vienna*.

[5] From a lost notebook of Schubert's, which his friend Bauernfeld knew and eventually published. This entry is dated March 1825.

[6] Marx's collaborator Friedrich Engels had long since laid down the line: culture must present not only the interesting but the typical. He wrote in 1888 to an English author, Margaret Harkness, about her story *City Girl*: the only fault he found was that it contained convincing individual characters but not typical ones. In a sense, and with honourable exceptions, Schubert study too has conformed to the natural human tendency to seek out things that are 'typical'. What is individual is harder by far to write about.

a relatively sophisticated musical technique, sequence.[7] Here already is a melody for the salon or concert hall rather than the streets, yet it counts as one of his most 'folk-like'. Matthias Claudius' poem *Abendlied* is likewise still familiar to very many Germans,[8] but sung to a simple, mostly conjunct melody from 1790 by the Danish composer Johann Abraham Peter Schulz (1747–1800); Schubert's song based on it (D. 499, 1816) is full of arpeggios and leaps of up to an octave.

Ex. 1 *Abendlied* (Claudius) as set by Schulz and Schubert

Melodies for mass participation are typified by the all-too 'accessible' *Hymn to Tito* learned for many years by the Yugoslav masses: consisting as it did of precisely two different notes, it could be and had to be sung, even by those so tone-deaf as to be literally unable to tell one note from another.

The 'Marx–Engels' view of Schubert was an anachronistic attempt to relate him not to his own time but to a future merely hoped for (and, whatever his Marxist biographers were bound to think, only marginally present even as they wrote). Since then, 'Schubert In His Time' has become the dominant theme in European writing about him. A complementary view is long overdue, a study of 'Schubert Out Of His Time', like a contrarian stock market programme buying and selling against current trends.

---

[7] Repetition of a phrase at a different pitch, usually a tone higher or, in this case, lower.

[8] A survey in the 1970s showed it coming first when those interviewed were shown a list of tunes and asked which they knew – nine out of ten knew of it, two-thirds had sung it – though when asked separately which tunes they knew best it failed to make the top twenty. (From the catalogue of 1990 Hamburg/Kiel exhibition on the 250th anniversary of Claudius' birth.)

The bumblings and fumblings of the DDR can, all the same, be relevant; it is all too easy to dismiss that curious country and all its not-inconsiderable works as do all too many British intellectuals, with the attitude, 'Know it? I don't even like it!' In search of a modern counterpart to the spectacle of very many decent, honest citizens trying to live some sort of sensible life under an obsessively supervisory, ridiculous regime, that of Chancellor Metternich and Police Chief Sedlnitzky, one need look no further than the other end of Germany between 1949 and 1989 under the likes of First Secretaries Walter Ulbricht and Erich Honecker and their Ministry for State Security. Goldschmidt and the country's musical 'Pope', the composer/scholar/party luminary Ernst Hermann Meyer, began to write during the hopeful years of 'New Germany', before even the disillusion of the 1953 uprising against shortages and excessive work-norms.[9] Such men's condemnation of authoritarianism reflected experience of the 1933–45 Nazi regime (Meyer spent the war years as a refugee in England, and produced a classic study of early chamber music), and the fervent belief that something better could and must be built. What their own country turned into was what they had most condemned about Schubert's Austria, where the cultured and sensitive Mayrhofer had had to support himself as a censor.[10] Yet in the one place as in the other, things of value still flourished: 'the authorities didn't understand the art we practised, so they left us to get on with it'.[11]

In England, Wilfrid Mellers[12] adopted a comparably sociological if more conciliatory approach, but rather than press-ganging Schubert to serve the Dictatorship of the Proletariat, he saw him more plausibly as in search of 'salvation in a communion of kindred spirits' and his circle as part of 'an intellectual minority, awaiting their doom, if not calmly, at least with their eyes wide open'. It is certainly true at least in part that Schubert is 'a composer of Friendship as Bach had been a composer of the Church and Handel a composer of the State'. His circle saw the need for changes in society, but were triply constrained – by the State and its supervisory apparatus, by their salaried status as its servants, and by their awareness of the destruction and evil that had attended a serious reform of the established order in France. No wonder they fell back on self-improvement and the higher disciplines of art and the intellect.[13]

---

[9] Bertolt Brecht said of that uprising that 'the people, having let the Government down, should be dissolved and a new one appointed'.

[10] In the DDR, too, 'the literary intelligentsia also staffed the censorship department' (Edgar Mittenzwei, in *Die Intellektuellen, Literatur und Politik in Ostdeutschland 1945–2000*, Leipzig, 2001, which offers a dispassionate account of relationships between eastern Germany's rulers and intellectuals in DDR times and after).

[11] Private communication to the author from Siegfried Lorenz, apropos his forty-four years living in the DDR. Anything with words was, of course, subject to far closer scrutiny.

[12] In *The Sonata Principle*, 1957.

[13] Many of the papers in *SSF* touch on this, notably Ilja Dürhammer's 'Von den lachenden Fluren des Ideenreiches', which stresses the disillusion that overtook Schubert's serious-minded friends once they had turned into bureaucrats looking back wistfully on the creative days of their youth.

Any such flattering unction seems wiped clean in a recent account of Schubert's Vienna by Leon Botstein (see note 1). He takes perhaps the blackest view of all, throwing in an ever-worse shortage of life's necessities, whereas according to Alice Hanson's sociological study 'good food [not to mention good wine and beer] was readily available in Schubert's Vienna, as one of the few creature comforts in an otherwise insanitary and over-crowded city'. According to Botstein, the Viennese even had to spy on their own circle of acquaintances: the parallels with the DDR grow and grow. Even Postl/Sealsfield and the DDR commentators went less far: the vast army of spies needed to perform Sedlnitzky's work of supervision was recruited from what Goldschmidt called 'the demoralised strata of the city's population', while Sealsfield reported some 10,000 such 'Naderer', from the 'lower end of the tradesmen class, messengers, working men, even prostitutes, forming a network which runs through the whole of Viennese society like the red thread that runs through the British navy's towropes'.

Amid all that misery the remark by Schubert's dramatist friend Bauernfeld, in his diary for 8 March 1826, 'for him, the world is beautiful', could suggest a degree of naivety unprecedented before Jaroslav Hasek's Good Soldier Schweik, who had his own private anti-Habsburg agenda. Botstein's positive point is that for those very reasons culture became immensely important and music, in particular, 'the one virtually incorruptible means of communication', given occasions such as the evening gatherings, with music and dancing, that came to be known as Schubertiads.

For the West German commentator Frieder Reininghaus, in *Schubert und das Wirtshaus* (Berlin, 1979), as for the DDR theoreticians a generation earlier, Schubert and his entire circle were victims of political repression. Reininghaus at least comes over as refreshingly eccentric, with 'evidence' such as five 'attempts to compose *Die Forelle*' (in fact five copies for friends who understandably loved the song). That is taken to show an obsession with its lyric, where a political message could underlie the conventional warning to girls to beware of young men's wiles: 'don't trust the rulers, they'll come after you' – it had in fact happened to the song's poet, C.D.F. Schubart. At least some of Schubert's friends (for example Senn) would have known that, but the connection with his music is the more tenuous since the warning comes in a final verse which he didn't even set.

Not that one should totally write off the political background. By 1813 France's days as dominant power in Europe were clearly numbered, the 'wars of liberation' (Befreiungskriege) having culminated in victory for the Allies at the battle of Leipzig. That year represented a peak of hope for many enlightened Austrians, after a decade and more seeing the reforms of Maria Theresia and her son the Emperor Joseph steadily whittled away by her grandson Franz and his ministers. What happened next was a gross betrayal of those hopes.

What one should not do, however, is interpret politically each and every expression of discontent and 'Weltschmerz' in the Schubert circle. There is more to life than that. In a sociologically conditioned view of him, any sense of wonder and awe, not at worldly power whether Imperial or ecclesiastical, but at the grandeur of creation itself, can find a place only as a politically tinged feeling for nature. An immense amount is now known about him as 'child of his time', and the assumption is always that the time conditions the way the child composes. Which leaves out of account the man and his individuality.

With more-recent speculation about Schubert's sexual constitution one confraternity gives way to another. Pathfinding articles in *Nineteenth-Century Music*[14] seemed to be saying Schubert was homosexual, though they also emphasised the completeness of his artistic persona and its logic in its own terms. The initiator Maynard Solomon eventually felt he must stress that a great deal of his original piece addressed the element not of homosexuality but of hedonism in Schubert's character. And there recent biographies support him.

To make the idea of a specifically homosexual music more widely intelligible, analysis would need to show not only the things about Schubert's genius that make him different (something that has been attempted to the point of exhaustion), but how they are correlated with a homosexual constitution (and that is still at an early stage). Nor is it ruled out that there could be what philosophy calls a category mistake in attempts to treat sexual orientation and musical make-up as interdependent. What could be overlooked, as in the politicisation of Schubert, is the crucial role of fantasy in creating things not present in the 'real' world. To insist, as prime mover, on reactions to those that are present, reactions determined by 'inclinations and constitution', could be to overlook the role of creativity and imagination in human life.[15] There is, after all, such a thing as free will.

The blending of the elements in human character referred to by a convenient shorthand as 'male and female' is complex, and a male's way of coming to terms with his own percentage of 'femaleness' by no means predictable. This will be of the essence in considering the theme of Schubert and love, but it is a

---

[14] The initial article (all the articles appeared in *Nineteenth-Century Music*) was Maynard Solomon's 'Schubert and the Peacocks' (XII/3, 1989). Issue XVII/1 (Summer 1993) was dominated by the controversy. Rita Steblin countered sceptically in 'The Peacock's Tale, Schubert's Sexuality Reconsidered'; Kofi Agawu tried to hold the balance in 'Schubert's Sexuality'; Susan McClary weighed in pro-Solomon with 'Music and Sexuality: The great debate'; James Webster contributed 'Pathology, Sexuality, Beethoven, Schubert'; Solomon elaborated and elucidated his ideas in 'Schubert, Some Consequences of Nostalgia', and the editor Lawrence Kramer made a plea for examining homosexual aspects of Schubert's art. That was to be thoughtfully expanded in his book *Franz Schubert, Sexuality, Subjectivity, Song* (Cambridge, 1998). Such speculations have so far been of interest mainly in America; in Europe even the newest generation of music historians still seems obsessed with the social and political background, to the extent that the Viennese publisher of Hanson's *Musical Life in Biedermeier Vienna* altered its neutral title to *Die zensurierte Muse. Musikleben in Wiener Biedermeier* (The Censored Muse, Musical Life in Vienna's Biedermeier Period) when it appeared in German.

[15] 'O imagination! thou greatest treasure of man, thou inexhaustible wellspring from which artists as well as savants drink! O remain with us still, by however few thou art acknowledged and revered, to preserve us from that so-called enlightenment, that hideous skeleton without flesh or blood!' (Schubert's Lost Notebook, 29 March).

field beset by the crassest misunderstandings and distortions; best perhaps to leave it that

> The one important thing is the aesthetic effect on his work of an artist's inclinations and constitution. Whether Goethe 'had anything' with the youthful love of his old age, Marianne von Willemer, is as irrelevant to the researcher as his love for her is important, since the latter inspired his Suleika in the *Westöstlicher Divan*, and so one of the most beautiful books of lyrics in German literature. Schubert's creative work is as unimaginable without his affection for (*inter alia*) Joseph von Spaun, Johann Mayrhofer and Franz Schober, and of course Therese Grob and Caroline Esterhazy, as Goethe's without his relationships with the women who were at various times his muses.[16]

Any serious analyst of great composers is after a clear picture, not of the man 'in his life' but of the man *in his music* – the 'artistic persona'. The argument for going into questions of sexuality is part of a still more basic one – that music is not what an older aesthetics called autonomous but ties in with many other aspects of what is most important in a person's life. That may seem self-evident once you look at it at all, yet it carries enormous dangers.

The composer and scholar Hans Gal had no intention of falling into the trap of regarding Schubert as a mere child of his time, a packet of sociologically conditioned reflexes. He stressed the sheer force of genius, and Schubert's joy in creation. Gal knew about political oppression, for like his fellow-composer Meyer he spent the war years in Britain as a refugee from Nazism, but he wrote as the final words of what must be the most beautiful of all books about Schubert:

> He is the only one of the great who could idealise the everyday world. Anyone who is too unimaginative to be grateful for and enjoy this aspect of Schubert's idiom, this delight in the gift of life and its expression in the homeliest colloquial terms, lacks an essential organ of perception. Fate, which thrust this precious vessel of grace defenceless into the world, gave him the capacity to rejoice, and this it was that made him rich. From this wealth he drew the love that lives in his melodies, the love he never received and always so lavishly poured forth. Since then the world has not stood still. The sounding brass and the tinkling cymbal have made amazing progress. But what has happened to love?[17]

For each new generation, Schubert has new things to say. The post-1945 avant-garde had its moments of finding him congenial and inspiring, less on sociological grounds than out of a feeling that he had been the first to set foot in the new world to which they had open access. Dieter Schnebel, interestingly enough a former priest, called the beginning of the late B♭ piano sonata

> the record of a dissociating life, feeling its way rather than taking hold, no longer able to find a form, its courage that of hesitation or despair. Development leads to

---

[16] Dürhammer, 'Der Wandel des Schubertbildes'.
[17] Closing words of *Franz Schubert and the Essence of Melody*.

a snarl-up and ends in an explosion, out of whose smoke the episode with the second subject rises like steam.[18]

In the background here is a view at one time said to underlie, for example, the entire work of Karlheinz Stockhausen; that since music consists simply of pulse, of vibration, manifest (depending on its number, wavelength and rhythmic organisation) as duration, pitch and timbre, all three may legitimately be handled in comparable ways. At one time the predominant way was 'total serialism'; one is free to look on that as the crudest and most theoretical 'me-too-ism' after Schönberg's formulation of a serial technique applied to pitch only, but the principle of omnipresent vibration is yet one more allotrope of an age-old insight common to most religions as to many substitutes for religion such as Theosophy, which Schönberg found fascinating,[19] and symbolism. Whether it even offers a sound-based justification for the post-1945 essays in total serialism, let alone touching on Schubert's musical thought-processes, is a moot point, but clearly Schnebel, like his successors down the same apparently far-fetched line, loves his Schubert and can produce his evidence, particularly when entering the muddy waters of the 'popular'.[20] His time will come.

Any assessment of a great mind and its work, like any performance of great music, is likely to pass over some facet or other, though to Hans Gal one bows the knee in face of such insight. Most of the other approaches outlined offer one or other sympathetic feature but leave a gap that needs filling. No more than partial understanding is to be expected of any one commentator; even given the available wealth of informed comment and deeply musical sympathy, sides of Schubert still await elucidation.

---

[18] 'Auf der Suche nach der befreiten Zeit', written in 1968–9 and published in *Musik-Konzepte*, Schubert volume, Munich, 1979.

[19] See Rudolf Stefan, 'Über die Klangvorstellungen Arnold Schönbergs', in *Klang und Komponist, Ein Symposon der Wiener Philharmoniker*, Tutzing, 1992.

[20] 'Schuberts Ländler', in *DOE*.

2

Wonder and Submission

Right and True Devotion

Das Schaudern ist des Menschen Bestes.
Awe is the best of man.

Goethe, *Faust*, Part 2

There is nothing of the morbid or the occult in our awe before Him; but in that awe is the very stuff of worship and of religion itself.

William Temple

Ave Maria! Maiden mild!

Sir Walter Scott, *The Lady of the Lake*

String Quartet in E♭ (D. 87); Symphony No. 1 in D; Geisternähe; Mass No. 1 in F; Salve Regina No. 2 (D. 106); Deutsches Salve Regina; Stabat Mater (Jesus Christus schwebt am Kreuze); Salve Regina Nos 4 (D. 386), 5 (D. 676), 6 (D. 811)

A fly on the wall would have had much to observe as and when the Schubert family's conversation came round to religion. Schubert Senior was bound by his calling of local schoolmaster, as by his nature, to be a pious pillar of society; eldest son Ignaz was something it was very dangerous to be at the time, a freethinker relentless in his hatred of clerics (Franz called him the 'iron man').[1] For that reason the second brother, Ferdinand, who worked contentedly for the church as organist and choirmaster, in due course became head of the family, though Ignaz did finally take over his father's school. As for Franz, his textual omissions when he set the Ordinary of the Mass have already been mentioned. Many composers mangled those texts, but as a boy he had sung them every day, and he left bits out with a curious consistency hard to credit as random or the result of memory-lapses. It would scarcely have escaped his notice that the Catholic church went hand in hand with the regime in keeping the populace in its place and thought to a minimum.

We should, however, remember that religion is more than dogma, church,

---

[1] Letter from Zseliz to his brothers and stepsister, 29 Oct. 1818.

liturgy; it also involves intimations, greatly varying from person to person, of some force greater than oneself. They are not concepts reserved for an educated elite, but basic perceptions that can be experienced by anyone, intellectual or not. The 'Linz Circle' of Schubert's middle adolescent years was enormously beneficial in the development of his intellect and talent; its high-minded reading had the strongest influence on his literary tastes and so on his choice of texts to set to music, but it would be a mistake to imagine that it helped form his religious side. He was neither a theologian nor a mystic but a musician of genius, translating into sounds, not what he had learned about but what he most deeply felt and sensed – his 'irrational perceptions'. Hence his occasional impulse of 'right and true devotion', which would (as he wrote in that letter) 'catch him unawares'.

And once it did, what music resulted! Where a text truly spoke to him, he responded. In parts of the two final Masses in A♭ and E♭ he gave of his best as he set the liturgy, and there is truly characteristic Schubert in 'lesser' works too – the earlier Masses, or those invocations of the feminine as advocate and help in time of trouble, the *Salve Reginas*. Six are in Latin and one in German (though to me the piano Adagio in G, D. 178, written one month after the Mass in the same key, is like a further member of the family, with its opening motive that so suits the words SAL–ve Re–GI–na, and its ensuing variety of moods. The earlier of its two versions is dated 8 April 1815, the day his half-sister Maria Theresia was born, and it has been charmingly suggested that its 'prayerful mood' has something to do with the new arrival.)[2] The *Salve Reginas* are scored for a variety of forces and date from as far apart as 1812 and 1824. There are also numerous songs that one could term his 'Geistliche Lieder'. The greatest of those, *Die Allmacht*, was a product of his 'harvest' year, 1825, and took as its text pantheistic lines from an epic poem by a senior churchman, Pyrker.[3]

The *Salve Regina* hymn is addressed to the Virgin Mary, and Schubert's first setting of it dates from even before his first Mass. Places where there have been well-documented manifestations of the Virgin become world-wide objects of pilgrimage and may say things even to people not of the Roman faith; a Buddhist known to me visited Medjugorge in Yugoslavia, where she is said to have appeared to children in the 1980s, and reported feeling there a strong sense of something profoundly good. Her cult at its strongest has at times down the centuries amounted to a 'private army' within the Roman church, while the

[2] By the pianist Simon Nicholls, programme of a London South Bank concert, 18 Sep. 2002.

[3] Hungarian churchman (1772–1847), in turn Abbot of Lilienfeld, Bishop of Zips (Szepeshely), Patriarch of Venice and Archbishop of Erlau (Eger). In his biography by Roland Dobersberger, *Johann Ladislaus Pyrker, Dichter und Kirchenfürst*, 1997, a 'second subject' and source of much-needed light relief is Pyrker's immense ambition and self-belief as epic poet – he was in his own view a German Homer – together with his pathological sensitivity to criticism; clearly the type of man who never lets anyone else have the last word, he proved tireless in his efforts to extract the first, as in the comedy of his repeated attempts to secure acknowledgment from Goethe.

Once Schubert began to appear in society Pyrker became an admirer. Their cordial relationship is immortalised in two great songs (*Das Heimweh*, D. 851; *Die Allmacht*, D. 852, 1825) to texts from Pyrker's voluminous literary work.

extremes of conduct – call it compulsion neurosis, call it saintliness – resulting from a total involvement with the Virgin are on record in many a life; outstanding young men have been so consumed by it as to achieve the ultimate feat of dying on one of the crucial days in her story.[4] Vienna, however, has been only average in its devotion to her, and no Schubert biography records any such preoccupation, beyond a remark in his 1816 diary that at an art exhibition in Vienna the only picture to appeal to him strongly was a Madonna and Child by a painter named Abel. So his predilection for the *Salve Regina* hymn and the impulses behind his other Marian pieces were personal rather than having to do with his social milieu or its religious practices. The music, however, remains and speaks; it could be that Schubert preferred to pray to a human mother-figure rather than a divine father-figure.

Salve Regina

Salve Regina, Mater misericordiae,	Hail, queen and mother of mercy,
Vita dulcedo et spes nostra, salve.	Life, sweetness, and hope: hail.
Ad te clamamus exules fili Evae,	To Thee we cry, the exiled sons of Eve,
Ad te suspiramus gementes et flentes	To Thee we sigh, mourning and weeping
In hac lacrimarum valle.	In this vale of tears.
Eia ergo, advocata nostra,	Therefore hail, our advocate,
Illos tuos misericordes oculos	Turn upon us those
ad nos converte	pitying eyes of Thine
Et Jesum benedictum	And hold out to us
fructum ventris tui	after this our exile
Nobis post hoc exilium ostende.	Jesus the fruit of Thy womb.
O clemens, o pia, o dulcis	O merciful, pious and
Virgo Maria.	sweet Virgin Mary

The offertory[5] Salve Regina dates back to the early twelfth century. It was first included in an antiphonary in 1140, recommended shortly after for the Procession during the Feast of the Assumption, and then associated first with Vespers and later with the evening service, Compline.[6] It gave composers a chance 'to conclude the office with music in the nature of a finale'.[7] Its theme is the Virgin Mary's intercession on behalf of mankind 'mourning and weeping in this vale of tears'. Schubert's first setting, in F major (D. 27, June 1812), was written either for a school-friend (see Werner Bodendorff, *Die kleineren Kirchenwerke Franz Schuberts*, Augsburg 1997) or as a display piece for Therese Grob, a neighbour's daughter with a remarkably well-developed soprano voice. After an Imperial decree in 1806 women were supposed not to sing in the Mass

---

[4] C.C. Martindale, *Christ's Cadets*, 1913.

[5] The offertory was part of the Proper, that is to say its text varied day by day; it came between the *Credo* and *Sanctus*, to accompany (as its name suggests) the offering of bread and wine.

[6] See Marina Warner, *Alone of All Her Sex*, 1976: the hymn even features in Dante's *Paradiso*, 'sung by princes in the flowery valley of neglectful rulers, wailing and sighing'.

[7] Maurice J.E. Brown, 'Schubert's Settings of the *Salve Regina*', *Music & Letters*, 1956, pp. 234–49. Though alive to the quality of much of the music, Brown ascribed Schubert's repeated setting of the text to purely practical considerations – 'an opportunity presented itself whereby a sacred work of his composition could be performed'.

unless they were in some way close to the director of music, but Therese evidently qualified – her parents did at least own a silk factory.

Before Schubert set the text again he matured a great deal. His first symphony (D major, D. 82), completed on 28 October 1813, shows how attentively he had listened to music by Haydn, Mozart and Beethoven: Gülke[8] perceptively suggests that particular echoes of those composers are intentional rather than merely showing him up as 'derivative'. Schubert was not just 'absorbing a style' (as that supremely imitative monkey Mozart had done in his formative years!); these works by his great predecessors were particularly close to his heart, and all part and parcel of his overriding passion – music.

Newbould's analyses[9] of the 1st Symphony can be recommended and his perception of both its models and its originality accepted, but there is a little more to say. The first movement's reuse of its introduction 'up to speed' may have precedents in Spohr, but could equally suggest that the Seminary orchestra had played Mozart's 'Posthorn' Serenade of 1779, whose first movement shows precisely that formal innovation. And Schubert's Minuet and Trio (see below) tips the balance strongly in favour of the Mozart as model.

The two middle movements deserve attention, the second not just for its melody echoing yet another D major work, again by Mozart, the 38th (*Prague*) Symphony, but for its subtle refinements on sonata form, extending right down to the micro-level in the detail of an ever-more chromatic harmonisation of its curiously asymmetrical[10] principal melody as it reappears. This movement is a piece to treasure, an early manifestation of something utterly basic in Schubert's approach to form, namely a way of letting the processes of 'development'[11] spill over, both backwards into his exposition sections, where melodies are elaborated with a strong sense of 'I like being where I am', and forward into recapitulations. What is good and to hand is seized on and made to stay, even if it was supposed to go away and come back later. His sonata-form recapitulations can be literal to the point of tedium, but are sometimes astonishingly different and new, like the one in the 1st Symphony. What Schubert did there, still not yet seventeen, looks forward both to his own mature work and to that of Bruckner.

The second minuet in Mozart's Serenade has not 'a trio' but two, and the second has given the work its nickname, for in it a posthorn shows what (little!) it can do. At the end of the trio it has a repeated figure that rises higher each time; something very similar occurs both in the episode of Schubert's slow movement and at slightly greater length in the trio of his minuet. Eighteen months later came the first of a series of further references to the posthorn

---

[8] *Schubert und seine Zeit*, p. 58.

[9] In *SandSy* and *SMM*.

[10] A continuation at bar 8 overlaps with the end of the opening melody, as in the 'Dona nobis pacem' of the 1828 E♭ Mass (see 'Pride of Performance' for that work's architectonic subtleties).

[11] Newbould (*SandSy*, pp. 149–50) distinguishes usefully between two types of 'development': restatement, perhaps in different harmonic areas (which is also found in many of Schubert's exposition sections), and 'real' development (modulation and transformation) as in sonata form's development sections.

figure, in the Kosegarten setting *Der Abend* (D. 221); he returned to it in the melody of another 'evening song', *Abendlied* (D. 499, 1816, see Ex. 1, p. 13) and again at the outset of *Widerschein* (D. 639, 1820).

There is one more anticipation of later music in the 1st Symphony; after a fermata near the end of the slow movement's recapitulation, the music continues in a way that looks forward to moments ('O clemens, O pia') in both the second *Salve Regina* eight months later and the fifth one, composed in 1819. When the latter is considered later in this chapter, a further Mozart connection will be suggested.

The symphony's tributes to earlier masters may seem to have little or nothing to do with Schubert's 'right and true devotion', but they emphasise the range of his sense of wonder: it was set ringing not only by nature's splendour and by people, but also by music, his own and other composers'. In this book's chapter 'Pride of Performance' it will be seen that at the end of his life his mind still turned to Mozart as he wrote the E♭ Mass.

In his next symphony (No. 2 in B♭, D. 125, 1814–15) Schubert seems to have been less sure of himself, for in its first movement he made hard work of getting away from his home key and first subject; the latter insists on being there even once he has laboriously climbed into the dominant. This apparent regression illustrates the process memorably described by Schönberg in his *Harmonielehre* (chapter 'Fourth Chords'), whereby a genius' true originality first shows itself through 'his inability to bring off something any old craftsman would have done immaculately'.

By the time of the 3rd Symphony (D. 200, 1815) we find at least one pattern that will recur in a great mature work (see Harvest for a comparison of the opening of the 'exposition' in the 3rd and the Great C Major symphonies). It is an entirely engaging piece, as are its successors No. 4 in C minor (D. 417, 1816), which Schubert too portentously called 'Tragic' when it merely has the charm of a young man taking the world unusually seriously;[12] No. 5 in B♭ (D. 485, 1816), where Mozart reigns supreme; and No. 6 in C (D. 589, 1817/18), which blends Haydn with the fashionable Rossini. These early symphonies are underrated, and have something to do with 'the inmost Schubert', but it would be naive to look for more than the very occasional shadow or sign of awe and terror in music written for his former colleagues at the Seminary to play. A sudden almost alarming outburst of rejoicing at the end of the 6th Symphony's finale looks forward to the Great C Major (via the 1817 D major Italian Overture, D. 590 and 1820 *Zauberharfe* Overture, D. 644: see 'Harvest'), and its euphoria should act as a reminder that the sense of the Divine brings with it wonder at the 'Mirum' as well as terror at the 'Tremendum'.

All of that has involved running on ahead; between the 1st Symphony and second *Salve Regina* (28 June–1 July 1814. D. 106 and thus the immediate

---

12 Newbould (*SandSy*) interestingly spots a reference (not literal but with a similar atmosphere and 'ductus') to the 'Chaos' Prelude from Haydn's *The Creation* as early as the opening bars of the first movement's introduction. Haydn's masterpiece, and especially its opening few minutes, will later be seen to have played a significant role in Schubert's inspiration at various stages.

successor in Deutsch's thematic catalogue of the F Major Mass) lay eight months during which, despite the demands of teacher-training, he composed an opera (*Des Teufels Lustschloss*), two adventurous string quartets (E♭, D. 87; D major, D. 94), the Mass in F and numerous songs. The new *Salve Regina* gave the solo line to a tenor. It is no longer than the first setting but musically more substantial, a vigorous piece in an active tempo (Andante), with a good deal of light and shade. The text's contrasts with the earthly vale of tears are emphasised by a jabbing repeated-note-triplet figure found in other music from the same time; there is a vigorous call to attention in the first movement of the E♭ quartet (Ex. 2a), and a gentler one in the slow movement (Ex. 2b); then in perhaps the best of Schubert's very early songs, *Geisternähe* (D. 100, from half a year later, June 1814, but likewise in E♭), it is heard in the left hand of the piano at 'er sehnt nach dir' (he longs for you, Ex. 2c), becoming quite menacing in the brief interludes between the verses of the song. Ex. 2d shows various forms assumed by this figure in the second *Salve Regina*. The sighs at 'suspiramus' are very Schubertian, whereas a falling phrase at 'hac lacrimarum valle', though equally so, could reflect youthful experience of Haydn's oratorio *Die Schöpfung* (*The Creation*): this is an important strand in Schubert's work, to be examined later.

Ex. 2a D. 87, I

Ex. 2b D. 87, II

Ex. 2c *Geisternähe*

Ex. 2d *Salve Regina*, D. 106

A year later Schubert turned again to the theme of the Virgin Mary, in a short *Stabat Mater* (D. 175, April) and three months later a third setting of *Salve Regina* (D. 223, F major, another piece for Therese Grob). The *Stabat Mater* hymn goes back to the fourteenth-century Franciscan movement, and its full version, with two dozen three-line strophes, has provided the basis for major musical works ever since the Eton Choirbook at the turn of the sixteenth century. By the time of Verdi's outstanding 1898 setting (No. 2 of *Four Sacred Pieces*) the *Stabat Mater* had became a concert genre, but Schubert's could still expect an ecclesiastical outlet, at the local Lichtental church. He set only the first four strophes, to dignified, expressive music, with one or two 'fingerprints' such as an S-curve linking-figure for the strings also found in slightly different forms in the G Major Mass and the song *Das war ich!* from about that time (see the section 'Schubert in Love?' later in this chapter). After a first setting of his version of the text he repeats and varies the music; some of his intensifications are of interest to anyone concerned with niceties of composing technique. From the outset he springs minor surprises; for example, the beginning gives no clue whether the music will go on in the major or the minor. In its slightly impersonal impressiveness this early piece belongs with the late Eb Mass rather than the matchless, 'testamentary' one in Ab from 1819–22. Both those major works are discussed at length later.

The third *Salve Regina* shares its common-time tempo and briskness with D. 106, but not the same range of emotion. Though much of the second strophe, from 'Eia ergo' onward, is omitted (did nobody around the church notice or object?), the piece is just as long; its main purpose again seems to be to show off Therese's voice, complete with top c-s. It was revised with the addition of wind parts, performed and published in 1825.

The fourth and sixth settings (Bb, D. 386, early 1816; C major, D. 811, 1824), are in simple four-part texture. D. 386 demonstrates Schubert's priceless ability to write a far better tune than his fellow-composers. D. 811 is the one *Salve Regina* that belongs in the world of the male-voice quartet (he specifically marked it 'Quartetto'), and seems designed for domestic devotions, whereas the others would find their place in the liturgy. (Schubert even allowed for an organ accompaniment to D. 386.) The sixth *Salve Regina* has an important successor in *Das stille Lied*, from 1827, which shares its idiom and at least one of its techniques, the use of echo (see 'Pride of Performance'). This *Salve Regina* was defended by a great Schubertian, Maurice J. E. Brown, against those who called it unctuous and jejune: to him, it 'overflowed with humanity . . . belong[ing] heart and soul to the early nineteenth century'.[13]

---

[13] 'Schubert's Settings of the *Salve Regina*'.

Around the time of the fourth setting Schubert composed a 'German Salve Regina' (D. 379, 21 February 1816), dignified and hymn-like and definitely a choral piece (with organ accompaniment), also a half-hour-long oratorio amounting to a 'German Stabat Mater' (D. 383, February 1816). There the text is by the greatest religious writer of the German Enlightenment, Klopstock, whom Schubert revered and set to music in fine songs (notably *Dem Unendlichen*, D. 291, September 1815, and *Das Rosenband*, D. 280, probably from earlier the same month: the latter is a reminder that the magisterial author was also at home in the tenderest love-poetry). In *Jesus Christus schwebt am Kreuze*, to give the 'German Stabat Mater' its more appropriate title, Schubert achieves majesty and a measure of beauty, without often sounding identifiably himself; it could be a worthy but not outstanding late Haydn work. The succession of twelve short movements recalls Haydn's *Seven* [plus Introduction and Earthquake] *Last Words of the Saviour on the Cross*; that had been heard in Vienna as soon as a month after its 1787 Cadiz premiere, while the version adding voices to the original purely orchestral score was also familiar in Vienna, where it had received its first performance.

The third number in *Jesus Christus schwebt am Kreuze* seems to model the opening of its melody on the end of Haydn's 'Emperor's Hymn'. High-flying horns are used poetically in the latter part of the fifth, as sole accompaniment to the ethereal sound of the female voices, and then against the entire choir. This imaginative use of pure choral sound is a reminder that Schubert's time saw the start of a move away from 'concerted' church music and towards a renewal of the old *a capella* (= unaccompanied) style. The subtle and seemingly effortless Palestrina was to become the ideal even in the eyes of a master of artifice such as Wagner. Schubert lived too early to feel the full impact of that 'Cecilian' movement, but passages such as No. 5 in *Jesus Christus schwebt am Kreuze* show which way the wind was blowing. In the tenth section earthly joys and sorrows are touched on with a pleasing lightness, and the imaginative use of wind instruments brings one close for a few moments to the real Schubert. He remembered that music when he came to compose *Lazarus*.

The jewel among the *Salve Regina*s is No. 5 in A major (D. 676, November 1819, soprano and strings), with less light and shade than No. 2, but unforgettable nuances of shade! It is the immediate neighbour in the Deutsch catalogue of the A minor–major song *Die Götter Griechenlands* (D. 677), germ-cell for the great A minor string quartet from five years later, and a close enough neighbour of *Lazarus*, where A major is likewise the home key. Still closer to it in time is the Mass in A♭ (D. 678), also begun in November 1819 but not finished for three years. The tempo is stiller and more obviously devotional than in Nos. 2 and 3 – it recalls Mozart's Marian pieces[14] in his Litanies and Vespers (and Schubert had already seemed to quote one such work near the end of the Kyrie of his B♭ Mass three years earlier), as well as anticipating *Lazarus*' quietist

---

[14] Mozart's religious strain continued to fascinate Schubert – see 'Pride of Performance', apropos the E♭ Mass.

world.[15] There could also be a brief quotation at 'O clemens, o pia', just before the middle point and at the corresponding one near the end, of the supplicatory 'Cum vix justus sit securus' in the *Dies Irae* of Mozart's *Requiem*. As in No. 3, the structure is binary, but this time the piece accommodates almost the entire text (give or take the name Jesus?), on which it constructs something of a verbal fantasia, and is musically far more elaborate and resourceful. Brown's sympathetic account of the music's progress ends with an apt comment on its final reiterations of 'Salve Regina' – that the soft tone of the music is suited to 'Vale, rather than 'Salve' – not 'hail' but 'farewell'. If this was a piece for Therese Grob, one might well wonder to whom Schubert in 1819 was saying goodbye (see 'Schubert in Love?'). For a perfect and haunting example of his 'right and true devotion', one need look no further.

The Early Masses

> It is with faith that one first comes into the world, and it long precedes intelligence and knowledge; for in order to understand anything, one must first believe in something . . . Intelligence is nothing but analysed faith.
>
> Franz Schubert

Masses in F, G, Bb, C

What do the words 'a Mass' signify? To a churchman *The Mass* is the entire sequence of events at whose centre lies the transubstantiation of bread and wine into Christ's body and blood on their consecration by the celebrant at the Eucharist. This is an age-old mystery, codified by the Fathers of the Church during the dark ages. For a Roman Catholic churchgoer, too, *Mass* is clearly that, but it can be anything from a prescribed weekly social ritual to a profound act of spiritual nourishment. The same goes for members of other denominations, who share in the same mystery under different forms and under different names – the Anglican 'service' or 'communion', the Lutheran 'Gottesdienst', and so on.

To a musician, *a Mass* is a sequence of pieces setting to music those parts of the liturgy that recur in all celebrations of the Eucharist (the Ordinary) rather than those particular to the day (the Proper, which will be recited, chanted or sung in one or other composer's setting). Such a mass setting will normally have been composed with an actual 'service' in mind, so its component movements, in performance, would have been separated by all the other events of the Eucharist; even if conceived as a continuous musical whole, it

---

[15] Quietism: Passive attitude towards life with devotional contemplation and abandonment of the will, as form of religious mysticism (*Concise Oxford Dictionary*).

would not have been heard as such. In Schubert's Austria it was, indeed, illegal to perform a Mass except in a church, and the concert performance of masses developed only from the mid-nineteenth century onwards, when the Choral Society movement was one element in the growth of middle-class culture. But by the 1820s, with three movements of Beethoven's *Missa Solemnis* given at a concert in the Kärntnertortheater, there were signs how things were going.

A musician of no denomination, or even of no religion, is also very likely to find engrossing things in the Mass, as set to music by one or other master. Feelings of supplication and gratitude, an occasional sense of being something that only an act of overwhelming kindness can save from disgrace, wonder at things too great to comprehend, professions of belief – none of those are specific to one religion, for they form part of human nature. Schubert lived as a Roman Catholic in a Roman Catholic country, so the available channels for such intuitions were for him in the first line those offered by the Roman church, and the liturgical works considered in this book were part and parcel of his self-expression.

A musical setting of the Ordinary for concerted forces has always been a major undertaking, since in its fullest form, prior to the modern practice of singing the text in the vernacular, the 'Mass' consisted of the Greek invocation 'Kyrie eleison/Christe eleison/Kyrie eleison' (Lord have mercy on us, Christ have mercy on us, Lord have mercy on us); a lengthy Latin text (the remainder of the Ordinary is entirely in Latin), whose opening lines are thoroughly familiar to English speakers since they also occur in Handel's *Messiah* – 'Glory to God in the Highest, and peace on earth, good will towards men': there is a great deal more. Then come the Nicene Creed; the text sequence 'Sanctus, Sanctus, Sanctus . . . Pleni sunt coeli et terrae gloriae Tuae . . . Osanna in excelsis, Benedictus qui venit in Nomine Domini, Osanna' (Holy, Holy, Holy . . . Heaven and earth are full of Thy glory, Hosanna in the Highest, Blessed is he that cometh in the name of the Lord, Hosanna); and 'Agnus Dei qui tollis peccata mundi, miserere nobis . . . Dona nobis pacem' (Lamb of God, who taketh away the sins of the world, have mercy on us . . . Grant us peace). A composer will most likely engage with all of that only if there is some call for it, some hope of the result's being performed. He may set about his task as devout churchgoer, as creative artist fascinated by the text's ethical content, but most likely as both.

A short form of the mass, known since the sixteenth century as a Missa Brevis, originally consisted of very concise settings of all the movements, sometimes with different parts of the text sung at the same time; after the Reformation it might take the form, in the Lutheran service, of music to only the two opening movements, the *Kyrie* and *Gloria*. Schubert's masses set the entire text of the Ordinary, Nos 1, 5 and 6 being 'Missae Solemnes', 2 and 4 Missae Breves, with No. 3 something of a hybrid.

Attendance at Mass, not to mention active participation in it, was basic to Schubert's life as a chorister; given his father's moral standing as local schoolmaster it is hard to credit his having later been allowed to absent himself, even if he wanted to, while he still lived at home. But once he lived elsewhere he was no longer a willing churchgoer.[16]

In 1783 the Emperor Joseph had banned elaborate, instrumentally accompanied church music except at the Imperial Chapel and certain specified churches. Vienna's cathedral (the Stephansdom) was commented on as having fallen behind in repertoire and standard, for example by Vincent and Mary Novello in their *Mozart Pilgrimage* of 1829; fortunately Schubert's local Lichtental church was one of several in the suburbs where concerted music was allowed. It dated back a century and had a prosperous congregation well able to support a modest ensemble. The choir that sang there at the first performance of Schubert's earliest mass setting in 1814 is thought to have numbered between twenty-five and thirty including the soloists, the orchestra very slightly more.

The Mass in F major has been undervalued in accounts of his early life and music.[17] Some of its more extravert sections – what one might call its public face – are a shade conventional in the best sense, that of reflecting an obvious knowledge of and affection for the masses, notably Haydn's, which Schubert had sung so often. But wherever intimacy and tenderness are in place, something personal points far ahead, to his mature masterpieces. That is so in the *Kyrie*, and in a remarkably quiet, inward-looking confession of faith in the *Credo* (from which at seventeen he already saw fit to omit 'unam sanctam catholicam et apostolicam ecclesiam', one holy apostolic church). A discrepancy between a somewhat empty 'public' manner and a richly communicative private voice became apparent later in his career, clearly and deleteriously so in the score of *Fierrabras*;[18] it would even show itself in aspects of his final mass (E♭, 1828). In the one in F there is just the first hint of it, no more, for even a 'set piece' such as the fugal 'Cum sancto Spiritu' at the end of the *Gloria* has vitality and directness, as well as meeting the technical demands of fugue in exemplary fashion.

Of the nine and a half weeks it took Schubert to compose the F major Mass, more than three (30 May–22 June) were spent on the *Credo*, where like all his predecessors he made a clear musical break before the text that begins 'et incarnatus est' (and was incarnate). There, after a predominantly choral opening section, he used the solo voices. Where he was individual is that for 'Crucifixus etiam pro nobis' (He was crucified also for us) he reverted to a choral texture, whereas it was traditional to give the solo voices the entire middle section and reintroduce the choir only at 'Et resurrexit'.

The F major Mass is, all in all, a gentle, sunny work. Passages in it suggest that he had in his ears the sound of Mozart's *Ave Verum Corpus* (an influence first felt near the opening of the *Credo*, and later at bar 40 of the 'Dona nobis pacem') and of Beethoven's 6th ('Pastoral') Symphony (evoked in the wondrous string interludes in bars 74–7 of the closing 'Dona nobis pacem', and then

[16] McKay, *Franz Schubert.*
[17] Newbould (*SMM*) gives a sympathetic account of it.
[18] See 'Schubert and the Composition of *Fierrabras*'.

in its orchestral postlude). And yet one totally unexpected thing shows Schubert thinking hard and feeling deeply: at seventeen, he evidently felt a sense of terror at the thought of Christ's Second Coming, for after 'et resurrexit tertia die' (and on the third day He rose again) he set the words 'et iterum venturus est' (and He shall come again) to unexpectedly dramatic, violent music for the baritone soloist such as can be found in no setting by his great predecessors, nor in his own subsequent masses. The more obvious cues for strong expressiveness in this portion of the text are 'cum Gloria' (with Glory) and, particularly, 'judicare vivos et mortuos' (to judge the living and the dead). One or two Mozart masses show a slight rise in tension at this point, but purely with an eye to the longer text and 'vivos et mortuos'; Schubert is in with his 'shock-horror' chord the moment the Chosen One appears (glory or no glory), rather than waiting for the more rationally terrifying thought of Judgment. His final examination for the Teacher's Certificate assessed his religious knowledge as 'poor', but this music conveys an intuition of something 'tremendous' – a highly individual reaction suggesting monotheism, direct confrontation with an all-powerful force, rather than the pantheism that often seems to underlie his later music of loving acceptance.[19] Here is the soul's 'tremor' in face of the Absolute. For the pious listener such sounds might indeed have offended against Pope Benedict XIV's 1749 encyclical inveighing against 'operatic' church music, *Annus qui*. But behind it lies one of Schubert's earliest impulses of 'right and true devotion'.

At this point the 'Tremendum' is felt particularly through one unusual chord[20] (Ex. 3a) that creates confusion by offering a dissonance and its resolution simultaneously. Schubert knew what he was doing, for the same harmony breaks into the quiet music near the opening of the later subsection of the *Credo* devoted to the Holy Ghost ('qui ex Patre Filioque procedit', Ex. 3b). It looks ahead to the 1818 *Einsamkeit*, where a mountain stream thunders as it overcomes obstacles (und donnernd über Klippenhemmung/ Ergeht des

---

[19] A distinction put to me by Brother Thomas Joseph, formerly of the Community of St John, Notre Dame de Rimont, Fley, France.

[20] It can be viewed either as a dominant thirteenth in its last inversion, or as a dominant seventh under which the third of the resolution chord has been placed. In the G major Mass 'et iterum venturus est' shows a curious treatment of a dissonance (the 9th), which resolves in an unusual way. The effect is mildly disconcerting but not on the level of the F major Mass. The closely related harmony in *Der Einsame* differs (Schubert being too sensitive a craftsman to crack a peanut with a sledgehammer) in that the root of the dominant-seventh chord, e, which otherwise sounds throughout the passage in question, is not actually heard in the crucial chord (nor for that matter is the fifth, b), though it is there again in the upper part immediately the dissonance is resolved (fourth beat). On the other hand, as a delicate further touch of colour, the (rootless) dominant seventh is enhanced to a (rootless) dominant ninth by the inclusion of f.

Ex. 13 F major Mass, *Der Einsame*

Giessbachs kühner Strömung), and the chorus *Gott in der Natur* (D. 757) written for the singing-pupils of his friend Anna Fröhlich in August 1822; there it matches ideas of terror and power (Sein Wagen Sturm, und donnerndes Gewölk und Blitze sein Gespann).[21] A few weeks later it figured in a haunting lead-back in the Unfinished Symphony's slow movement (bars 130 and 132), and then in the scherzo of the 1824 Duo for piano duet (bars 37–8, and matching point 36 bars back from the end of the principal section), where it adds a *frisson* to an otherwise ebullient movement. A near-relative of it appears rather curiously in the 1825 song *Der Einsame* (The Solitary, D. 800, Ex. 3c, whose determined, more-than-stoical good temper comes nearest to showing signs of strain at its climactic moment, the text (addressed to the domestic cricket)[22] being 'Wenn Eu're Lied das Schweigen bricht/ Bin ich nicht ganz allein' (When your song breaks the silence/ I am not quite alone). At this touchingly wistful moment the harmony is very akin to the one that conveys existential terror in the early mass: the poet's 'prospect of total solitude' may have been more unsettling to the composer than he cares to admit. In all of that we find one of Schubert's subcutaneous 'red threads', that tell of a soul caught up in 'le Devenir'.

Of the F major Mass's four solo singers, the soprano is given a prominent but not dominating part. She makes an early appearance in the *Kyrie*, returns with similar music near the end, and is the first soloist heard in the *Gloria*, but after that she merges into the background. Silent in the *Credo*, she is on no more than an equal footing with her partners (second soprano and two tenors, for Schubert chose his soloists from the choir with no need to worry about fees for extra star singers) in the round that makes up the *Benedictus*; after the tenor and bass have contributed to the sombre *Agnus Dei* she reappears as merely one of the quartet in the closing 'Dona nobis pacem'.

Schubert later confirmed (see 'Schubert in Love?') that this music for soprano had first been sung, and very beautifully, by Therese Grob. He had written self-indulgently for her voice in his first *Salve Regina*, and his third, from a full year after the composition of the F major Mass, was another such display piece. The soprano writing in the mass is of a different order, fitting its context perfectly without making her show off, and it is a measure of the young composer's professionalism that he could turn any personal feelings for a singer to such impeccably good account. He would have had a precedent in Haydn's 'Missa in Angustiis' (or 'Nelson' Mass: we English like to remember the ones we won); that, in view of the special circumstances of its composition, was the great man's most vigorous, assertive liturgical work, dominated by a soprano soloist who

---

21 In many ways the chorus is also like a first draft for the great 1825 song *Die Allmacht*, to a more generally pantheistic text, but in its final section the choir abruptly changes tempo where the song continues as it was.

22 'There are not in the unseen world voices more gentle and more true that may be so implicitly relied on, or that are so certain to give none but tenderest counsel, as the voices in which the Spirits of the Fireside and the Hearth address themselves to human kind.' Charles Dickens, *The Cricket on the Hearth*.

Ex. 3a F major Mass, *Credo*

Ex. 3b F major Mass, *Credo*

Ex. 3c *Der Einsame*

'ran the show' in a way surpassing anything Schubert had occasion to invent for Therese! Had Schubert submitted to an overriding urge to give her a specially prominent place in his early mass, it would be more prominent by far; we shall see in 'Schubert in Love?' that in the *Benedictus* sections of the Mass in B♭ and especially the one in C he was inspired to write remarkable things with her in mind.

The F major Mass's *Sanctus* anticipates those of his final two Masses in its wave-like build-up of power over the threefold invocation, 'Holy, Holy, Holy'. A year later, soon after composing another in G major, Schubert wrote an Offertory, 'Tres sunt qui testimonium dant' (There are Three who bear witness. . . and those Three are One, D. 181), where both the middle section and the recapitulatory final one throw in a quite unexpected, loud dissonant chord (a 'mere' diminished-seventh, as if he had just experienced *Don Giovanni*'s mortal battle between the Don and the Commendatore, but still mightily effective). So the Trinity, too, seems to have touched a sensitive spot in the young composer. His very late *Tantum Ergo* offers a similar but more sophisticated shock at much the same points.

In the *Benedictus* Schubert adhered to Viennese tradition and called upon the solo voices, but specified two sopranos and two tenors rather than the customary soprano, alto, tenor and bass. That worked well, since the same slightly asymmetrical melody was to be delivered by each soloist in turn, with more-or-less-identical music heard four times over; a S – A – T – B quartet could have made that harder to write. The second, third and fourth vocal entries, and resourceful reorchestration of the accompaniment, provide variety. Schubert returned to that idea in the *Benedictus* of the G major Mass, where he solved any problems in writing a line equally suitable for soprano/tenor and baritone by confining his melody to a relatively close compass. Maybe he felt after the F major's performance that four statements were too many; certainly he confined himself to three in the G major, the alto remaining silent. It nonetheless becomes crystal clear that the musical model is the (four-part) quartet in canon from Act 1 of Beethoven's opera *Fidelio*. In the F major Mass, one could without the benefit of hindsight point as plausibly to a round such as the A♭ section in the Act 2 Finale of Mozart's *Così fan Tutte*; in particular, the five-bar opening phrase runs counter to a totally symmetrical pattern in Beethoven's melody.

Schubert also tried to give the F major Mass touches of a hitherto-unattempted cyclic form: the main motive of the *Credo* turns the line of the *Kyrie*'s introductory two bars upside down. Still more significantly, the main theme of the concluding 'Dona nobis pacem' reuses and varies the beginning of the *Kyrie* proper.[23] That movement's two bars of introductory orchestral chords are still in the air, for Schubert varies their harmonic progression at the end of both *Kyrie* and 'Dona nobis pacem'. Schubert here enchants his hearers, seeming to conjure up some idyllic landscape.[24]

---

[23] Süssmayr's completion of the Mozart *Requiem*, not unknown in Vienna in Schubert's day, had fallen back on the opening music to round off the work; though a *faute de mieux* solution, this could have interested Schubert.

[24] The A♭ Mass strikes a similar note of rustic idyll, again in F major, not in 'Dona nobis pacem' but in 'Pleni sunt coeli'.

Ex. 4a *Kyrie*: opening

Ex. 4b *Kyrie*: ending

Ex. 4c *Agnus Dei* (Dona nobis pacem): ending

On a more purely technical level, some chromaticisms in the descending top line of the *Kyrie* are removed in the 'Dona', while a perhaps even more important simplification is that the latter is composed mostly in rounded two- or four-bar phrases, where the *Kyrie* dropped in a significant number that were of uneven length. Such flexibility of phrase-structure was to stay with Schubert throughout his life, and would be crucial in giving the late E♭Mass its special contour.

There may be one very small touch of Haydn in bars 48–9 of the *Agnus Dei*, where an expected major chord (dominant) is replaced by its minor version, a reminiscence of the old 'church modes' also found in the spinning song in

Haydn's *The Seasons* (*Autumn*) as the text speaks of outward beauty combined with inner purity.

In 1822, eight years after composing the F major Mass, Schubert showed signs of wanting to round off the one in A♭ in the same way, though with nothing like so literal a repetition. It was certainly not an idea absorbed from Haydn, whose concluding pleas for peace show a euphoria like a self-fulfilling prophecy. For Schubert, peace and mercy already seem identical; but (as in Beethoven's 'Pastoral' Symphony) the peace at the end of the F major Mass is of this world, not the next. An acknowledged sub-genre at the time was the 'Pastoral' Mass, emphasising the rustic mood most famously exemplified in *Messiah*'s 'Pastoral Symphony'; a 12/8 time-signature (replaceable by 6/8 + 6/8) is an essential part of that, and Schubert's first essay, though emphatically a Missa Solemnis, has touches of it.

In April 1815 he replaced his magical closing section with an energetic and rather longer fugal 'Dona Nobis Pacem' (D. 185). It too is in 6/8; the original consists of 87 bars in an Andante tempo, the replacement of 139, Allegro moderato. A more outspoken plea for peace, it could have been composed for a service during the public alarm over Napoleon's escape from exile on Elba, even as the Congress of Vienna continued to divide the spoils of supposed victory; it has interesting features such as a repeated 'grinding to a halt' followed by a dramatic high soprano invocation, 'pacem', but it is hard to imagine its generally weaving the original's spell.

Between 2 and 7 March 1815 Schubert made his second setting of the Ordinary (D. 167, in G major), a Missa Brevis. Its completion within six days, where its predecessor had had nine weeks devoted to it and been ready three months before its performance date, argues an urgent commission, almost certainly for the same Lichtental church, where Ferdinand was unpaid organist. The mass has aroused comment on account of a Beethoven reference[25] at the start of the *Credo* – a resemblance between the First Prisoner's solo in Act 1 and Schubert's *Credo* theme, the common idea being unwavering faith.

Ex. 5 Upper line, 1st Prisoner's song (Fidelio), lower line, G major Mass

[25] David Cairns ('Schubert, Promise and Fulfilment', in *Responses*, 1973) pointed to the resemblance between the *Credo*'s opening ('I believe') and the First Prisoner's song – 'We will trustingly build on God's help'. Schubert encountered *Fidelio* for the first time while composing not the G major but the F major mass, probably on 23 May 1814 when the final version was first performed. McKay detects a clear influence of *Fidelio* on Schubert's early

A different musical connection between *Fidelio* and another section of the G major Mass, the *Benedictus*, has already been hinted at. There are enough stories of great musicians' incredible aural retentiveness to make it plausible that a single hearing of the canonic quartet from *Fidelio* would have been enough to keep it at the back of Schubert's mind for the rest of his life. Don Fernando finally arrives in the name of the law, meaning here the feudal lord, the King. It would be no surprise if an inventive, impressionable young genius associated rescue with the idea of 'qui venit in Nomine Domini'. Beethoven's canonic quartet would be a highpoint in any work, though nobody can say just why Schubert picked on it in quoting *Fidelio*. Like the First Prisoner's song, it is in G major, and that could have influenced Schubert's choice of key for his new mass. The ramifications of his second *Fidelio* quotation in the G major Mass are examined in 'Schubert in Love?'

The G major Mass has been popular for almost two centuries since its composition. It was first published with another composer, Robert Führer, claiming authorship: there are known to have been performances at the great monastery of Klosterneuburg, a few miles up the Danube from Vienna, in 1831, 1842, 1843, 1844, 1846, 1855, 1856, 1857 and 1859. The Hofburgkapelle itself did not use the setting by its former member until his old friend Randhartinger, by then Imperial Director of Music (Hofkapellmeister), had it performed under the Deputy Director, Johann Herbeck, on Christmas Day 1865. That completed a remarkable double for Herbeck, who had eight days earlier conducted the forty-years-overdue first hearing of the two completed movements of the B minor Unfinished Symphony. The 1945 *Schubert* by Arthur Hutchings, written from the standpoint of one challenging the 'givens' of mid-century English musical life (does any other book on Schubert find reason to invoke the Victorian church composer John Bacchus Dykes, 1823–1876?), called the G major Mass 'a grand little service ... banished from Westminster [Roman] Cathedral but nourished at [Anglican] St Paul's'.

Such affection for a 'minor' work springs from something more than its generally song-like[26] character; listeners unversed in the technicalities of composition respond to the loving care Schubert took over its every detail. There is the endearing way the *Credo* turns to account the dry pizzicato bass that accompanied its opening; the line returns subtly modified as a sinuous melody high in the first violins, accompanying the text 'qui propter nos homines et propter nostram salutam descendit de coelis' (who for us men and for our salvation came down from Heaven). It would be hard to imagine a finer intuitive reaction to the idea of the incarnation of the Deity. And in the canonic *Benedictus* the counter-subjects, not only for the voices but also in the instrumental parts, are worked out with great sensitivity and expertise. It could have been done in a far more routine way, but Schubert is always alive to

operas *Des Teufels Lustschloss*, whose second version was completed on 22 October 1814, and *Fernando*, completed on 9 July 1815.

[26] The word applied to this in the authoritative study of Schubert's Masses, Hans Jaskulsky's *Schuberts lateinische Messen*, 1986, is 'liedhaft'.

melodic possibilities, playing off his basic scalewise movement against one variant after another of broken-chord and S-curve melodic figures. Here, from whatever motivation, he was working at something that engaged his strongest sympathies.

In a Mass intended for Lichtental it would have been logical to have Therese Grob in mind for sections such as the *Benedictus* where the soloists traditionally came to the fore, and although in that section of the G major Mass she simply leads the way, he made her the leading soloist in the *Agnus Dei*, where she has two solo passages, the bass one, and the middle two soloists none.

This jewel of a Missa Brevis found an echo a few weeks later when on the 26 March Schubert set to work on a group of settings of the poet Theodor Körner, with whom he had spent an unforgettable evening two years earlier. They had seen and heard Gluck's *Iphigenia in Tauris*, and Körner had given the adolescent musician firm advice about sticking to his intention to become a composer. Körner himself was only in his early twenties, but already working successfully as dramatist at the Vienna Burgtheater. He very soon went off to join in the war of liberation, and in August of the same year he was killed. Schubert waited two years before he began to set his poetry to music. One song from March 1815 was *Das war ich!*, where he set out from a verbalisation of an idea of love. The song throws light on Schubert at what may have been a unique moment in his life; its full significance is considered in 'Schubert in Love?'

Schubert's third mass, in B♭ major (D. 324), was begun on the eleventh of November 1815, a month after the probable composition date of *Erlkönig*. He marked the *Gloria* '6.12.1815'. The full score of his Mayrhofer opera *Die Freunde von Salamanka* is dated as soon after as the 18th of that month, so the mass may well not have been completed until early in 1816. This time nothing is known about any commission. The B♭ has the dimensions of a Missa Brevis but is scored like a Missa Solemnis, with oboes, bassoons, trumpets, timpani and even a passage in the *Kyrie* for three trombones, which can hardly have been the only one he intended. A surviving organ part calls the work a 'missa solaimne'. This is by some way his most 'Haydnesque' mass, concise and gentle and with more than one reflection of the world of Haydn's string quartets. Schubert was familiar with their wealth of fine music from the family's chamber-music sessions and from working with the Seminary orchestra, where they were played in orchestral transcription. Tactful touches of colour from trumpets and timpani enhance the Haydn resemblance – and it should be remembered that Schubert knew the latter's 'Nelson' Mass intimately. There could be an echo of its *Benedictus* (not the only one in Schubert's output, see 'Harvest') in the latter part of the *Kyrie*, where the trumpets are given some curiously menacing dotted rhythms, first with a falling octave followed by repeated notes, repeated notes, and towards the end seeming to revolve like windmills. The B♭ Mass's position halfway between simple Brevis style and a grander tradition is apparent as the second 'Kyrie eleison' section develops the music of the first, rather than simply reverting to it; a Missa Solemnis may at this point offer new music, though even in his grander masses Schubert still preferred simply to elaborate on that heard earlier. A series of rising sequences is a pointed quotation from the 'Nelson' Mass.

Structurally, the movement relies greatly on reappearances of its opening music, with a quite individual instrumental theme repeating in sequence its bar-long opening motive. It is an exuberant figure, and this *Gloria* has been called 'theatrical';[27] Schubert was probably writing it at the same time as *Die Freunde von Salamanka*. His devotion to *Fidelio* persisting, he clearly quotes that Beethoven opera's final chorus, where Leonore is hailed as her husband's saviour, in the music for 'Laudamus te'. For the first time in his masses he omits from this section the words 'suscipe deprecationem nostram' (receive our prayer), an omission he repeated in his final three.

As in the two final masses, the 'Domine Deus, Agnus Dei' section is long and serious. Of the customary points for fugal elaboration, 'Cum sancto Spiritu' (with the Holy Ghost) to some extent conforms to tradition, but is a curiously round-like fugue that uses to engagingly different effect the traditional way of beginning;[28] here again there is a model in the 'Nelson' Mass, in fact in its corresponding section, though the theme itself seems taken from Beethoven's Mass in C. Schubert's round is all the more endearing for its accompaniment of whizzing string figures, unusually fleet even by the standards of Viennese concerted church music; a quite sizeable assertive coda in a quicker tempo opens quietly after an interrupted cadence that evokes yet another and very dramatic point in Beethoven's opera, the moment at the climax of the dungeon scene when Leonore pulls her gun on Pizarro.

The *Credo* is concise indeed. At the choral opening the strings are still going full tilt, and as in the *Gloria* there is a strong feeling of a 'cantus fermus' from traditional plainchant. 'Et incarnatus' is, for a change, a bass solo, followed by a hushed choral 'Crucifixus', a contrast of mood and resource found in Haydn's *Mariazell* and *Wind Band (Harmonie)* masses. Once again Schubert runs counter to the general Viennese tendency to give this entire middle section to the solo voices. 'Et resurrexit' literally recapitulates the opening music, as does the quite brief, non-fugal 'Et vitam venturi saeculi' (and the life of the world to come). At 'qui locutus est per prophetas' (who hath spoken by the Prophets), choir and orchestra are in unison, as they will be at the same point in the A♭ Mass. This can be sensed as 'a prophet's voice';[29] Schubert's passages in unison are often of interest.

---

[27] By Ronald Stringham in his pioneering 1964 dissertation on Schubert's Masses.

[28] Statement-and-answer on tonic-and-dominant.

[29] Jaskulsky. Other choral unison or octave passages in the A♭ Mass are in the *Credo* at 'descendit de coelis', 'et iterum venturus est', and 'qui locutus est per prophetas' (a striking line of falling thirds), and in the *Agnus Dei* the two choral 'miserere nobis' phrases after the opening 'Agnus Dei, qui tollis peccata mundi'. 'Unison' choral writing (I adhere to the convention that 'unison' means the same note or line, not only at precisely the same pitch but at two or more different octaves, see *Grove* entries 'unison', 'all' unisono') can produce a most effectively solemn or mysterious effect. One of the most famous such uses is at the *a capella* opening of the *Agnus Dei* in Verdi's *Requiem*. When in the concluding chorus of Bach's *Actus Tragicus* (Cantata No. 198, Funeral Ode in memory of Saxony's Queen Caroline) the libretto speaks of the poet's epitaph

The *Sanctus* opens with a great crescendo and rising choral line, *pp* to *ff*, B♭ to G, something Schubert was to repeat and even overdo in the late E♭ Mass. At the end of the main *Sanctus* section the 'Osanna' continues in the same *Adagio maestoso* tempo. That was something Schubert had also done in the F major Mass, where the 'Osanna', with exactly the same tempo marking, was kept as short as possible. Here it runs to seven bars. The other four masses adhere to the usual practice of breaking into a quicker tempo, reusing the ensuing music when 'Osanna' is repeated after the *Benedictus*. Curiously, the repeat of 'Osanna' in the B♭ Mass is marked to be performed at the rather quicker tempo (Andante con moto) of the *Benedictus*, despite the fact that the music is identical. A good conductor's sleight-of-hand will be able to make sense of this apparent lapse of concentration on Schubert's part.

Of greater musical interest, indeed the most striking feature of this movement, is that the *Benedictus* occupies about three-quarters of it. Here Schubert for the first time in the work spreads himself in Missa Solemnis style; the section is entirely for the soloists, the top (soprano, Therese!) line naturally dominating since it mostly carries the melody. It opens with a passage for the strings that could be from a Haydn quartet slow movement; a brief, tender figure beginning with a violin trill returns many times to form a bridge, bring about a cadence or offer an interlude. The vocal melody sets out with a rising and falling fourth (see Ex. 6), a figure already met in the 'Domine Deus, Agnus Dei' of the G major Mass, and reminiscent of Cherubino's 'Voi che sapete' in Mozart's *Le Nozze di Figaro*.[30] There seems a further *Figaro* reference, to that *ne plus ultra* of reconciliation, the quiet ensemble before the final scurry and flurry. All in all, this leisurely section offers the most alluringly Schubertian music in the entire B♭ Mass; Haydn has been charmingly and originally absorbed, even if there is nothing so strange or new as to make one detect future greatness. With the echo of this movement in the corresponding section of the next mass, in C major, it will become clearer still that here, as in so many of Schubert's 'self-referring' passages, we find a link in a longer chain that usually culminates in something remarkable – in this case the slow movement of the Great C Major Symphony (see 'Harvest').

The *Agnus Dei*'s opening two bars for the strings are another hint of the world

---

for the beloved queen, 'which we would read' (Der Dichter spricht, Wir wollen's lesen), Bach makes his choir sing the ensuing tribute with the same vocal line in all the voices at three different octave levels, giving an effect of impressive public unity. A strange example in Schubert comes in the 1826 Seidl setting *Widerspruch* (Contradiction) for voice (or male voices) and piano, where within a seemingly carefree, vigorous song the middle strophes, capturing a moment at the top of a mountain, are composed entirely in unison: the literal 'narrowing down' occurs at the very point where agoraphobia momentarily sets in ('Ach, wie beschränkt, wie eng/ Wird mir's im Luftgedräng' – Ah, how limited, how narrowed I feel, hemmed in by the air). This is the more enigmatic since unison is also briefly used near the beginning when the text speaks of the opposite, of 'the walls expanding' as one gets into the country. The textual prompt thus appears to be change rather than a specific mood.

30 Brown detected an obvious echo of the latter in the opening 'greeting' of Schubert's first *Salve Regina*.

of chamber music; then a series of brief solo entries[31] is tactfully supported by the choir. Schubert sensed that, as the final section, the ensuing 'Dona nobis pacem' must be of more considerable proportions. A nicely judged binary form brings this Haydnesque mass to a fittingly cheerful, untroubled close; soloists and choir amiably co-exist almost throughout, only the very end being purely choral. A brief passage of D minor 6/8 is a faint reminder of the spinning-song aspect of *Gretchen am Spinnrade*, or (more likely) of the spinning song in the *Autumn* section of Haydn's *The Seasons*, already briefly invoked in the F major Mass's 'Dona'. Schubert is still alive to the possibility of heightening a work's conclusion, for at the start of the coda a previous treatment of the choir's 'pacem' in echo now becomes a double echo, first in the orchestra and then for the soloists.

The B♭ Mass was noticed outside Vienna. On the sixth of October 1824 Ferdinand wrote to Franz about visiting Hainburg, on the Danube just the Vienna side of Pressburg (Bratislava), where he was coopted to play the organ in a mass 'by a well-known and famous composer' whose name escaped them; it turned out to be his brother's third mass, in an almost exemplary performance.

The 1816 C major Mass was the only one of Schubert's published in his lifetime, in 1825, with a dedication to his early teacher Michael Holzer, choirmaster of the Lichtental church. It appeared again soon after his death, with a replacement *Benedictus* for chorus, and was one of the pieces with which he seemed on his way into the established church repertoire. It is scored for violins and continuo, without violas, i.e. a 'Salzburg' scoring:[32] the middle months of 1816 were a time of great involvement with Mozart, as Schubert's diary entries show, and after the song-like Mass in G and Haydnesque one in B♭ the C major 'comes nearest to the world of Mozart's Missae Breves' (Jaskulsky). Another considerable Salzburg figure had been Haydn's brother Michael, whose church music figured alongside Joseph's at the Hofburgkapelle; in Salzburg in 1825 Schubert made a point of visiting his grave, and wrote of him in the warmest terms.

The soprano soloist is prominent throughout the C major Mass, and it takes little intuition to point one yet again towards Therese Grob. Whereas the solo-quartet passages in Schubert's liturgical works usually come in alternation to a choral texture, here the choir seems there almost as occasional relief from and for the soloists. In the *Credo* Schubert did something most uncharacteristic, forgetting (or for some other reason omitting) to set the important words 'Ex Maria Virgine' (of the Virgin Mary) after 'Et incarnatus est' – the last thing one would have expected of him, and perhaps the only argument supporting the idea that his omissions arose from forgetfulness. Two striking anticipations of the Great C Major Symphony are considered in 'Harvest' – a descending phrase

---

[31] Two for soprano, then with tenor and soprano in imitation.
[32] Schubert later added optional parts for trumpets and timpani, and (before the work's publication) for two oboes or clarinets.

in the *Gloria*, and the opening line of the *Credo*. In the *Sanctus* the theme at 'Osanna' is very like the main subject of the 4th Symphony's slow movement.

For the second time in Schubert's masses we find a connection between two *Benedictus* sections. In the C major, he takes up a thread from the Bb, retaining the key (F major) and the opening melodic outline.

Ex. 6 Openings of *Benedictus* vocal line in Bb and C major Masses

(See also Ex. 7.) Here the soprano soloist comes most fully into her own, for the whole section is hers, whereas in the previous mass she had the other solo singers for company. Her undulating line, accompanied by obbligato parts for the two violins and cello,[33] makes up one of Schubert's typical 'walking' (gehend) movements: the introduction and slow movement of the Great C Major Symphony are but two of the finest examples. Here is a heartfelt Therese piece, but of a new kind, lyrical rather than coloratura, with an enterprising use of wide intervals. The C major Mass was not performed until 1825, so this movement's evident preoccupation with the soprano voice, and probably one particular soprano voice, had to do with Schubert's inmost feelings, not with a prospective performance. It is considered in more detail in 'Schubert in Love?'

By the time Schubert wrote another mass, he had seen a great deal more of the world, and it proved a major work, in many ways summing up and rounding off the first half of his career. Some biographers view the years between the C major and Ab Masses as a time of 'crisis' for him, but that is a curious term to apply to a time of steady development before the real crisis of 1822–3. What stands beyond doubt is that between 1816 and the beginning of work on the Ab Mass late in 1819 he gave every sign of the most thoughtful interest in things of the spirit.

The music that resulted is considered in Chapter 3, but there is more to say about his late teens, and for that matter about the *Benedictus* of the C major Mass. Like Beethoven, Bruckner and Brahms, Schubert never married: the enormous role played in those three composers' lives by the idea of woman is a matter of record, and it is time to see where Schubert stood.

---

[33] And, in the final published version, the first oboe.

Schubert in Love?

Half our literature, highbrow and popular, for the past three hundred years, has assumed that what is probably a rare experience is one which almost everybody has, or ought to have; if they do not experience it then there must be something wrong with them.

W.H. Auden

Benedictus of C major Mass; Das war ich!

It may seem strange to admit erotic links to other humans into a consideration of 'right and true devotion' – but who save a total misanthrope can fail to sense a mysterious attraction to others, having little to do with reason, achievement or even obvious sexual chemistry, and everything to do with irrational perceptions, intuitions that defy conscious formulation? Another person, too, can be 'mirum', so one cannot omit from a search for 'the inmost Schubert' the complex of problems and opportunities summed up in his century as The Woman Question – nor, given the tenor of recent speculation, what the century just ended neglected to call The Homo Question.

Biographical evidence about his relations with women is, to put it mildly, confusing. When music came into it, he reacted warmly; the actress Sophie Müller, for example, was also a good enough singer to perform his songs, and they counted as at least good friends. The tutelary deities around his circle, notably the four singing and music-teaching Fröhlich sisters, kept an eye on him and knew what he was about. But Anselm Hüttenbrenner recalled him as clumsy and unforthcoming in his general relations with the opposite sex, as he had reason to be once he was ill. At times one finds him behaving or using words to meet at least the minimum requirements for being thought (whether sincerely or as cover for something else) 'normally' heterosexual, a sensible precaution in days when even an aristocrat like the poet Count Platen had to be very careful to camouflage his homosexuality. The most notorious source is the light-hearted remark in a letter home from holiday, 'there are eight girls in the house where I live, nearly all of them pretty – as you see, one has plenty to do'. Such is the stuff of legend, and of Kitsch. On the other hand, not one love-letter from Schubert to a woman[34] has come down to us (which is less than conclusive proof that he wrote none). Many letters address his male friends in effusive terms. Such language was nothing untoward, for in Schubert's day emotions and tears flowed much more freely than they now do.

His 1818 visit to Zseliz in Hungary, as tutor to the children of a branch of the Esterházy family, introduced him to a refreshing figure, the Viennese-born

[34] A point made by Kramer in *Franz Schubert, Sexuality, Subjectivity, Song.*

chambermaid/lady's maid Pepi Pöcklhofer,[35] who was already thirty if Schubert judged her age correctly. She could have been anything from friend in need to partner in affair ('the manager [is] my rival', he wrote to his friends on 8 September). A return visit in 1824 marked the effective start of a rather mysterious relationship with the younger Esterhazy Countess.

His principal known feminine friend during his teens was Therese Grob, already met as performer of the first *Salve Regina* and the early masses. His friends' late-in-life reminiscences of their relationship must be taken with a mountain of salt. One from Seminary days, Anton Holzapfel, said forty years after the event that Schubert wrote to him in 1815 about his deep love for Therese, and that he made a 'bombastic and absurd' attempt, likewise in a letter, to talk him out of it. Anselm Hüttenbrenner claimed, again in the 1850s, that after Therese's marriage Schubert said he had been deeply in love with her, that she loved him too, that for three years *she hoped he would marry her* (an idea whose unreality is compounded by the recent discovery mentioned in the next paragraph), and that the fact of her eventual marriage 'still hurt him'. Holzapfel recalled her as 'by no means a beauty, but well-built, rather plump and with a fresh, childlike round face [and] a lovely soprano voice', while Hüttenbrenner had Schubert referring to her as 'not exactly pretty' and with a pock-marked face, but 'a heart, a heart of gold . . . She sang the soprano solos in my mass most beautifully and with deep feeling'.

A recently discovered memoir in the Austrian National Library by Robert Franz Müller (1864–1933), *Franz Schubert und die Familie Grob*, makes clear, on the other hand, how close the entire Grob and Schubert families were. Müller, grandson of one of Therese's best friends, emphasised that Schubert seemed as close to her cellist brother Heinrich as to her, and that Ferdinand and Ignaz visited the Grob house oftener than he did. The researcher Rita Steblin, who discovered all this ('Therese Grob, New Documentary Research', *Brille*, Jan. 2002) stresses that it by no means disproves the idea of his being strongly attracted to Therese, rather that it confirms his friends' impression of an inability to express his deepest feelings except in music. Müller was also categorical that even in old age Therese had no inkling of Schubert's having been 'in love' with her, until Kreissle von Hellborn's pioneering biographical work conjured up the charming phantom of a romance between them. As for the 'Therese Grob album' into which in 1815 Schubert copied out seventeen of his songs, it seems as likely that it was handed to Heinrich (perhaps in the hope that he would pass it on to her) as to the singer herself. It certainly passed into the possession of his heirs.

Franz's failure in 1816 to secure a well-paid teaching post in Laibach (Ljubljana) must have put an end to any fantasy of his marrying Therese; whoever won a silk-factory-owner's daughter must have prospects. When in 1827 Schubert came across Wilhelm Müller's poems and made them the text for

---

[35] A true Susanna-figure, she was promoted from 'Stubenmädchen' to 'Kammerjungfer' the year he visited Zseliz, later married (sure enough) the count's valet, and her final title was Kammerfrau (Lady in Waiting).

Winterreise, the loss of his health rather than of a loved one (let alone of the prospect of social democracy) would have weighed heaviest on him; yet he could have noted with grim approval the line in *Die Wetterfahne*, 'Ihr Kind ist eine reiche Braut' (their child is a rich bride), for his relations with Therese had had the final line drawn under them on 21 November 1820, the day of her marriage, right under his nose in the Lichtental church, to a master baker, Johann Bergmann. A baker would always have the prospect of eager customers. Hüttenbrenner alone recorded a reaction; five years since the compilation of the song-book was a long time for so active a mind at so formative a stage, and Schubert's comments, if authentic, suggest warmth and a degree of regret but scarcely a broken heart. However, a great composer's heart is in his music, and the weeks after the marriage produced two remarkable outbursts, a String Quartet, never completed, in C minor (D. 703) and a turbulent setting of a poem by the arch-Romantic Friedrich Schlegel about creative inspiration, *Im Walde* (D. 708). The fever continued well into 1821.

If we are to worm ourselves deeper into Schubert's soul in the matter of Therese, it is worth turning the clock back to his earliest years. He was born into a district something between village and suburb, only lately assimilated into the city of Vienna, in an age when the working day began at sunrise, to end at sunset, and he was thrown into a house full of competing siblings, where his father also taught a whole lot more children. His mother was pregnant for about a third of his first four years,[36] and the streets of his home district would have been a safe place to play and wander. Goldschmidt[37] picked up Schubert's sister's recollection that one person the young boy attached himself to was a carpenter's apprentice who spent some of his time in a piano workshop; there Franz Peter would have first got his hands on a keyboard. The area where he spent his first years, the Himmelpfortgrund (loosely and quite unsuitably[38] translatable as Heaven's Gate) lay between two streams and on a slight slope with a good drying wind, so among the workers congregating there were Vienna's washerwomen, long-standing and dynastic as, for example, the present-day costermongers on west London's Portobello Road, and given to singing as they worked on the laundry. There was a wash-house very near to where Schubert was born; the women serviced not only the public but even the Emperor, at an address in the Säulengasse near the house bought by Schubert's father when Franz was four. The ideal of the 'Waschermadl' 'embodied qualities the Viennese of both sexes would have been glad to claim for themselves: humour, charm, a natural attractiveness, the right approach to

---

[36] Franz Peter, born 31.1.1797; Aloisia Magdalena, conceived 3.1799, b. 17.12.99, d. 18.12.99; Maria Theresia, conceived 12.1800, b. 17.9 01.

[37] *Schubert, Ein Lebensbild*, p. 47.

[38] It consisted of 86 properties housing 3,000 people, a mixture of workers at the new factories owned by middle-class entrepreneurs such as the Grobs, craftsmen who in many cases had lived in the area for generations, and day-labourers. The district 'swarmed with children' (Goldschmidt). The factory-owners also owned the apartment houses so could make a further good living from rent. These new out-of-town areas became the proving-ground for the aspirations to a freer life that finally broke loose in the 1830 and 1848 revolutions.

working and to enjoying themselves'.[39] Something resembling that freshness and charm (rendered in German by the untranslatable word 'Schmelz') is found in Renoir's extraordinary painting in the Baltimore Art Gallery, 'Washerwomen': they are idealised figures, perfectly round as roses. A more down-to-earth picture of Viennese 'Waschweiber' is in the Historisches Museum der Stadt Wien.

It takes little imagination to see the infant Franz Peter in his element with cheerful, vocalising Viennese femininity, and made something of a fuss of. Where better to inhale the mixed breath of melody and the common folk than among the washerwomen of the Himmelpfortgrund? Here was a matrix for later reactions to the opposite sex.

An early attachment to the female singing voice would have found its natural continuation when a decade later he came to know Therese. Whether a powerful reaction of that kind has any bearing on the controversies over Schubert's sexuality is a moot point, but something could be learned from the story of the undoubtedly heterosexual Mozart and the soprano Aloysia Weber, even though their relationship started well after the composer's years of puberty. By the time they met in Mannheim in 1776, Mozart, on his way to Paris with his mother to seek renewed fame and lasting fortune, was all of twenty. With him the loved one's person and voice were as one. As he became deeply involved with Aloysia a new inventiveness pervaded music such as the set of violin sonatas he began to write in Mannheim. It was as if with his total command of violin and piano he felt two sides of himself coming together; as if he were playing both instruments at once. In that respect Schubert, with his passion for singing, was in an even better, in fact ideal position: he could and did sing his songs to his own accompaniment, and it has been plausibly argued[40] that a singer's approach is in place throughout his music, with a range of performing implications not immediately apparent from his notation. Mozart's 'Mannheim' sonatas show an exuberance, a feeling of 'anything can happen', like that in the mind of a young man sensing a total identification with someone in the outside world who has come to embody a whole hidden side of himself.

Once he was back from Paris, bereaved and unsuccessful, Aloysia had no further immediate use for Mozart, who took it very hard; but in the course of 1779 his creativity staged a man-size fight-back with the composition of the Violin–Viola Sinfonia Concertante, Concerto for two pianos, the 'Posthorn' Serenade, the Singspiel *Zaide* and possibly the Violin Sonata in Bb, K. 378. His reactions to her evolved over his final twelve years: his labile verbalising faculty, ever on the *qui-vive* to say what his partner or correspondent wanted to hear, made him write of her to his father as a 'cold woman with a nasty mind' (she being by then safely married to the actor Lange), after which second provisional conclusion they were in contact for a few years more. The glowing music he wrote for her in Vienna is what in the true Hofmannsthal spirit I prefer to trust. It even strikes me that the

[39] Helga Maria Wolf, *Damals am Alsergrund*, Vienna, 1991.
[40] David P. Schroeder, 'Schubert the Singer', *The Music Review*, Vol. 49, 1988.

florid *Et incarnatus* of the 1782–3 C Minor Mass is far better suited to the supreme singer Aloysia than to her differently endowed sister Konstanze, who was supposed to sing it as part of the 'conciliation' with her future father-in-law Leopold Mozart. Here could be a case of 'the second-best bride'.

Aloysia's reactions to Mozart were still more enduring; throughout a career fraught with pregnancies, collapses, sick-leave and amazing recoveries she remained one of the great Constanzes in *Die Entführung* until well into the nineteenth century, revering his memory even as she herself came to be revered as a fine artist and superb colleague. So much for coldness and nastiness: the self-preservative instinct takes whatever form it must.

As with Mozart and Aloysia, a musical ear should acknowledge in Schubert's perception of Therese Grob a strong element of being in love with the voice, whether or not the actual person involved him on the same earth-shaking level. The soprano-solo *Benedictus* of the 1816 C major Mass was mentioned at the end of the previous section; there could be few more intimate acts for a young musical genius than to dedicate the best of himself to a voice he had fallen in love with, and this *Benedictus* is like a moment of contemplation, trying to capture the essential qualities of the well-loved voice ever more clearly and for good. He doubles back and back on himself, with at times an odd hesitancy of harmonic movement; harmonies change on each quaver of a 2/4 bar and circle within F major. After four clear four-bar phrases, two for the orchestra and two for the singer, the bass begins to repeat itself at the end of the next four bars, running over the mid-phrase caesura and effectively suggesting an extension: without the two 'static' bars, where the singer holds a top g over the repetitive bass, this would be a seven-bar phrase, but the two static bars extend it to nine. More to the point, by staying on one long-held note, they bring into action one of the human voice's most alluring features.[41]

The pattern is repeated in the second half of the movement. In his late E♭ Mass Schubert was to work wonders with such architectural ambiguities of phrase-length, and it shows the calibre of his musical mind at nineteen that these subtleties are found in a movement that is also a record of his feelings for Therese. Something of it was to reappear in the episode theme of the Great C Major Symphony's slow movement (Andante con moto, 2/4, F major. See 'Harvest').

At the very end of his life Schubert replaced that music with a surprisingly stern contrapuntal piece for chorus, but gave it a second subject of (with hindsight!) downright Verdian warmth. Schubert never permitted himself the luxury of a Mass setting where the soprano soloist would be the motive force and leader she is in Haydn's 'Nelson' Mass; and yet music such as the C major Mass's solo *Benedictus*, and for that matter its replacement, is the best record of his feelings for and about Therese. The letters to and from Holzapfel are lost, the

---

[41] See Robert Musil on the famous soprano Geraldine Farrar: 'this rise-and-fall, *this squeezed-out holding of a single note*, and this way of flooding over – flooding and being seized by ever-new convulsions and streaming out yet again: that is lust'. (Diaries 1916–18: in *Tagebücher, Aphorismen und Essays*, Rohwolt, pp. 187–8.)

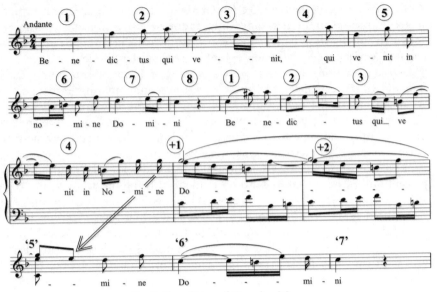

Ex. 7 *Benedictus* of C major Mass

scores survive and are written in Schubert's first language, music. If their orientation on but one 'incidental' feature of the young woman is found disappointing when there might have been an 'amour folle', that is a problem for the onlooker rather than for Schubert.

1815 appears to have marked the start of the intensest obsession with Therese; it was also the time when he began to set Körner's poetry to music, having lived for over two years with his indelible memory but not set a poem by him. The setting of *Das war ich!* is apposite at this point. It is at first sight unremarkable – one 'strophe' of music for all six stanzas (printed editions reproduce only the first four), with the music never even modulating out of the home key, G major. Pentameters, with their five stresses, are going to offer a composer a problem and opportunity, and the song's rhythm and barring are a little less straightforward, but overall the sense of eight-bar periods is retained. There is a constant pull between piano part taking its departure from the first

Ex. 8 *Das war ich!*

beat of a 3/4 bar and vocal part entering halfway through the bar to push forward towards the next strong beat; it is as if the first bar were a prelude and the piece itself began with an upbeat to the second. In that way, Schubert admirably avoids squareness in what is going to be a song without variation of the strophe itself. There is also a clear borrowing from the *Benedictus* of the G major Mass – not from the Beethoven-inspired opening, but from the second half of the paragraph. Bars 9–13 of the song almost reproduce the melody and harmony (including a poignant turn to the minor in the third bar, with E♭ in a middle part), and almost exactly the bass-line, of bars 8–11 in the *Benedictus*. (See Ex. 9.) As we shall see, the poem, like the liturgical text, speaks of rescue, of someone coming with superior power.

Ex. 9 Upper treble stave, *Benedictus* of G major Mass, lower treble stave *Das war ich!*

All of that could be enough to lift a song above the run-of-the-mill, but still leave ample room for something of real and striking interest. Any deeper fascination here is to be sought in the text. The oldest pitfall for anyone writing about or making programmes with song is to concentrate overmuch on the words, as if they were somehow identical with the composer's inspiration but had the advantage of being easier to talk about. To take one of the most obvious examples: for all Wilhelm Müller's qualities, *Winterreise* as masterpiece is Schubert's. Pain and loss in the text are unforgettably reflected in the music, while the circumstances occasioning them, whether in the author or in the composer, are less relevant. But now and again it makes sense to look more closely at a text, to find what so attracted the composer to it. In the poem of *Das war ich!* a dream offers the vision of coexisting worlds – male strength and activity, feminine brightness and goodness to which the male is drawn: he is stronger, able and obliged when necessary to protect and rescue, but on a lower spiritual plane. Whereas in the *Salve Regina* text the feminine principle intercedes and saves, on this lower purely physical level it is male strength. Nor is Körner dreaming merely of the particular person who engrosses him (and there were many in his late adolescence, before the great love of his short life), though she is like his dream-figure: what enters his dream is an idealisation, an angelic entity on 'luminous heights'. The dream is followed by feelings of the triumph of universal love, and then of a new start in a better life, with the dream-lady leading the way – but the poet's moment of participation has passed, and at the end he can only hope to be the one she chooses as partner. The sobering truth is that the 'power to strive' is concentrated not in him but in her. That is not what one will ever gather hearing the song performed, unless some exceptionally conscientious singer went so far as to seek out the two final verses, but Schubert would have seen the entire poem before setting it.

Its reproducible content accords with Körner's comments about his fiancée in a letter to his father – he had 'found his goal in life, a place to drop anchor', and 'without her I should have sunk in the whirlpool about me'. It dates, however, from before he met her, forming part of a collection *Knospen* (Buds), published when he was nineteen. (Spaun was a friend, and that may have been how Schubert came to see *Knospen*.) As if to underline that it is a genre-piece it was followed by *Das warst du*, and one must seek out a totally complete edition of his works[42] to find it reprinted. That is a measure of its purely literary merit. He was a personable and talented young man and had an almost alarming fluency with words, but only his love for a young Burgtheater colleague, the actress Antonie Adamberger, first met at the dress-rehearsal for his comedy *Der Grüne Domino* in January 1812, lifted his poetry from the superficial and naive to a level where it could reflect profound first-hand experience.

Antonie was a prime instance of theatrical talent transmitted down the generations. Her grandfather Karl Jacquet and two of his daughters, Maria Anna (Nanny) and Katharina, had been among Vienna's favourite theatrical performers between 1750 and the turn of the century. Maria Anna married the tenor Valentin Adamberger, Mozart's first Belmonte in *Die Entführung*, and their daughter Antonie, like her contemporary Sophie Müller whom Schubert came to know better, was not merely an outstanding actress but a singer good enough to perform any songs forming part of her theatrical roles. She thus became the first person to sing, as Klärchen in Goethe's *Egmont*, Beethoven's

---

[42] The same goes for more than half the sixteen Körner poems Schubert set: five (*Trinklied vor der Schlacht, Schwertlied, Gebet während der Schlacht*, duets *Jägerlied* and *Lützows wilde Jagd*) were among those reflecting the poet's military service in 1813 and soon published under the title *Leyer und Schwert*, seven (*Sängers Morgenlied, Liebesrausch, Amphiaraos, Der Morgenstern* (Stern der Liebe, Glanzgebilde), *Das war ich!, Sehnsucht der Liebe, Auf der Riesenkoppe*) came from *Knospen*. From *Schwänke und Scherze* Schubert chose *Das gestörte Glück* and *Liebeständeley*. *Wiegenlied* (Schlumm're sanft) and *Mailied* (duet) appear in other collections or none.

songs *Freudvoll und leidvoll* and *Die Trommel gerühret*. After ten years (1807–17) at the Burgtheater, the final four in mourning for Körner, she surprised her friends by marrying the historian and numismatist Josef Cales von Arneth, assistant curator of the Emperor's collection of coins and antiques. Her retirement from the stage was widely regretted, her histrionic talent thenceforth confined to occasional recitations for the Empress, following a recommendation from Pyrker, who had heard her recite from his *Tunisias*. Antonie Arneth took over the function from Sophie Müller, whose health had begun to fail. That in turn led to Antonie's being made Overseer of the Empress's foundation for the education of soldiers' daughters, the Karolinenstift.

The Arneths are on record in the diary of Schubert's young friend Franz von Hartmann as present at a number of Schubertiads, such as the one painted by Schwind, who did not include them. The previous October she had sung some of the *Schöne Müllerin* songs and settings of poems from *Wilhelm Meister* to Grillparzer at the monastery of St Florian, and, the same evening, *Ellens III. Gesang (Ave Maria)*, accompanied on the monastery's organ; and on 20 April 1827 she sang Schubert songs and recited Schiller poems ('enchantingly', Hartmann commented) at another Schubertiad at Spaun's. Like Schubert, Antonie was buried in the cemetery at Währing, though her remains were later removed to lie with her husband's in the Central Cemetery.

One or two of Körner's pieces for 'Toni', such as *In der Nacht*, are genuinely touching and touchingly genuine, with an emotional accuracy that shows *Das war ich!* to be merely drawing a bow at a venture. It is in fact the kind of self-revealing deep fantasy that can, given a certain unusual type of nature, become a self-fulfilling prophecy. The kind of visionary relationship adumbrated in the poem of *Das war ich!* may or may not have come Schubert's way: if it did, then Therese Grob and Caroline Esterhazy were the most likely people to have been involved. In Therese's case, what his biography tells us is more prosaic though endearing: that he developed for a well-liked family friend and colleague from pre-pubertal years a strong attachment arising from a combination of burgeoning sexual energy, enthusiasm for a voice and the musicianship with which it was used, and pleasure in an evident 'heart of gold'. His music tells us more, but whether about his innocence or his experience is a moot point: he had already 'encompassed' the emotions of Goethe's Gretchen in that great song composed a few months before *Das war ich!*, while in the 1816 *Stimme der Liebe* (D. 412) both the unprecedented exploratory modulations and the loving care lavished on the song's detailed construction[43] could suggest an amazing ability to sublimate, or indeed simulate, amorous exaltation.

Any discussion of Schubert and love needs to bear in mind the word's countless meanings and implications. Just as 'carbon' takes in the entire range from graphite to diamond, so 'love' runs from the most platonic fellow-feeling to the fiercest, most destructive possessiveness. One, extreme in its way, is what W.H. Auden called the experience of another person as numinous, clothed in

[43] See Leo Black, 'Schubert, The Complete Voice', *Musical Times*, Dec. 1997.

glory, charged with an intensity of being, an intense being-thereness – what mystics have called The Vision of Eros. He added that 'half our literature, highbrow and popular, for the past three hundred years, has assumed that what is probably a rare experience is one which almost everybody has, or ought to have; if they do not experience it then there must be something wrong with them'.[44]

Schubert's creative reaction to *Das war ich!*, and his *Salve Reginas*, touch on a concept formulated by Carl Gustav Jung, whose researches into human psychology unearthed the archetypes 'Anima' and 'Animus', the unconscious female and male principles in male and female psyche respectively. In his lifelong survey of the world's civilisations and practices Jung showed himself not over-concerned with music, and least of all with Western European classical music; the archetypes appearing in *The Ring* are mentioned in passing in *Mysterium Coniunctionis*, which also contains an intriguing suggestion that in *The Art of Fugue* Bach was composing out the fantasy images that came to him at a late stage in the individuation[45] process. But Jung was engaged with the anarchic, potentially life-giving forces of the collective unconscious, and accustomed to highly educated patients whose culture in no way helped them avoid psychic disturbance but rather inhibited the release of their deepest energies. He noted at one point that in some legends the Anima can appear as an animal, for example a cat, but the idea of her as the art of music would have been too Western, too civilised: not for him Martin Luther's identification 'Frau Musica'. And yet it conforms with one of his ideas:

> The Anima believes in . . . the 'beautiful and good', a primitive conception that antedates the discovery of the conflict between aesthetics and morals. It took more than a thousand years of Christian differentiation to make it clear that the good is not always the beautiful and the beautiful not necessarily good.[46]

Jung suggested at one point that man's apprehension of the Virgin Mary approximates her to the more-or-less universal 'Great Mother' figure, but untypically makes her non-sexual; he saw her as part of a possible 'quaternity' – good and bad male, good and bad female – and commented that Catholicism (to its advantage over Protestantism) includes her as the good female. In his very late *Answer to Job* (1952) Jung's feeling for widespread deep movements of the psyche led him so far as to declare the Assumption, after its infallible Papal definition in 1950, the most important religious event since the Reformation.

The Anima is found

> as a nixie, a siren, *melusina* (mermaid), wood-nymph, Grace or Erlking's daughter, or a lamia or succubus, who infatuates young men and sucks the

---

[44] 'Shakespeare's Sonnets', first of two broadcast talks reprinted in *The Listener*, 9 July 1964.

[45] Individuation: 'the development of the psychological individual as a being distinct from the general collective psychology . . . Before it can be taken as a goal, the educational aim of adaptation to the necessary minimum of collective norms must first be attained. If a plant is to unfold its specific nature to the full, it must first be able to grow in the soil in which it is planted.' (*Psychological Types*, ch. XI, Definitions.)

[46] *Psychology of the Unconscious*, p. 2.

life out of them . . . changes into all sort of shapes like a witch, and in general displays an unbearable independence . . . Occasionally she causes states of fascination that rival the best bewitchment, or unleashes terrors in us not to be outdone by any manifestation of the devil. She is a mischievous being who crosses our path in numerous transformations and disguises, playing all kinds of tricks on us, causing happy and unhappy delusions, depressions and ecstasies, outbursts of affect, etc.[47]

Some of that can be found reflected in the poetry Schubert set; as regards him personally, a little can be inferred from the realistic account of his cycloid temperament found in recent biographies (notably McKay's), to replace older simplistic idealisations and distortions. But it would appear to have virtually nothing to do with his music's technical perfection and balance. Jung saw a coming-to-terms with the Anima as the major achievement in a man's individuation. It corresponded to the 'master-piece' with which a craftsman made the transition from journeyman to master, and it demanded a high degree of realism, especially in personal relationships; some of those risk having little if anything to do with the object, and being all to do with the sensor subject. Bearing in mind Ferdinand Hiller's 'Schubert did only music, and lived by the way', one could look upon the last day of October 1814, when he composed *Gretchen am Spinnrade*, as the moment when, still not yet eighteen, he achieved not only a musical masterpiece but a personal one. The crystalline clarity of thought in the work of a young master is a reminder that nobody's universal conclusions, not even Jung's, are so universal as to cover the entire range of humankind.

To become conscious, the Anima (referred to variously by Jung as 'she' and 'it') may be 'projected' on to the outside world, in which case 'it always has a feminine form with definite characteristics' – perhaps anarchic and pagan, perhaps in the admirable form of a living person known to the subject. This latter projection is unlikely (as, for example, the poet Verlaine found[48]) to lay the foundations of a successful relationship; nothing, surely, irritates a woman so infallibly as being placed on a pedestal and made to feel she is a function rather than a person. But with patience and great good fortune it can lead to inner development.

Rilke's exhaustive deep survey of man's inner life in the *Duino Elegies* contains near its start a perfect formulation of the process of coming to terms with the Anima:

---

[47] Ibid., p. 25.
[48] The Verlaine poems of Fauré's *La bonne chanson* were addressed by a man to a woman, yet something about the female voice can make it seem the more natural one to perform them; certainly I have not experienced in any performance by the 'correct' tenor or baritone voice the other-worldly beauty of recordings by Suzanne Danco or (for the BBC) Norma Burrowes. Verlaine's poetry, initially and prophetically in *Mon rêve familier* (Section *Mélancolie* of *Poèmes saturniens*, mid-1860s), and later in the poems of *La bonne chanson* (1871) inspired by Mathilde Mauté and immortally set to music by Fauré in the latter's greatest song-cycle, are a *locus classicus* for 'self-revealing deep fantasy' as harbinger of domestic disaster once acted out in real life. Schubert and Körner were for different reasons spared Verlaine's devastating fulfilment; whether Schubert was ever in danger of it is arguable.

Sollen nicht endlich uns diese ältesten Schmerzen
fruchtbarer werden? Ist es nicht Zeit, dass wir liebend
uns vom Geliebten befrein und es bebend bestehn:
wie der Pfeil die Sehne besteht, um gesammelt im Absprung
mehr zu sein als er selbst? Denn bleiben ist nirgends.

Must not these oldest pains at last become
more fruitful for us? Is it not time that in loving
we free ourselves from the loved one and endure it, a-tremble;
as the arrow endures the bowstring, then springs in its balance
to add up to more than itself? For there is no abiding.

                                                    Elegie I

The idea of an accommodation with the Anima can be at best a speculative contribution to the story of Schubert and Therese Grob, despite music such as the C major Mass's *Benedictus*, which shows that for Schubert the singer, too, 'comes in the name of the Lord'. It could, on the other hand, provide the key to his later relationship with Countess Caroline. The younger of the two Esterhazy countesses was only twelve when during his first visit to Zseliz as tutor he described her in passing as a 'nice child'.[49] On his return in 1824 something about her at eighteen clearly made the deepest impression, or else something of the kind developed over the ensuing years as he gave her piano lessons during her visits to Vienna. Neither socially nor geographically could she be a 'member of the circle' or attend Schubertiads, but Schwind placed her portrait at the centre of the back wall when many years later he recreated his memories of those occasions (*A Schubertiad at Spaun's*, Museum der Stadt Wien, Vienna). It is now less certain than it once seemed that she was simple-minded, though some profoundly sensitive musicians are so much better at music than with people as almost to count as that; and clearly music played a central role in Caroline's life. She had an excellent knowledge of the piano and its repertoire,[50] far beyond the purely social accomplishments required or for that matter tolerated as part of a well-bred young woman's 'femininity'. There has been much simplistic thinking about this episode in Schubert's life – an extended one, for his dedication of the late piano-duet Fantasy shows it continuing till the last year of his life – as if male–female attraction must at all costs be couched in terms of sexuality, however impossible, and the practicability of marriage. *Mutatis mutandis*, recent speculations tempt one to draw a similar distinction in respect of Schubert's male friends, and to bear in mind Dürhammer's example of Goethe, Marianne and the *Buch Suleika*. Schubert's August 1824 letter to Schwind contains a crucial expression that needs to be translated precisely: 'so aber verspüre ich eine verfluchte Sehnsucht nach Wien, *trotz des anziehenden bewussten Sternes*' (but as it is, I long damnably for Vienna, despite the lodestar you know of). A mariner can

---

[49] Letter to friends, 8 Sept. 1818.
[50] Why else should Schubert in 1824 have asked Ferdinand to send to him at Zseliz Bach's '48', which appears at no other stage in his biography?

navigate by a magnetic or lodestar,[51] but would scarcely expect to embrace it. (Though one should recall Hamlet's 'Here's metal more attractive'.)

If music can project the Anima, it can surely also project the corresponding function in woman. The Animus subsumes the female's latent maleness; like the Anima, it can be negative, and is so all too often when it appears in Jung's work. It can, however, be positive,[52] and that is where Countess Caroline's strength evidently lay. When Schubert told Caroline that 'all his music was dedicated to her anyway'[53] he spoke truer than he knew, or at least truer than anyone else knew.

Lyric Intermezzo: *The Secret*

Geheimnis; Aus Heliopolis (D. 752, 753); Wanderer Fantasy

An Franz Schubert[54]

Sag' an, wer lehrt dich Lieder,
So schmeichelnd und so zart?
Sie zaubern einen Himmel
Aus trüber Gegenwart.

Erst lag das Land, verschleiert,
Im Nebel vor uns da[55] –
Du singst – und Sonnen leuchten
Und Frühling ist uns nah.

Den Alten, Schilfbekränzten,
Der seine Urne giesst
Erblickst du nicht, nur Wasser,
Wie's durch die Wiesen fliesst.

So geht es auch dem Sänger,
Er singt und staunt in sich;
Was still ein Gott bereitet,
Befremdet ihn, wie dich.

To Franz Schubert

Speak – who teaches you songs
So flattering, so tender?
They conjure up a heaven
'Mid drab reality.

First the land lay veiled
In mist before us;
You sing, and suns glitter
And we feel spring is near.

The old man crowned with reeds,
Watering his urn,
You do not see – just water,
As it flows through the meadows.

So it is for the singer too,
He sings, he is amazed in himself:
What a God quietly prepared
Takes him aback, like you.

[51] Lode-star: star that is steered by, esp. the pole-star; (fig.) guiding principle, object of pursuit (*Concise Oxford Dictionary*).

[52] See the account of 'Miss X' in *Animus, A Study in the process of Individuation*, p. 290.

[53] Anecdote from Schönstein's memoirs.

[54] Mayrhofer's text before Schubert's few emendations (M. & L. Schochow, *Franz Schubert Die Texte seiner einstimmig und mehrstimmig komponierten Lieder und ihre Dichter*, Hildesheim, 1997).

[55] Mayrhofer's poem seems to contain a topical reference: 1816 was the 'year without a summer', following the greatest known volcanic explosion, that of the volcano Tambora in the Java Sea. McKay, in 'Schubert and the "Year Without Summer"', *Brille*, June 2001, concludes like Mayrhofer that Schubert's good humour was proof against bad weather.

There are still a few mysteries for Schubert's biographers to solve, should they be thought important enough. When Johann Baptist Mayrhofer first met him at the end of 1814, the composer, at almost eighteen the younger man by ten years, had just set to music one of his poems shown him by their mutual friend Spaun. Mayrhofer had trained in theology at the great monastery of St Florian, then turned to the law, and he became yet another of the serious-minded senior figures who saw to it that Schubert added to his store of knowledge in all fields. A year later, he was already writing a libretto for him (*Die Freunde von Salamanka*), and by 1818 things had reached the point where he offered him a share of his rented room to live in.

One sign of his admiration was the poem reprinted above. It dates from early in their friendship, so it is unlikely that its obscure references to an old man crowned with reeds, 'watering his urn', and to water flowing through meadows, were the kind of purely private code that close men-friends like to build into their verses, as much as anything to tantalise the outside world.[56] If one is prepared to speculate wildly, it might reflect the crucial moment when Mayrhofer realised the full depths hidden within his new friend.

As a biographical document, *Geheimnis* is a riddle wrapped in an enigma. The 'Schubertians' certainly liked to go on trips up the Danube to Atzenbrugg, twenty-five miles west of Vienna; somewhere along the way there could have been a statue of a river-god with an urn. But for Schubert in 1816 those excursions still lay in the future. The river-god could have figured in some painting the two men saw, or reflect the kind of rough, quirky statuary in gardens such as those of the Vienna Belvedere; but that would make it hard to explain its reappearance to a Danubian fisherman in a different poem considered below.

Whatever his context, the old man or river-god clearly engaged Mayrhofer's attention, and it was typical of him to read into him something Schubert construed differently – perhaps a symbol of mortality, of life flowing by, like the river through the meadows, recalled with regret by those who dwell in the past as if minding the urns of the dead. There, to judge by the poem, he and the nineteen-year-old composer disagreed;[57] Schubert saw only the beauty of flowing water amidst all nature's other beauties. Mayrhofer's was not a temperament to generate such instinctive wonder at the natural world, but being a poet as well as a classical scholar and theologian he found it natural to celebrate his gifted new companion in verse.

Wonder begets wonder; the creator amazed at the world finds himself in turn amazed – disconcerted,[58] even – at what nature has inspired in him. Schubert is

---

[56] An intriguing suggestion thrown out in conversation by Graham Johnson, who had the Auden–Isherwood circle of the 1930s particularly in mind.

[57] Christopher Gibbs' excellently sober-minded *The Life of Schubert* points out that his letters and other writings 'mix joy and sorrow', and 'even when they do not explicitly declare this theme, they often demonstrate it by turning from melancholy topics to more hopeful ones'.

[58] 'If we look for an expression to match the special inward reaction to the Mysterium or to the 'Mirum', only one for the moment occurs . . . something like "Stupor". There is a clear difference between Stupor and Tremor – it signifies blank amazement, a state of being absolutely

taken unawares by his own musical genius, as he is by the world's beauty – or so it seems to a perceptive friend; and for all the wise things written about his professionalism, all the wondrous craftsmanship identified in him down the two centuries since his time and Mayrhofer's, a core of wonder should be acknowledged as fundamental to his perception of the world. He could be angry and bitter at the state of the musical profession, he had every reason for dismay at the state of society, he later plumbed his own depths of guilt and despair, but the counter-balance was always present and made itself felt in his music, time after time.

What more natural than for a young composer paid a compliment such as Mayrhofer's to return it with interest by setting it to music? But how! For his setting, *Geheimnis*, is typical of Schubert's utter originality. Its unique features have scarcely been noticed.[59] The opening curlicue, winding its way down in the piano's upper register (Ex. 10a) – did a song ever start so mysteriously and innocently?

Ex. 10a *Geheimnis*

Ex. 10b Duo, D. 574

Ex. 10c Symphony No. 6

disconcerted' [*auf den Mund geschlagen*, literally if anachronistically translatable as 'gob-smacked']. Otto, *Das Heilige*. Mayrhofer's theological training would have familiarised him with the terminology quoted a century later by Otto, but the thing itself was something Schubert could only discover on his own account.

59 E.g. Richard Capell, *Schubert's Songs*, 1928: 'Mayrhofer in *Geheimnis* pays Schubert the most handsome compliments . . . which Schubert at once sets to music, like everything else his friend writes.' Capell's much-admired book for the 1928 centenary shows perfectly how little the gift of writing wonderful things about acknowledged masterpieces marches with the ability to identify unrecognised wonders. Song after amazing song is dismissed as of no interest, whereas the evocations of the great cycles are still well worth reading.

Here is the perfect symbol for something appearing inexplicably like Schubert's inspiration, and for Mayrhofer's 'where *do* these songs come from?' It is not the only time he eases us into a work; he does so as early as the first of his two settings of Körner's *Sängers Morgenlied* (D. 163), from February 1815, while the 5th Symphony (D. 485, 3 Sept.–3 Oct. 1816), composed only a few weeks before *Geheimnis* in the identical key of B♭, does so very winningly, if with a counterpointing line of chords against the flowing string figure. An early violin entry in the A major Duo Sonata (D. 574, Aug. 1817) has something similar though accompanied (Ex. 10b); bars 17–30 at the end of the slow introduction to the first movement of the C major 6th Symphony (D. 589, Oct. 1817–Feb. 1818) repeat that idea (Ex. 10c).

Then there are the figures that come winding up from below – most famously the brief piano introduction to the great song *Suleika I* (D. 720), and, in a totally different mood, the double-bass figure that opens the unfinished B minor symphony (see Ex. 26, p. 99).

Another vintage Schubertian moment comes as he responds to 'you sing, and suns glitter'; his ear for piano texture is all-important as the instrument emerges from the nether regions where it has growled for a few bars. There is a comparable passage in *Auf der Riesenkoppe* at the lines about 'Three kings' fortunate realms' (Dreier Könige glückliche Länder), glinting in the sunshine, with pulsating chords and a repeated-chord figure in the topmost part. Music such as the late Piano Impromptus (especially the F minor D. 935 No. 1, Dec. 1827) is here on the way.

The transition to the second section comes at 'so it is for the singer too', and very odd it is – scarcely prepared for except by a moment or two of silence. A transition from E major to the distant key of F major is mediated only by a pause and the single shared note e – that is to say, it is so abrupt as to have any self-respecting harmony-teacher reaching for his red pencil.

Ex. 11 *Geheimnis*

Three notes follow the pause: first c, then d and g entering below it. The c would be comprehensible enough as third of the subdominant minor (A minor), but the others make this a virtual rather than substantive bridge to a far-distant key, and the next 'harmony' is incomprehensible with E major still in our ears: not only are all three new notes after the pause chromatic in the key we have just left, but they don't even make an intelligible harmony until the accented passing-note c resolves onto b♭. Here there appear to be 'incompatible harmonic planes' of a kind identified in Schubert by a modern scholar (see 'Harvest'); what the composer is after is pure alienation-effect, strangeness speaking for strangeness, in an intentionally far-fetched piece of composition, which like the song's inspired arpeggio opening could mark the birth of expressionism – in 1816! Indeed, much of *Geheimnis* (the beginning, the hole in the middle, the 'progressive tonality' that has it ending in, rather than simply 'on', the dominant of the key where it began) scarcely 'illustrates' so much as standing in its own right as a token of remarkable things within. Those remarkable things emerge elsewhere in his music, often in less alienating form; it is more than useful to have a poetic summary of them delivered by so authoritative a source as Mayrhofer.

There was to be an important postlude to *Geheimnis*. In the late summer of 1821 Mayrhofer sent a collection of twenty poems, *Heliopolis* (City of the Sun), to Schubert and Schober in St Pölten, where they were working on their opera *Alfonso and Estrella*. Schober had by then supplanted Mayrhofer as Schubert's closest literary collaborator, but the collection was sent all the same, and even with a dedication to him. It was calculated to interest them both, for it contains fascinating ideas about artistic creation as a means of improving man's lot in an oppressive age. The first poem's third strophe mentions the figure of a river-god, observed by a fisherman on the Danube:

Der Flussgott auf dem Hange	The river-god on his slope[60]
Sah seiner Urne zu.	Looked toward his urn.

The admiring fisherman is one of Mayrhofer's not infrequent healthy outdoor figures, and the poem as a whole offers an antidote to the hand-wringing in an earlier piece set by Schubert in 1817 as *Auf der Donau*. There, a journey along the river prompts reflections on how the world has gone to the dogs, with castle ruins and no enlightened river-god to offer wisdom in bad times.

Heliopolis was not made up entirely of new poems; it was rounded off, for example, by one Schubert had already set; there another water-borne figure, seaman rather than fisherman on the river, greets as his protectors in stormy weather a pair of twin stars (Castor and Pollux? Goethe and Schiller?). He promises to hang up his oars in their temple once they have seen him safely home. That song, *Lied eines Schiffers an die Dioskuren* (D. 360), is another 1816 piece.

In April 1822 Schubert set three more poems from *Heliopolis*, turning the melancholy No. 4 into the supremely beautiful *Nachtviolen* (D. 752); the other two (No. 5, 'Im kalten rauhen Norden', which became D. 753, and No. 12, 'Fels

---

[60] 'Hang' has also been translated as 'ledge' (David Gramit, 'Schubert and the Biedermeier; The Aesthetics of Johann Mayrhofer's "Heliopolis"', *Music and Letters*, 74/3, 1993, which offers a valuable assessment of Mayrhofer's contribution to both the society in which he lived and to Schubert's development).

auf Felsen hingewälzet', D. 754) he called simply *Aus Heliopolis* without numbering them I and II. They are important in his development, for *Fels auf Felsen* crucially anticipates the piano texture at the opening of the Wanderer Fantasy. The relationship between the two pieces has been largely overlooked because of another song reflected in the Fantasy – the Schmidt von Lübeck setting *Der Wanderer* (D. 489), whose best tune is used as the basis of the slow section's free variations. Being so so much more famous,[61] it has diverted attention from the at-least-equally-important influence of *Fels auf Felsen*, but both songs unmistakably underlie different parts of the Fantasy.

Ex. 12a *Aus Heliopolis* ['II'], D. 574, end

Ex. 12b Wanderer Fantasy, opening

[61] See 'Oaks and Osmosis'.

Ex. 12c *Der Wanderer*, D. 489

Ex. 12d *Wanderer Fantasy*, 2nd section

Schubert's music from 1817, the year after the composition of *Geheimnis*, was dominated by a renewed relationship with the piano as a solo instrument, manifested in several sonatas, and by his ever-present gift of song. This took on remarkable depth and gravity in *Der Tod und das Mädchen* and *Gruppe aus dem Tartarus*. By 1818 his mind was turning more and more toward inwardness and reflection, and from then on, for four years, he produced a series of works that clothed such thoughts in some of his most characteristic music. Some of them are considered in the next chapter.

3

Years of Reflection
Lazarus and the A♭ Mass,
background and foreground

Und was die innere Stimme spricht,
Das täuscht die hoffende Seele nicht.

And what the inner voice pronounces
Does not mislead the hopeful soul.
                    Schiller, *Hoffnung*

An den Mond in einer Herbstnacht; Piano Sonata in A minor (D. 784); Grablied
für die Mutter; Einsamkeit (D. 620); Das Marienbild; Vom Mitleiden Mariae; Die
Gebüsche; Himmelsfunken; Der Wanderer (Wie deutlich des Mondes Licht);
Abendbilder; Bertas Lied in der Nacht; Nur wer die Sehnsucht kennt (male-voice
quartet, D. 656); Ruhe, schönstes Glück der Erde; Marie; Nachthymne; Mass in
A♭; Lazarus

The Reflective Schubert

Schubert rarely let people see how deeply he reflected on life, and even
nowadays the depth of his thinking about the world is no more generally
appreciated than the sophistication of his musical thought processes. He was
in contact with a wide range of German literature, thanks to voluminous
reading with his educated circle of older friends (the *Bildungszirkel* or 'Linz
circle' of the years leading up to 1820), and later through the reading evenings
(*Leseabende*) initiated by Schober. Some of what he read was very new. All
that knowledge was not acquired to pass an examination, but in case it had
something to say to him: and, sure enough, it often gave a local habitation
and a name to the musical ideas teeming in his brain. It is easy to take as his
own certain views absorbed from a lifetime of reading or from cultivated
friends, hard to imagine what really emerged of its own accord in his head,
apart from music. Such a man's work must be a more accurate pointer than
any words he set down on paper. But just occasionally he opened his heart,
and his mind, when the time and the company were right – as they clearly

were when in 1825 he astonished his Linz friends the Ottenwalts with a late-
night discourse:

> We sat together until not far short of midnight, and I have never seen him so, nor
> heard: serious, profound and as though inspired. How he talked of art, of poetry,
> of his youth, of friends and other people who matter, of the relationship between
> ideals and life, etc! I was ever more amazed at such a mind, of which it has been
> said that its artistic achievement is so unconscious, hardly revealed to and
> understood by himself, and so on. Yet how simple it all was! – I cannot tell
> you of the extent and unity of his convictions – but there were glimpses of a
> world-view that is not merely acquired, and the share worthy friends may have in
> it by no means detracts from the individuality shown by all this.
>
> (Letter to Spaun, 27 July 1825)

The years 1819–20 mark a first high point in Schubert's reflections on
questions of life and death. Two major works make that apparent, the Mass
in A♭ (D. 678, Nov. 1819–Sep. 1822) and *Lazarus* (D. 689, early 1820). They did
not, however, spring from his forehead 'fully disarmed'. For a year and more he
had been seeking out reflective texts. As early as April 1818 he made the first of
four settings of poems by a Baden professor and theatre-critic named Aloys
Schreiber, whose poetry had appeared the previous year. *An den Mond in einer
Herbstnacht* (To the Moon on an Autumn Night, D. 614) combines a floating
vocal line with a piano part whose steady tread could put one in mind (not for
the first time in Schubert's music) of Bruckner. It was one of the songs Brahms
intended to orchestrate. It also contains a prophetic passage. Just before the final
resumé of its opening melody the song comes virtually to a halt, like Gretchen's
at her spinning-wheel, and the flow of melody turns briefly into something
more declaimed, like a recitative. Schubert rarely does that in his mature songs,
and it can be a sign that his melodic invention has been defeated by words
defying even his lyrical powers: bars 75–81 of the Novalis *Hymne* (I) from
February 1819 certainly give that impression. But here it is a legitimate mixture
of elements, an extension of the palette, like later composers' introduction of
'speaking-voice' or 'speech-song'.

The poet has been addressing the moon, which has long kept watch over his
life and given it radiance, and the words set in recitative run 'But your light does
not pierce the dark rooms where they [his dead friends] lie at peace, and where
I, too, shall soon rest.' Those words clearly spoke to Schubert, who was twenty-
two and in the most robust health. His attention was caught, not for the first
time, by an acknowledgment of an ineluctable, superior power. The song is in A
major: key, sentiment and mixture of vocal styles all look forward to *Lazarus*,
begun almost two years later. (See Ex. 14.)

The end of the song marks the start of another short but fascinating chain of
connections. Schubert adds a striking phrase for the piano (see Ex. 15a). It is the
kind of new idea found in certain Mozart codettas,[1] as if at the eleventh hour

---

[1] In the last of his great string quartets dedicated to Haydn, the one in C major (K. 465), Mozart
introduced a new idea at the end of each movement.

Ex. 14 *An den Mond in einer Herbstnacht*

Ex. 15a *An den Mond in einer Herbstnacht,* postlude

Ex. 15b D. 784, 2nd movement

some fresh view, not previously stated, needed to be considered. Mary's first scene in *Lazarus* would contain at least a hint of such a new postlude-idea, and all of five years after composing the song, at the time of his illness, Schubert gave a similar outline to the principal theme in the slow movement of an extraordinary piano sonata (D. 784 in A minor, see Ex. 15b).

Far nearer in time, *Grablied für die Mutter* (D. 616, from June 1818 and so a fairly close successor of the Schreiber song) was written after the mother of Schubert's former schoolmate Ludwig von Streinsberg had died. It is elegiac, a cameo of a grieving father and family at the graveside, yet it ends with a consolatory piano-postlude, not in the obvious minor mode heard up to that point, but in the major. The two song-postludes are similar, not so much in their melodic outline as their way of shedding new light on questions asked by the reflective soul.

When Schubert went to Hungary and the Esterhazys in the summer of 1818 he evidently took with him his slim volume of Schreiber, a volume of Petrarch, and Mayrhofer's poem *Einsamkeit*. That he made into a vast song about a pilgrimage through life; it ends with some of his most endearing nature-music, in which cuckoo and blackbird exchange calls. An interest in Petrarch's blend of love-poetry and mysticism suggests Schubert's continuing fascination with themes of reflectiveness and devotion, and in Zseliz he set to music two Petrarch sonnets (No. I, D. 628; No. II, D. 629),[2] also another Schreiber poem, *Das Marienbild* (The Madonna, D. 623). This tells of a wayside shrine, cut into the trunk of an oak – 'without columns, without threshold' – and Schubert matched it in a melody and harmonies of unaffected warmth. He could express his 'impulses of devotion' in such music, even as he derided the local priests in letters home: a reminder there that life is one thing, art another. A 6/8 Adagio in E (D. 612) for piano dates from the same time. It has a predecessor already mentioned, the 1815 piano Adagio in G. Schubert began that piece as if it were an instrumental *Salve Regina*, and, in the same way, parts of this later Adagio in E suggest the mood of devotion that pervades *Das Marienbild*. The Adagio in E is a minor jewel in Schubert's output of piano music, full of intricate arabesque and decorative detail. Here, too, we could be hearing bird-song.

Back in Vienna in the autumn, he set a further Petrarch sonnet (No. III, D. 630, 1818), and produced another Marian piece, the Friedrich Schlegel setting *Vom Mitleiden Mariae* (Of Mary's Shared Suffering, D. 632, December 1818). That is almost self-consciously archaic, in pure three-part counterpoint, a successor to the domestic 'geistliche Lieder' from the latter part of the previous century. (*Die Perle*, D. 466, from August 1816, had been comparably archaic in manner, combining a genuine, wistful lyricism with a three-part texture that could almost be an exercise in species counterpoint.)

Die Gebüsche (D. 646, January 1819) sets another poem by the same Schlegel brother. Its harmonies wander almost alarmingly and show again Schubert's readiness to modulate or explore every harmonic nook and cranny within his home key; that was already apparent in such songs as *Stimme der Liebe*[3] (D. 412, April 1816). Reviewers tended to home in on it as a bad habit, even if they recognised its purpose, to convey the text. It is seldom more marked than in *Die Gebüsche*, where the poem speaks of a world through which, for all its

---

[2] A priest, Karoly Kovacs, working in Zeliezovce in the 1960s, ascertained that these songs believed to date from after Schubert's return to Vienna were composed in November 1818 while he was still in Hungary. Kovacs' ms disappeared, but came to light in 1995 (see Geza Horvath, 'Franz Schubert in Zeliezovce', *Lilium Aureum*, 2000).

[3] See 'Schubert: The Complete Voice'.

multiplicity of sights and sounds, there runs 'a single soft note, for one with ears to hear'. *Die Gebüsche* was one of the countless unknown pieces posthumously left to Ferdinand's tender care. Schumann spent New Year's Day with him during his 1838–9 visit to Vienna that resulted in the discovery of the Great C Major Symphony. The song remained unpublished till 1875; Schumann had meanwhile incorporated the Schlegel line quoted above, as superscription to his Fantasy in C for piano, Op. 17: there the 'just audible tone' is a musical quotation from Beethoven's *An die ferne Geliebte*, but it is conceivable that the slow arpeggiation at the opening of the Fantasy's third movement reflects *Die Gebüsche*.

That song's mystical overtones were matched a month later, in *Himmelsfunken* (D. 651), by the sense of a divine presence. There is in the latter song the suggestion of a wind band, and an anticipation of the piano part of the 21st song of *Winterreise, Das Wirtshaus*. *Himmelsfunken's* poem comes from an 1819 collection, *Die heilige Lyra*, by a professor of French, Johann Petrus Silbert, another 'Cecilian' figure on the highest wing of the Church associated with the leading religious enthusiast of the day, Clemens Maria Hofbauer. In 1823 Schubert reverted to *Himmelsfunken* for a chorus of captive knights in *Fierrabras*, also quoted at the opera-overture's opening (see chapter 'Hard Sayings').

A number of strikingly reflective songs date from February and early March 1819. In the Schlegel setting *Der Wanderer* (D. 649) the vocal line follows the bass in a characteristically submissive way throughout the first of its two strophes. Here we find an important Schubertian 'fingerprint', VDB, which is examined later in this chapter. Another Silbert setting, *Abendbilder* (Images at Evening, D.650), passes from the wistful evocation of a dew-laden evening to a final outpouring of affirmation at the words 'Ruht, o Traute, von den Wehen,/ Bis beim grossen Auferstehen/ Aus der Nacht/ Gottes Macht/ Einst uns ruft, in seiner Höhen/ Ew'ge Wonnen einzugehen' (Rest, o dear one, from your sorrows, Till at the great Resurrection God's power calls us to enter into eternal heavenly joys). The opening is yet another variant on Schubert's way of trickling gradually into a piece. The rolling broken sixths in the piano part will permeate the entire song, whose pictorial effects are memorable – the cawing of ravens deep in the piano's left hand, the moon reflected in the river by means of a falling line in the same register, the insistent sound of the church bell summoning the faithful at evening. And the music at the song's culminating stage is truly personal Schubert, to set alongside comparably affirmative A major music in songs such as *Abendröthe* (D. 690), a very important piece discussed in 'The Complete Voice'. The end of *Abendbilder* also shows that whatever his personal doubts about physical resurrection, Schubert was not proof against the emotional power of a good poem by a poet who believed in it.

Other outstanding songs from early in 1819 were the exceptionally still and beautiful *Bertas Lied in der Nacht* (D. 653, his only *Lied* to a text by the new star of Vienna's literary scene, Grillparzer), and the Mayrhofer setting *An die Freunde* (D. 654).

Schubert composed relatively little in April 1819, but one piece from then is a male-voice-quintet[4] setting (D. 656) of Mignon's *Nur wer die Sehnsucht kennt* from Goethe's *Wilhelm Meister*, in the kind of texture the modern age calls 'close-harmony'. At times it echoes the melody of the E major Adagio from the previous year. There is also another gem of a male-voice piece, *Ruhe, schönstes Glück der Erde* (D. 657), which sets to music an unknown author's prayer that peace may descend and silence the 'storms of the heart' and the 'vain dreams' whose burgeoning brings such pain. The soul is to rest 'as if in a grave filled with flowers', until it rises, healed. This choral piece's harmonic intricacies are structural, but also add colour in a seductively sensual way: yet again Bruckner springs to mind, while the 'resurrection' even seems to hint at Mahler's 2nd Symphony (as at that work's 'bereite dich/ Zum neuen Leben'). *Ruhe, schönstes Glück*, with its textural smoothness, was a worthy forerunner of the songs Schubert produced in May, when his mood deepened into an overtly religious strain in his first setting of the supreme mystical poet of the day, Novalis. The chorus also anticipates the powerful Schlegel setting *Im Walde* from late 1820, and the 1821 *Gesang der Geister über den Wassern*.

As Schubert came to set Novalis, he was first drawn, yet again, to the theme of the Virgin Mary. *Marie* (D. 658) tells of an 'inward image' of her, which the poet can nowhere in the world find realised, and it is no surprise that the modest poem prompted one of Schubert's divinely simple melodies. Other more ambitious Novalis settings from May 1819 were the four 'Hymnen' (D. 659–662). (The new *Schubertgesamtausgabe* gives the title *Hymne* to only the first of the four, each of the other three appearing as *Geistliches Lied*.) In *Hymnus* (I) he struggled unprofitably with the poet's obscure metrical schemes; the other three are simple strophic songs, II and III ringing the changes on the same pair of keys, B♭ minor and major. The texts of these 'hymns' invoke and worship a male Saviour, something that perhaps came less naturally to Schubert than his reaction to the feminine principle in the *Salve Regina* hymn.

He was back on more familiar ground early the next year in a vastly more successful Novalis song, *Nachthymne* (D. 687). By early 1820 his mind was occupied with the A♭ Mass and *Lazarus*; *Nachthymne* shows him going forward from *Ruhe, schönstes Glück*, and in a different direction from the one he took when he immediately afterwards began to set the Protestant Niemeyer's *Lazarus* poem. Novalis' text is no mere genre piece. It reflects Last Things – not his own premonition of an early death, but reflections on the death of his fiancée. That gave rise to the *Hymnen an die Nacht*, where Schubert found the text for *Nachthymne*. Mystics' fascination with the dark, and with its obscure but intense sense of reaching out to the Unnameable, was not, on the whole, something for Schubert, whose 'better world' is one of light. (Survivors relating 'near-death' or 'out-of-body' experiences tell of moving into light, not darkness.) But he was obviously drawn to the profound emotions Novalis

---

[4] For a considered and full account of Schubert's male-voice part-songs, see M.J.E. Brown, *Essays on Schubert*, 1966.

associated with the transition from life to death, matching them with extra-ordinary harmonies and modulations. The harmony literally crumbles away at 'An jenem Hügel verlischt dein Glanz' (At that grave your splendour is dimmed), in sounds looking forward to two 1825 songs on poems by Craigher: the novice nun in *Die junge Nonne* (D. 828) relives the black night in her heart before she felt the call ('und finster die Nacht'), and the gravedigger in *Totengräbers Heimweh* (D. 842) expresses his world-weariness with 'es schwin-den die Sterne, das Auge schon bricht' (the stars disappear, the eye starts to fail).

In *Nachthymne* the vocal line is often tuneful and loose-limbed, and its occasional way of moving up and down through the 'harmonics' is a first step towards yodelling. In the final 'transfiguration' the piano breaks into rolling broken-sixths. At the opening of *Abendbilder* such figures were a symbol for dew falling, but in the course of that song they persisted as the text ran through a whole series of images, and by the end they helped underline the poem's consolatory message. At the close of *Nachthymne* they convey the departing soul's out-of-body ecstasy, swirling ever and ever higher as they do at the end of the Dionysian 1824 song *Auflösung*,[5] and they will be found again, with still other connotations, in the D major piano sonata from 1825, and the fifth song of *Winterreise*, *Der Lindenbaum*. The vocal line of the final section is a variation on the song's opening melody, and has at times a curious naivety that has been misunderstood. This ending has been dismissed as banal, by the ever-choosy Capell and also by so experienced an interpreter as Dietrich Fischer-Dieskau.[6] But Novalis is summing up his philosophy: by day he must believe and have courage, at night he 'dies in the holy fire'. There is here a childlike simplicity and purity ('Except you become as one of these'), which Schubert suggests with his prominent major thirds in the vocal line (Ex. 16c), the feature that provoked such criticism. They are also prominent in two Schlegel settings, *Der Knabe* (The Little Boy, D. 692, from a mere two months after *Nachthymne*, Ex. 16a) and *Der Schmetterling* (The Butterfly, D. 633, date uncertain, Ex. 16b).

Ex. 16a *Der Knabe*

Ex. 16b *Der Schmetterling*

---

[5] A resemblance pointed out by Marie-Agnes Dittrich in the *Schubert Handbuch*.
[6] In *Schubert, A Biographical Study of his Songs*, London, 1978.

Ex. 16c *Nachthymne*

All in all, *Nachthymne* is a major achievement, and it is not surprising to find that in the major works from the period that began around the time of its composition Schubert attained new heights in his treatment of reflective themes.

As a pendant to the pieces considered above, two sizeable works could convey something of Schubert's keen delight in the countryside and its beauty. That was already apparent in the 1818 *Einsamkeit* composed in Zseliz; in the summer of 1819 he went for the first time to Steyr and Linz (Upper Austria), where he and Vogl began their long series of visits to Vogl's music-loving friends. Sociability dictated that there was little time for composition, and what there was went mostly on a birthday cantata for Vogl, but the A major piano sonata (D. 664) almost certainly dates from then; for all the ambiguities of its slow movement (see chapter 'Grace under Pressure') it counts as predominantly relaxed and high-spirited. He dedicated it to a young lady friend of whom he wrote approvingly to his Viennese friends (this was the holiday when he wrote the famous or notorious letter about the eight pretty girls, whose surface attractions clearly complemented the beauties of the countryside.[7]) The 'Trout' Quintet (D. 667) also arose from that time away from Vienna in 1819; it was commissioned from him by a Steyr mine-manager and keen amateur musician, and composed once Schubert was back at his desk in Vienna and into his professional routine.

---

[7] One of them was Karoline Eberstaller, daughter of a French general but later adopted by a doctor living in the house. It has been reported that in the early 1840s she befriended the young Anton Bruckner, playing Schubert piano duets with him, which impressed him enormously. She lived to a great age, dying in 1902 (Ernst Hilmar, 'Schubert und Bruckner', *Brille*, June 2001).

The Mass in A♭

Music is spirit, spirit leading into obscure distances beyond the
reach of consciousness; its content can hardly be grasped with
words . . . and, before all else, with feeling and sensation . . .
Music admits us to the depths where spirit and nature are still
one – or have again become one.

Emma Jung

Did Schubert recognize the liturgical meaning of *Pax*? Not he.
Pax was the gift of happiness.

Arthur Hutchings

Nothing is known of Schubert's reasons for writing his A♭ Mass. Unlike most of
his others, it was not a commission for a local church, and its composition took
him so long as to suggest that it had no immediate practical purpose. It dates
from the very years when Beethoven was at work on his towering Mass in D. For
whatever reason, Schubert cast his new Mass in a key as distant as possible from
that of the *Missa Solemnis*. Not a note of Beethoven's setting was heard in
Vienna until 1824, two years after Schubert completed his own. But it is
possible, given the conditions under which Beethoven had to work, that his
helpers spread abroad at least details of its key. That is speculation; what is fact
is that a large-scale Mass in A♭ by the Dresden composer Johann Gottlieb
Naumann (1741–1801) was published in Vienna in 1804 and reprinted more
than once, one of the reprints coming in the period when Schubert was a
chorister.

A♭ major is not the commonest key in Schubert; noteworthy pieces using it
between 1819 and 1822 are the 23rd Psalm and a clutch of songs (*Versunken,
Geheimes, Selige Welt,* the first version of *Der Musensohn* and *Schwanengesang*),
of which, for all the D.H. Lawrence-like symbolism of *Selige Welt*'s Mayrhofer
poem, with 'water breaking on the shore', only the last-named could be said to
concentrate on higher things. Later, as a key for devotional, reflective or tender
thoughts, A♭ would appear in *Im Abendrot* (1824?), *Fülle der Liebe* (1825), and
some fine 1826 songs including *Wiegenlied* (Seidl) and *Das Zügenglöcklein,* also
the choral *Mondenschein;* the last-named pieces, from the time when his mind
turned to revising his Mass in their key, perhaps show him determined to use it
elsewhere, just as during 1824 he had used it in the accompanied part-song
Gebet and his finest set of four-hand variations. For completeness' sake it should
be recorded that A♭ is also the key of the extraordinary 6th *Moment Musical,*
discussed in 'Grace under Pressure'.

A certain parallel can certainly be drawn between Beethoven's approach to the
Ordinary and Schubert's: both did precisely what strict church practice
deprecated, giving their own unique view and interpretation of the text
rather than simply enabling it to be delivered to the best advantage. For
which malpractice music-lovers remain eternally grateful.

Work on the Mass lasted from November 1819 until the autumn of 1822. One project after another intervened: first an opera, *Adrast* (never completed) and in February 1820 a setting of a dramatic poem, *Lazarus oder die Weihe der Auferstehung* (Lazarus or the Solemnity of the Resurrection), by August Hermann Niemeyer. In March Schubert was briefly arrested for cheeking the police, and only two of the poem's three acts were set to music. At about the same time two symphonies were left in sketch, he composed a sizeable score to accompany a play, *Die Zauberharfe* (The Magic Harp), and began another opera, *Sacontala.*

The A♭ Mass is unique in dating from a number of critical stages in his development. It is also the major exception to the rule that a work once left for any sizeable period was unlikely to be taken up again with much prospect of success. (Revision, as with the Great C Major Symphony, was a different matter; far more Schubert sketches and drafts exist than was once supposed.)

Not all the Mass is 'in' the key of A♭ (major). The outer movements (*Kyrie* and *Agnus Dei*) needed to be, to establish the key and leave it firmly in the mind, for a Mass of this stature, whether or not it will be heard continuously, is in its creator's mind also a symphonic work; but by the same token one or more of the middle movements will probably be in a different key. Here, the *Gloria* and *Credo* are in keys successively a major third lower (E major, C major); the *Sanctus* moves from the last-named key to its subdominant, F major. This brings a shift through one more interval of a third, to the A♭ major required for the closing movement.

'Mediant' key-relationships, such as the A♭–E [= F♭] and E–C that lead to the *Gloria* and *Credo*, had become steadily more important at the end of the previous century, thanks largely to Haydn, who more and more often cast his slow movements in the mediant or submediant of a work's main key. Such harmonies on secondary degrees of the scale were eventually treated by Schubert as on a par with the tonic and dominant that had ruled the roost until then, and took their place at the heart of his harmony. Thanks largely to them, it covers an unprecedented range.

Both the A♭ Mass and *Lazarus* are intriguing in their ways of grouping the orchestral instruments. In the Mass, the woodwind 'choir' (flute, two oboes, clarinets and bassoons, plus the two horns for the most part) is prominent, with the strings often used as if coming from another, contrasting world: two trumpets and three trombones weigh in at more-solemn moments, not all of them loud. In the *Credo* the mystery of the Incarnation is underlined by the sound of trombones, and a single trombone darkens the bass-line for '[to judge the living] and the Dead, and His kingdom shall have no end', while a single trumpet, answered by the timpani, casts an intriguing shadow over the pantheistic 'Heaven and earth are full of Thy glory', with mysterious quiet dotted rhythms in the background. In the *Kyrie*, answering two-bar figures for horns and trombones strongly suggest textures in the Octet four years later, an effect that recurs on clarinets and bassoons before the repeat of the opening. At the start of the *Credo*, as part of the movement's curious 'motto', a repeated C major chord teams up horns and trombones, followed by oboes, clarinets and trumpets.

Biographical evidence makes it clear that Schubert worked on the Mass as from November 1819, two months before he turned his attention to *Lazarus*. Certain resemblances between its *Kyrie* and music in the first act of *Lazarus* reflect that. The same kind of resemblance is found again in the *Gloria*, which he may have sketched immediately after. It is unclear precisely when the *Credo* and *Sanctus* were written: a sheet of paper with a draft of an 1821 song, *Die gefangenen Sänger*, also contains ideas that found a place in the *Credo*. The *Agnus Dei* is supposed not to have been written till near the date when according to Schubert the work was completed, September 1822. It is, however, of interest that in rounding off the Mass he reverted to a mood found at the pastoral conclusion of the *Kyrie*.

Down the centuries the invocation 'Lord have mercy on us, Christ have mercy on us, Lord have mercy on us' has been treated in every way, from the jewelled conciseness of Byrd's Mass in Three Parts to the contrapuntal complexities of the vast double-choir *Kyrie* presented by Bach to the new Elector of Saxony in 1733.[8] One could ask for no more inviting doorway into both the liturgy and the twenty-two-year-old Schubert's inner world than this *Kyrie*. Only in the B♭ Mass had he made the opening prayer an outspoken 'have mercy'; the ones in F, G and C opened quietly, but without the sense of coming from somewhere else that he conjures up here.

The 're-entrant' melody at the start of the *Kyrie* is part of a nexus of Schubertian connections. A similar curve appears in a different theme from the Mass, the *Gloria*'s 'Gratias agimus tibi' (Ex. 17b, which like Exx. 17c–g is here transposed to A♭ to make the themes' audible similarities more visible), and in the 'parallel' work of the time, *Lazarus*, Jemina's important narration opens with yet another such figure (Ex. 17c). The theme could also put one in mind of second subjects in two slow movements of important chamber works, the A Minor String Quartet (D. 804, 1824, Ex. 17d) and later the C Major String Quintet (D. 956, 1828, Ex. 17f: there the melody in question is in E♭ in the exposition, A♭ in the recapitulation). Another 1828 work, *Hymnus an den heiligen* Geist (D. 948) opens with a similar outline (Ex. 17e).

Ky - ri - e   e - le - i - son

Ex. 17a *Kyrie* of A♭ Mass

---

[8] Along with a *Gloria*: both movements found a place in the B minor Mass, which contains a completely different movement for the return of 'Kyrie eleison', something not always found even in a Missa Solemnis.

Ex. 17b *Gloria* of A♭ Mass

Ex. 17c Jemina's aria (*Lazarus*)

Ex. 17d   D. 804, II

Ex. 17e *Hymnus*, D. 948

Ex. 17f String Quintet, I

Ex. 17g *Salve Regina*, D. 677

Philosophy and religion associate rounded- and wave-forms with ideas of perfection and completeness,[9] and 'circular' and wave-like figures such as these play a striking role in Schubert's songs and instrumental music, whether as melody or as accompaniment. Most of the melodies shown above turn upwards after an initial downward move. That was no mere tag used by Schubert to match any religious idea, for contrast is at hand in the main theme of a piece

---

[9] Peter Tenhaef, 'Der Kreisfigur in der Musik Franz Schuberts', *Brille*, Jan. 1999.

that could scarcely be closer in time and spirit to the A♭ Mass at its outset, the 1819 *Salve Regina* in A (Ex. 17g above). Together with its continuation, this sets the Marian invocation as two almost perfect circles, in fact a Q then an inverted Q, with the second higher than the first.

Schubert was well able to keep the different worlds of the A♭ Mass and *Lazarus* separate, and there was nothing new about a great composer's working on more than one major work at once. Beethoven regularly did so. And yet Schubert insinuates himself with equal delicacy into the cantata's dark world and the Mass' realms of light. In *Lazarus'* opening instrumental paragraph, which rises and falls over the space of twenty-three bars, the second half contains a long falling violin line, wonderfully harmonised and seeming already to express in sound what the hero will shortly put into words: that the soft rustling of the natural world about him is a voice gently saying 'dust to dust'. Bars 25–33 of the A♭ Mass's *Kyrie* outline a faintly similar falling curve, and Schubert, like Lazarus, seems 'already there'. If this *Kyrie* is a prayer, it is one prayed with a smile, one that expects to be heard or even knows it has already been heard. Schubert does not so much begin this Mass as flow into it; were one to seek a *fons et origo*, it might lie in Mozart's late choral piece *Ave Verum Corpus*, a piece reflected at all stages of Schubert's religious music from the 1814 F major Mass to an 1828 *Tantum Ergo*.

Another subtle link between *Lazarus* and Schubert's Masses is a type of gradual, hesitant leadback to a restatement. An early case was the passage before the repetition of 'Kyrie eleison' in the G major Mass, where the dissonant minor ninth eventually resolved upwards into a rising scale culminating on the tonic. That is a first hint at a highly expressive moment in *Lazarus* (likewise a leadback) before the recapitulation of the main section in Mary's first scena, but in the interim the A♭ Mass offers another if simpler instance. As in the G major Mass, it leads back to the recapitulation of the *Kyrie*.

In the A♭ Mass the clarinet's brief filling-in scales during short breaks in the solo line form another feature that suggests *Lazarus*, where there are countless brief woodwind echoes of, or comments on, vocal phrases. A long choral phrase ends with a figure very like the one that plays an important role at the end of a main phrase in Mary's second aria, at the words 'fasst er dich und wanket nicht' (he takes hold of you and does not waver). As this expressive coda develops, another figure in an inner part (bassoon, then viola) audibly resembles an idea heard twice in the middle section of Mary's second solo (its second appearance, at 'die atemlose Brust' (the breathless breast) is even more striking than the first, with an ominous echo on the trombones). In the Mass, this figure feels like a question, memorably answered when it reappears in the major to help the movement towards its pastoral-sounding conclusion. The same passage also has a zigzag descending broken-chord found in the G major Mass and *Das war ich!*, as later also in *Geheimnis*, and in general it shows so striking an affinity with the end of the entire work as to raise the odd question about the A♭ Mass's remaining chronology. If one examines it and *Lazarus* from that point of view it seems, given the resemblances just mentioned, that the cantata takes over musical ideas from the Mass, rather than vice versa.

The *Gloria* is unrestrained in its initial hymn of praise to God in the highest, the violins rush about as they so often do in Viennese church music (see 'Harvest'), with the choir by turns forthright and restrained, as the text dictates. All the while, the woodwind and (when not rushing about!) the strings are in intimate dialogue, as they have been since the outset of the *Kyrie*. But the truly memorable and characteristic Schubert begins as we reach the hymn of gratitude in the second section.

In Viennese church music the *Gloria* was often subdivided into five. Here two sections in neat A–B–A form are followed by two that are more 'end-directed', and then by the long 'Cum sancto Spiritu', which rounds off the movement with a fugue, as was expected in a Missa Solemnis. Schubert dwells particularly on the passages of praise and gratitude. In the section that runs from 'Gratias agimus tibi' (We give thee Thanks) to 'Domine Deus, Rex Coelestis' (Lord God, heavenly King) the opening for solo quartet, with a couple of choral responses, shares a 'walking' 2/4 time-signature with the extraordinary *Benedictus* of the C major Mass. It also offers the soprano soloist one effective high entry to show off her upper register. That solo was composed while Therese and her voice were still a recent memory, though by now the soprano is not the all-important 'object of desire' put on show, merely *prima inter pares* as one quartet-member.

Not the least endearing feature of this generous, almost obsessively repetitive 'Gratias' is that it starts and for a long time remains in pure two-part counterpoint, filling out only at a return of the opening phrase. That was exactly what Haydn had done, to wondrous effect, in the slow movement of his last completed string quartet, Op. 77 No. 2 in F. The two passages are in closely related keys (Schubert's in A, Haydn's in D). A string-player who grew up performing chamber music with his family and at school is most unlikely not to have known Haydn's late masterpiece; Franz played the viola in the family quartet, so would have been one of the two members who in Op. 77 No. 2 had to sit patiently awaiting their turn to contribute to the beauty. For a sensitive adolescent, the sense of finally losing himself in something wonderful can well be imagined. Here we find again the string-quartet influence already apparent in the *Benedictus* of the B♭ Mass.

There were adequate precedents for making 'Gratias agimus tibi . . .' an extended section featuring a soloist. Particularly fine examples are found in Haydn's late masses, though his text-division was different, in that he did not always make a caesura at 'Gratias agimus tibi', preferring to do so at 'qui tollis peccata mundi' (who taketh away the sins of the world). So it is something personal to Schubert that he chooses to build out this particular part of the A♭ Mass to such an extent. He even reverts, with dubious liturgical propriety, to a repeat of 'Gratias agimus tibi' after 'Domine Deus, Rex Coelestis'. The proportions within the *Gloria* of his final Mass in E♭ will again be different – strikingly so, indeed (see p. 180).

In 'Domine Deus, Rex Coelestis' Schubert uses the dramatic harmonic upward move through a semitone (a–Bb) associated with suffering since his great 1817 Schiller song about the endless torments of Hell, *Gruppe aus dem Tartarus*. It is as if the concept of God the Father entailed acceptance of a degree of pain.

'Domine Deus, Agnus Dei' (Lord God, Lamb of God) through 'Quoniam Tu solus sanctus' is a further example of Schubert's 'walking' tempo, with a reference to the *Benedictus* of Haydn's 'Nelson' Mass, which had been performed in Vienna in 1819, a year before Schubert himself conducted it. The vocal entries are separated by three appearances on the wind instruments of a motive that figured in *An den Mond in einer Herbstnacht*. This is part of yet another Schubertian chain of connection: after its appearance in the *Gloria* the song-figure will crop up once more in *Lazarus*, in Jemina's narration.

hol - der Nacht - ge - fähr - te

Ex. 18a *An den Mond in einer Herbstnacht*

Ex. 18b *Gloria* of Ab Mass

Mit En - gel - frie - den im blü - hen - den Ge - sicht

Ex. 18c Jemina's aria (*Lazarus*)

It is no exaggeration to say of *Lazarus* and the Ab Mass that there is a strong sympathy of mood between these two exactly contemporary works of religious inspiration meant for different contexts. Both offer a wealth of mainly conjunct phrases in a medium tempo, most of them winding gradually down to the tonic. 'Quoniam Tu solus sanctus' (For Thou alone art holy) opens quietly but grows and grows, leading to something remarkable for Schubert, eight bars of 'unison' choral march.[10] That in turn leads on to the fugal 'Cum sancto Spiritu',

---

[10] Of this transformation of the tune for 'Domine Deus Agnus Dei' Jaskulsky says that, as in the repeated setting of 'Tu solus Dominus', 'essential characteristics of the Ab Mass are here made apparent, such as the illumination of a particular passage of text from two contradictory sides, a result of the composer's deeply thoughtful attitude to the text . . . this is the very attitude which in other cases may have prompted Schubert to omit parts of the text'. One could demur and say rather that when 'Domine Deus' becomes 'Tu solus Sanctus' the same musical idea is looked at in the light of two different textual ideas, but Jaskulsky's further comment that 'the music offers – beyond all speculation – a clear view of the thoroughness and unconventionality with which Schubert made the text his own' compels full agreement. Such an appeal to the actual sound of the music is indeed the premise underlying this entire study of Schubert.

the only sizeable fugue in the A♭ Mass. As finally composed for the revision it takes up about a third of the movement in terms of time, with classic features, such as a stretto,[11] and pedal-points on tonic and dominant. This is not a reflection of Schubert's wish to impress in 1825, when he revised the Mass knowing he would apply for a senior post at the Imperial Court; the fugue in the first version is inferior in invention but only a little shorter, that is to say still very sizeable. It, too, jumps through the prescribed hoops towards the end.[12]

The *Credo*, in C major, strikes a different note from the *Kyrie* and *Gloria*, but shows similarities to Schubert's last setting, for male voices and a group of low stringed instruments (D. 714), of Goethe's *Gesang der Geister über den Wassern*. That piece is also in C and, in its first draft, from 1820, though a great deal later in the year. The *Credo* is tight and syllabic for much of its length, with 'Et incarnatus' and 'Crucifixus etiam pro nobis' much more expansive. There is no final fugue, nor are the soloists used till the very end. As usual, the Holy Catholic Church and Resurrection of the Dead get short shrift.

The cue word 'Credo' (I believe) occurs precisely once in the liturgy, but no fewer than twenty times in the course of Schubert's setting, as if the congregation or even the composer himself were being exhorted to believe. Or, in the composer's case, to keep at it and find ever-new ideas matching all the articles of belief. Again, this is not something unique to Schubert: but in the *Missa Solemnis* even Beethoven, the great repeater, said 'Credo, Credo' at the outset, and was content to list all the things believed in, until in the passage from 'et in Spiritum sanctum' to 'confiteor unam baptisma', he made each voice-part sing the word, on average, eight times.

All this could suggest that when Schubert wrote home about 'never forcing devotion' in himself, he was not being totally frank. A further allotrope of the Mass known as a 'Credo' Mass goes back to Neapolitan models, but nowhere else does Schubert go to such lengths in stressing that he, or someone, believes. Haydn had felt no need to do so; Mozart did it a couple of times, in his Mass in F (K. 196), where the 'Credo' motive, already familiar from earlier in the work, is identical with the tag that will reappear in the first movement of the Violin Sonata in E♭ (K. 481) and then, far more famously, to open the finale of the 'Jupiter' Symphony. 'Credo' is also stressed in Mozart's Mass in C (K. 257).

The *Credo*'s opening is marked by a striking antiphony of three instrumental

[11] In fugue, the introduction of two entries of the subject in close canon, i.e. the second coming in before the first has run its course.

[12] The original appears as an 'alternative' version in some modern editions, along with his final thoughts, and was in fact used when the publisher Schreiber first made the Mass available in 1875. In all other respects the publication represented Schubert's 'second' version; that was because only in the case of the vast and entirely new 'Cum sancto Spiritu' did he write down his revision separately, everything else being written into the manuscript over the first version and often rendering the latter indecipherable. Ferdinand had made a fair copy of the work as originally composed, but evidently this was not available to Schreiber (though by 1887 and the publication of the Complete Edition it was), so in following the ms he ended up with the first version of the fugue and the second of everything else. The new Complete Edition prints both versions in full in two volumes.

groups: chords on the horns and trombones, followed by oboes, clarinets, trumpets, and after the first choral phrase a concluding comment from the strings. The two wind chords punctuate the movement, being heard again at various structural points. The movement shows elements of sonata form, for something like a development section begins at the reversion to the main tempo for 'Et resurrexit', and something like a recapitulation at 'confiteor'. There the opening 'question-and-answer' section is literally repeated, so far as structure goes, but it is decorated, the initial stillness of the *a capella* voices being dispelled by the addition of a running bass-line for the cellos.

A profound contrast is created at 'Et incarnatus est de Spiritu sanctu ex Maria Virgine', the only setting of these words in Schubert's Masses not to use the solo voices according to long-standing Viennese tradition (for example, in the works of Caldara and Fux). Schubert divides the choir into eight parts, producing (with hindsight) a well-nigh Brucknerian mystery and solemnity. At the outset there is the sound of trombones, with bassoons. The music is not only very still and solemn, but harmonically and structurally ingenious. The section falls into two halves, each with the text as far as 'et homo factus est': the first modulates from its initial A♭ (the work's home key) to C (the movement's home key) – which might be taken in a more 'intellectual' composer or by a truly intellectual analyst as symbolising the transition from divine to human[13] – and then back again. There is also subtle variation of phrase-structure (4 + 3 + 5 bars answered by 3 + 4 + 5). Originally Schubert underlaid the text so as to elide 'ex Maria Virgine'. As we have seen, those important words were left out of his previous Mass, but given the intensity of his reactions to *Salve Regina* it is hard to take this as anything but a sign of haste, unlike his almost certainly deliberate variants elsewhere.

'Crucifixus' is a further, contrasting choral section. Schubert here departed from the Viennese tradition, which was to give the entire 'Et Incarnatus – Crucifixus' text to the soloists. 'Et resurrexit' has no special new idea of its own but simply brings a return of the opening quick music and of C major. One may briefly feel here that a recapitulation is under way, but it turns out that Schubert is beginning a kind of development section. Something similar occurred in the F and G major Masses, where the developmental return to the opening at 'et resurrexit' was not in the home key but in its dominant, and the text was underlined by a change from an initial *p* to a resounding *f*. In the B♭ and C major Masses, where the *Credo* sets out *forte*, he reverted to the original tempo and dynamic – in the B♭ work a literal repeat of the opening, in the C major with a new melodic line. For the E♭ Mass six years later he would hit on a new solution developing features of all those ideas. Jaskulsky goes so far as to maintain that a detectable and accomplished sonata form in this *Credo* predates Schubert's formal advances in masterpieces such as the mature string quartets.

---

[13] Gülke follows Jaskulsky in regarding this harmonic sleight-of-hand, with C major in fact representing the non-existent key D♭♭, as a symbol of the unfathomable mystery of the Incarnation.

'Et vitam venturi saeculi' is not the fugue that might have been expected; near the end, at a point where he could well be coming to an end, Schubert for the first time in the movement calls on the solo voices for an extra 'Amen' paragraph. The freshness of this long-delayed entry, like the sun coming out, makes one wonder whether it was a new idea that came into Schubert's mind when he thought he had completed the movement. Be that as it may, it undoubtedly sets the crown on his *Credo*.

For the *Sanctus* there is a further key-change to F major, with a reversion to the home key of A♭ in the *Benedictus*. This movement covers the widest range; it runs continuously as far as the end of the 'Osanna' and is kept very tight, yet there is time for one memorable moment after another. Both Isaiah (6,1–4) and the Book of Revelation (4,1–11) tell of the angels in Heaven praising the Almighty – 'Holy, Holy, Holy' – in tones that shake the Universe to its foundations. Such is the background of the *Sanctus* in the Mass, and Schubert's reaction to the angelic song touches on comparable depths.[14] Here he is drastically at odds with the gentle intimacy sensed in many Haydn settings of the same text. We sense his own awe-struck reaction to the liturgy, as we do in the music from 1814 to 'et iterum venturus est'.

The opening of this *Sanctus* goes far beyond anything in his previous settings. As the instruments build up the tension at the start, the harmony moves to the sharpened tonic (F♯ minor). This means that when the voices enter with their first cry of 'Holy', they are in the 'wrong' key. The pattern recurs twice, till the music finally settles on the dominant. Here is a classic case of Schubert riding the circle of thirds in a way that comes close to Bruckner: F – f♯ – (interrupted cadence) – D: D – e♭ – (i/c) – B; B – c – C – F, with all the upward semitone moves made by means of the augmented triad. Not surprisingly, it has been felt as Schubert's attempt to communicate the ungraspable. A Benedictine to whom I played a recording of it, a man unversed in classical music, found it 'spine-chilling'. Certainly it seems the perfect audible representation of the sense of awe, the 'irrational', numinous element in religious experience. And yet it all begins so modestly, so reassuringly, with faint horn-calls such as suggest a soporific summer day in the 'daytime lullaby' *Schlaflied* from 1817 (D. 527). That song (also known as *Schlummerlied* or even *Abendlied*) is, like this *Sanctus*, in F major.

The 'Sanctus' music passes directly into 'Pleni sunt coeli', a mere nine bars but with a weight out of all proportion. Although the 12/8 tempo of the *Sanctus* persists there is a major change in mood; the note-values shorten and swirling violin figurations are, for once, not the typical Viennese liturgical scramble but something more like one of Schubert's water-symbols; the burgeoning, explosive natural world of the 1825 D major Piano Sonata seems not so far

---

[14] Otto drew attention to the *Sanctus* of Bach's B Minor Mass as illustrating music's power to communicate Divine splendour, but not its terror; writing in 1917, he is unlikely to have been aware how perfectly Schubert had communicated his vision of precisely that in the *Sanctus* movements of his last two masses.

away. The choir is given a smoothly flowing melody, so that the 'glory in heaven and on earth' has a distinctly rural flavour. And yet there is unity in diversity, a mystery held over from the opening; the high voices, which just rose not only in loudness but in register to the final 'Sabaoth', are still in that zone of ecstasy as they sing 'coeli et terrae'. The joy is mysteriously punctuated by quiet throbbing figures on trumpets and timpani.

The horns reappear, with evocative rising-and-falling phrases that culminate in their long-drawn-out call at the junction into 'Osanna'. Schubert here seems to look forward years, to the fifth song of *Winterreise*, *Der Lindenbaum*. It would be no surprise were the tenor to enter with the crushing sadness of 'Nun bin ich manche Stunde Entfernt von jenem Ort,/ Doch immer hör' ich's rauschen,/ "Du fändest Ruhe dort"' (Now I am many hours' away from that place, And yet I still hear it rustle, 'You'd find peace there') – but for Schubert in the early 1820s paradise is not yet lost. This is one of the strange 'time-faults' in his music, where we are instantly carried forward from one year to a quite distant one.

The ensuing 'Osanna' in 6/8 is like a hunting scene out of the Autumn section of Haydn's *The Seasons*, with a totally human rejoicing worlds removed from the awe that engulfed us moments earlier. A delightful Schubertian subtlety gives the first bar of the opening four to the instruments, the first vocal 'Osanna' coming as an answer. Rarely in music can there have been so quick and total a transition from 'tremor' to 'admiratio'.

The Mass's principal key of A♭ reappears in the *Benedictus*, another of his 'walking' movements. A♭ is Schubert's 'tenderness' key: the nearest overtly religious counterpart is the 23rd Psalm (D. 706, December 1820), though the text of that piece takes it farther afield. The melody of the *Benedictus* relies on a simple major-second 'rosalia',[15] with uniformly regular four-bar phrases until the final extension, and there is a curious reference back to the 1819 Goethe song *Hoffnung* (Hope), which will be quoted again in *Fierrabras*. Here the solo quartet is heard first, with a bass-line for celli playing pizzicato, then for a choral reprise the double-basses are added. Yet again Schubert's mind seems to run back to the G major Mass and its *Credo*, as he writes the strings' accompaniment to this movement. As was usual, the 'Osanna' is repeated after the *Benedictus*.

The *Agnus Dei* returns to the overall tonic, A♭, as a work's finale should. Its sixteen-bar basic paragraph has a brief instrumental introduction with the strings carrying one of Schubert's rare 'con sordini' indications. The music achieves a fair measure of drama, for the soloists' smooth melody leads some way away from home, to E major, only for the choir's low-lying 'miserere nobis' to give a gentle tweak to the harmony so that the section completes by a typically circuitous Schubertian route a totally customary transition from tonic (A♭) to dominant (E♭). The pattern is repeated, complete with introduction, in a more-or-less literal transposition at the fifth.

---

[15] Rosalia: identical repetition of a melody or phrase a tone higher, held to be a somewhat crude composer's device, though Beethoven went in for it a good deal.

The third 'Agnus Dei' paragraph is left incomplete, for there is a different answer to its opening invocation – not 'miserere nobis' (take pity on us) but 'Dona nobis pacem' (grant us peace). The strings remove their mutes and the section follows a binary pattern. Again there is antiphony, with a lyrical phrase for the soloists answered by a forthright choral entry. The sopranos at this point introduce a characteristic figure, four repeated notes of equal length; that idea will be found at crucial points in Schubert's later work, above all in the finale of the Great C Major Symphony and another 'Dona nobis pacem', that of the E♭ Mass.[16]

Ex. 19 'Dona nobis pacem' of Mass in A♭

The four-equal-note figure breaks in forcefully, insisting 'pacem, pacem', then the choir rounds off the first subsection by climbing to the sopranos' highest note in the entire work, a top b♭. In a compressed rerun of the same music, fifty-two bars shrink to twenty-four, before the final, purely choral seventeen-bar coda entirely over a tonic pedal.

At last the hypnotic spell of seemingly endless four-bar phrases is broken. Schubert casually lengthens his stride, breathes deeper and dovetails his long phrases to make one begin even as the previous one ends. It is done unassumingly, but it is a bold, prophetic stroke.

The instruments have the very last word: a figure like the one at the end of the *Kyrie* transports us once more to the idyllic landscape that was glimpsed there and in 'pleni sunt coeli'. Years earlier, at seventeen, Schubert had aimed for a cyclic ending to his first Mass, and now he does so again. This concluding mood reappears a year later in some of the music for *Rosamunde*. One could also compare it with that at the end of the 1818 *Einsamkeit*; there, the picture of rustic idyll, appreciated at its true worth only as hard-won fulfilment after a lifetime of struggle, is the equivalent in music of T.S. Eliot's 'home is where one starts from'.[17]

In the A♭ Mass's 'Dona nobis pacem' the climax is built up to with less architectonic subtlety than one will find at the same point in the E♭ Mass, but in

---

[16] Fourfold repeated figures, rather than single notes, are strikingly apparent in the strange A minor piano sonata from 1823 and Florinda's powerful aria in *Fierrabras* from the same year. In the symphonic finale the four-note figure is not only part and parcel of a main theme, the second subject, but becomes, in the coda, a climactic point of the whole work. All this is latent as the choral sopranos in the A♭ Mass's 'Dona nobis pacem' sing their four equal minims.

[17] T.S. Eliot, *East Coker* (Four Quartets), London, 1940, Section V.

both works Schubert varies the size of his musical building-bricks to achieve a wonderful relaxation and feeling of *peace*.

Schubert wrote to Spaun on 7 December 1822, a few weeks after he completed the Mass, saying 'I still have the idea of dedicating it to the Emperor or Empress, for it has turned out well.' But with the onset of his illness he could not supervise a performance in 1823, which showed up certain impracticably difficult vocal and string writing and made little impression. Two years later, when the post of Court Vizekapellmeister was due to be advertised, Schubert revised the Mass with a view to making it part of his application. Contentious passages were simplified and he composed an entirely new 'Cum sancto Spiritu', much to the work's advantage; it is nowadays invariably used, and rightly so, though ironically enough even this fugue could not help to get the Mass performed at Court. The new Kapellmeister, Eybler, told Schubert 'Yes, His Majesty is partial to fugues – but only short ones'! Apart from that, very little real recomposition was involved – four extra bars in the *Kyrie* and the recasting of eight in the *Credo*; a curious attempt to take the fun out of the 6/8 'Osanna' by putting it into 4/4 time may also have been part of the revision (that seems likely from the manuscript paper on which it is written). Schubert also persuaded Diabelli to publish the *Tantum Ergo* (D. 739), *Totus in corde* (D. 136), F major *Salve Regina* (D. 223) and C major Mass (D. 452) in the summer of 1825.

Some of the finest music in Schubert's final two masses is inspired by the same portions of the text, but that is not the case throughout. The inner logic of this will become clear once there has been a chance to compare the two works in detail. The Mass in A♭ lets us share Schubert's intuitions before his illness, in religious music dominated by feelings of gratitude and glorification. Here the Creator only occasionally inspires awe, whereas his glory is ever-present and universal. Schubert seems certain that the prayer 'Lord, have mercy on us' has already been answered, and that 'grant us peace' surely will be. He carried through the composition of this major work over a long period fraught with interruptions, when many other projects were cast aside. It clearly meant something special to him, and so it should to us, as a major achievement rounding off his earlier career.

Lazarus

> Then said Jesus unto them plainly, Lazarus is dead.
> John, 11, 14

Even knowing a city well, one cannot know its every corner; there may be some old, quiet square, habitually missed not only by the casual visitor but even by the native of long standing. Ignorant of it, one may still call the place one's own and yet be overlooking something remarkable, something untypical yet in a deeper sense characteristic. So it is with Schubert's *Lazarus*: least practical of pieces, calling for six solo singers, and a small choir who must sit for an hour before delivering what little they have to sing, it is neither chamber music nor does it wholly suit the resources of a symphony orchestra. And yet more than almost any other work of his it shows us his hidden spiritual, reflective side.[18]

Lazarus sets a dramatic poem by a German scholar and theologian, August Hermann Niemeyer. Born two years before Mozart (1754) in the university city of Halle, he spent his entire life there and was still alive in 1820, when Schubert began to set his poem to music. He survived for a further eight years, dying in 1828, the same year as Schubert. The thought of his seventy-four years – more than Mozart and Schubert were granted between them – is ironic, since in 1778, at the ripe old age of twenty-four, Niemeyer had published a first volume of 'collected poems' much influenced by Klopstock's religious poetry. One was a three-act drama elaborating the story of the raising of Lazarus told in chapter 11 of St John's Gospel, but conflating it with the separate story from the other three Gospels in which Jesus restored to life the daughter of a 'governor of the temple'. Mark (5, 22) and Luke (7, 41) name him as Jairus; Niemeyer, Professor of Theology, doubtless had sanction for giving his daughter the name Jemina.

From the outset Niemeyer meant his poem to be set to music, as it very soon was. The year it appeared, the Magdeburg chorus director Johann Heinrich Rolle (1716–1785) took it as the text for an oratorio. During a visit to Vienna in 1811 Niemeyer left a copy of *Lazarus* with Ferdinand. According to Brown Schubert did not come across the poem until the winter of 1819–20. It now seems certain that his setting was meant for performance at Ferdinand's Alt-Lerchenfeld church, and that he completed two acts. Ferdinand conducted them, complete, in 1830 at the church of St. Anne in Vienna, but between then and the time the work was published (1865) the latter part of Act 2 disappeared. The reader in search of a detailed account of many aspects of *Lazarus* can scarcely do better than turn to Brown's 1966 *Essays on Schubert*.

What there is of the cantata tells a simple story, though it is based on a critical event, since in St John's admittedly somewhat visionary Gospel the raising of Lazarus is what finally makes the priests and Pharisees resolve to put an end to Jesus:

> Then gathered the chief priests and the Pharisees a council, and said, 'What do we, for this man doeth many miracles?' . . . Then from that day they took counsel together for to put him to death.
>
> (John 11, 47, 53)

In Niemeyer's poem Lazarus is one of a group of Jesus' followers during His lifetime. He is mortally ill, but having always dreaded the moment when he would have to leave the world he loves, he now feels calm and prepared. His sisters Mary (we have seen the warmth of Schubert's responses to that name!) and Martha react each in her own way. Martha feels only sorrow and

---

[18] See Gülke for a detailed account of its place within contemporary Romantic thought; and Leo Black, 'Raising the Dead', *Musical Times*, Jan. 1997.

apprehension, Mary is serene, impelled by a faith that comes from her contact with their 'Teacher'. A friend, Nathanael, brings a message from Him (John 11, 4, 'this sickness is not unto death, but for the glory of God, that the Son of God might be glorified thereby'). Martha is still overcome with grief, and Mary again calms her. Jemina, 'daughter of resurrection', hurries in, hoping to see Lazarus before he dies. He asks her to sing the story they have often heard from her on summer nights. She tells of her sleep, so like that of Lazarus, and this is where the music quotes again the figure from *An den Mond in einer Herbstnacht* that Schubert has already reused in the 'Domine Deus, Agnus Dei' of the A♭ Mass. Jemina then narrates her flight to heaven, where angels greeted her as a sister. But 'a voice called to me, Awake, Daughter – and I was back on earth, even as the last notes of the funeral chant died away'. After she has finished, Lazarus breathes his last, and the first act ends with music like a funeral march, pausing for each character to express sorrow in his or her own terms. As we shall see, Schubert ties this crucial passage together in a subtle and effective way that looks far ahead in his work.

Act 2 is set in the graveyard where Lazarus is to be buried, and the surviving portion of it is dominated by a new character, Simon the Sadducee. Lazarus looked death in the face, Simon cannot even look at a few tombstones without weeping and wailing. (He has his reasons, but Schubert never got as far as setting to music the text that tells what they are.) His long, conventional solo scene is followed by a little more music for Nathanael and Martha, and a touching burial chorus of Lazarus' friends. It is interesting that Schubert was still thinking in terms of musical ideas and motives from Act 1, but practically speaking this unfinished act is a write-off. The only real loss if it is left unperformed is the chorus, whereas Act 1 makes a fine self-sufficient piece offering room for a fascinating continuation. Schubert's surviving manuscript breaks off midway through a sizeable aria for Martha, who in the poem dominates Act 2 as her sister had Act 1. Niemeyer's third act takes up her meeting with Jesus (John 11, 21) when she tells him 'plainly' 'Lord, if thou hadst been here, my brother had not died', and Lazarus' actual resurrection is in reported speech, before he reappears. Simon has meanwhile emerged as a Job-like figure robbed of wife, children and even grandchildren – truly terrible blows since the Sadducees did not believe in the resurrection of the dead; now even he finds his faith restored.

Lazarus is scored for strings, double woodwind, two horns and three trombones. Schubert obviously felt there was no call for timpani in such a work. The wind instruments are used with the utmost economy and discrimination, and over long stretches only the strings play. The first clarinet is important in a way that looks forward to the sound of the Octet (which for all its conviviality has disturbing moments and wears what Aldous Huxley in a once-famous short story called a 'Gioconda smile'.[19] Its kinship with the deathbed world of *Lazarus* is significant. See 'Grace under Pressure'). The

---

[19] In *Mortal Coils*, London, 1938.

bass instruments' entry just before Lazarus' first lines, far below an expressive clarinet phrase, conveys a sense of awe like that at the end of the A♭ variation in the Octet's slow movement.

The first main section of Mary's first 'scena' is introduced by a pair of horns, as if Schubert were recalling the poetic third section of the Klopstock 'Stabat Mater' with its 'foretaste of Heaven'. In her second scena, bassoon and clarinet take turns with a disturbing accompaniment figure, rather as in the Octet's second variation paired strings exchange one in triplets.

In its colours, especially the use of the clarinet and lower strings separately and together, *Lazarus* also anticipates sounds of viola and celli found in the String Quintet (with the 1821 *Gesang der Geister über den Wassern* as an intermediate stage). The flutes are used sparingly and to great effect, while the horns and trombones never play together in Act 1. Schubert tends to score particular scenes for particular combinations of instruments: a table showing 'who plays when' looks rather like a football pools coupon! This treatment of the orchestra is more akin to the handling of instrumental colours in Baroque music than to the kind of orchestral writing that developed from the middle eighteenth century onwards, and one needs to look to the early twentieth century to rediscover the idea of creating subtle chamber-music textures through temporary groupings chosen from the range of instruments available in an orchestra. Schönberg made much of that from the *Gurrelieder* onwards. Some of the effects created by well-calculated and economical use of the wind instruments are striking indeed. The insidious sweetness of Jemina's near fatal sleep is perfectly conveyed by the combination of flutes and clarinets; the 'distant light, too powerful to bear' on her arrival in heaven by two flutes and an oboe in the upper register. Lazarus' blessing on 'the one who brings the tidings that I am to die' also uses the same high instruments, in a figure that could be out of Bruckner or even *Parsifal*.

The two horns play a leading role in Mary's first aria, and even the trombones are artfully used. They lend their weight to Martha's second outburst of fear, and again heighten the apprehensive mood when Mary speaks of the soul's struggles in this world. Their melodic role in the final ensemble of Act 1 is still more crucial, and hints at the important contribution they will make to all three main sections of the Great C Major Symphony's opening movement. As each character reacts to Lazarus' death there are the briefest interludes in which two trombones play a version of what has become a 'motto'. It is a brief snatch of melody that pervades the whole first act, or to be quite precise it is a new version of the act's initial complex idea. A year later Schubert returned to the same sequential layout for the end of a section, in *Gesang der Geister über den Wässern*, though without the solo interjections. Its purpose there is to illustrate water gently falling to find its own level – 'und leicht empfangen/ Wallt er verschleiernd/ Leisrauschend zur Tiefe nieder'.

But perhaps the most fascinating aspect of *Lazarus* is its musical prose, as distinct from poetry (though such a distinction would not be explicitly drawn for another century). Schubert's 'prose style' here is a worthy successor to

Bach's great ariosi and Mozart's accompanied recitatives. A quarter of a century later, Wagner developed what he called 'endless melody', but the scale and grandeur of passages such as the latter part of Jemina's narration shows Schubert already on the point of a comparable breakthrough. Vocal and instrumental lines blend with and echo each other, like voice and piano in the great songs, but the orchestra provides a more varied palette of subtle shadings than the piano ever could.

Apart from its 'prose' scenes, *Lazarus* does also contain a number of set pieces of a more conventional kind. Two are given to Mary, who is a worthy counterpart to her brother as principal figure: in her first, which one could follow operatic convention and call a 'scena' – part arioso, part aria – she prays that God may help him in his final struggle with death, so that he meets it 'with peace in his soul'. In the second she speaks of life's hardships and of their brothers who have already passed into the realm of light. Both contain brief passages where the vocal line doubles the bass rather than being its counterpole at the opposite end of the texture. This I abbreviate as VDB;[20] it is a significant procedure found occasionally in vocal music from most stages in Schubert's career.

His output is immensely varied, and yet it is no surprise to find many recurring features like fingerprints that make known an unmistakable presence. VDB has been less commented on than his ever-resourceful use of major–minor juxtaposition and contrast, or his rhythmic persistence, but it throws light on aspects of his psyche. The importance of the duality melody–bass in classical music can scarcely be overstated: the two must be well matched, yet in Schubert's songs there is no doubt where the spotlight is mostly directed – at the top of the texture, even during the piano's interludes. Brahms, a pastmaster not only at devising resourceful basses but also at thinking in terms of additional contrapuntal parts, was quoted by Schönberg as saying that one should be able to whistle any melody worth its salt, and such melodies will by their very nature lie in the most prominent register, the treble. The bass is a support, indispensable if the whole is not to be built on sand, but not the object of the most intense attention. This touches on all manner of dualisms in psychology, but has a physical basis: low notes vibrate slower than high ones, a low note of equal measurable intensity will sound softer than a high one, loudness and softness are in turn perceived partly in terms of near and far.[21] So it is not surprising that the Western European ear has increasingly tended to let the 'high', rapidly vibrating notes catch its attention, the 'low' ones being there rather to act as a stable 'base'. Here a pun may legitimately be intended!

Age-old Oriental wisdom refers to Yin and Yang: dark, unshakeable earth-energy resting under our feet; bright, restless heaven-energy streaming down

---

[20] See Leo Black, 'VDB', *Brille*, Jan. 2001, which lists two dozen such passages and draws attention to the themes (submissiveness, obedience to a higher law or an inner voice) common to their texts.

[21] See Helga de la Motte Haber, *Musik und bildende Kunst*, part I, 'Die räumliche Anschauung der Töne'.

from above. Schubert harboured enough and to spare of both. And various creation legends envisage the world before the Creation as a void gradually beginning to vibrate.[22]

It is therefore interesting to examine the passages in Schubert's vocal music where he deliberately reverses the polarity. It happens rarely (I have traced some two dozen instances in over four hundred songs, a significant one in the second *Salve Regina*, and three in *Lazarus*), but that makes it the more striking when it happens. Its effect is difficult and contentious to pin down in words, but the texts tell us something.

Whatever his contemporary critics may have said, Schubert was no 'clinger to words', as has been alleged of, say, Hugo Wolf. The basically well-disposed 1820 Viennese reviewer of his Singspiel *Die Zwillingsbrüder* called him 'too much wedded to details of the text', while G.W. Fink's equally well-meaning review of 24 April 1824 in the Leipzig *Allgemeine musikalische Zeitung* praised his almost invariable success in 'laying out the whole and each detail according to the poet's idea'. (Fink could not take the further step of accepting the results in a song such as *Auf der Donau*, but at least he got the point.) Words offered Schubert inspiration, he noted their images, and reacted primarily to their kernel of emotional truth, which could make him overlook literary shortcomings. He had innumerable different musical equivalents for the most frequently found poetic images, and above all for natural phenomena. A line of text could be his cue – but a cue is merely the signal for something to happen, it does not create the thing, which must in some sense be there already. It would be a mistake to regard the finale of Beethoven's Choral Symphony as 'inspired' by Schiller's Ode to Joy: there was music Beethoven had to write, and those stanzas offered him the occasion to do so. For Schubert, too there was music he had to write. Since he was so well read, passage after passage in poems played the same crystallising function for him that the Schiller Ode had for Beethoven.

VDB is fully effective only once it is a matter of a real melody doubled by voice and bass. To watch it develop from Schubert's twentieth year into his early thirties is to learn something about the workings of a unique musical mind. The texts in question show a close connection between this musical fingerprint and ideas of submissiveness,[23] subjection to superior force, abdication of the will, and of heeding an 'inner voice'. The actual words 'die innere Stimme' are set in VDB in the third verse of the Schiller setting *Hoffnung*.

The first VDB in *Lazarus* comes as early as the fourth line sung by Mary in her first 'scena', and could scarcely sum up more precisely an element of submissiveness in Schubert: 'ich verstumme vor des Weisen Führung' (I fall silent before the Wise One's leadership). There is another when she prays for Heavenly peace to enter Lazarus' soul (Dass voll Frieden Ihm die Seele sei), and

---

[22] For instances of vibration in creation legends see Jung, *Psychology of the Unconscious*.

[23] The early twenty-first century has developed meanings for 'submission' associated with a range of things from wrestling to sado-masochism, its ethical significance having meanwhile faded into the background along with much else of its kind. I have where possible used the alternative 'submissiveness'.

a third in her other scena, as she sings of the soul threatened by waves that swell to their peak (Ob die Wellen bis zum Gipfel schwellen). Here there is a threat coming from deep down, rather than submission to a benevolent power.

Lazarus is equally interesting when one comes to examine its techniques of composition. By Schubert's time, classical symphonic music was well advanced in transforming short themes and motives. Haydn's string-quartet movements were often made up of different versions of some minuscule idea given out at the opening. As for Schubert, he is prodigal with his melodies, like Mozart, but like Haydn he can prove a downright Scrooge when he needs to use his resources economically, and *Lazarus* shows him obsessed with one very simple scrap of melody also found elsewhere in his music both before and after 1820. At its simplest it is a mere snatch of major scale with a dotted rhythm (Ex. 20a), like the one that will later pervade the Great C Major Symphony (Ex. 20a'), but it soon takes on other forms. The listener can relate them to the original, insofar as the rhythm remains the same (Ex. 20b), but is more challenged once the long first note has been divided into two shorter ones (Ex. 20c). It can also be 'interverted', that is to say, the order of its notes can be altered (Ex. 20d), opening up a whole further range of possibilities. From the outset, *Lazarus* weaves a web of references to these figures in all their variety.

Ex. 20 Basic ideas in *Lazarus*

The work's first bars (see Ex. 21) contain not a simple melodic idea, but something more complex, an 'idea' in the sense propounded a century after Schubert in an article by Schönberg;[24] to his mind, which worked effortlessly in terms of simultaneous parts, an 'idea' was something made up of a number of different elements. Only the fact that they all appear at once gives it character, and that is precisely *why* they all appear at once. Schönberg's case in point was not from his own music, nor from the immediate past, but from the finale of a work composed when Schubert was six, Beethoven's *Waldstein* Sonata (in C major, Op. 53). Another famous example from later in Beethoven's work is the opening of his last string quartet, in F major, Op. 135. To approach a cantata in that way was bold and original. For the sake of balance it should be added that

---

[24] 'Comments on *Let there be Light! – Hugo Riemann's Metrical-Accentual Scheme* by Theodor Wiehmayer' – ms, 1923.

since *Lazarus* is, after all, by Schubert, not Schönberg, much of it is more loose-limbed, with quite literal repetitions of whole sections.

Ex. 21

Why did Schubert take to this libretto with such unforeseeable intensity? Why was he overtaken by one of his impulses of 'right and true devotion'? He lived among friends – artists, civil servants, few musicians – but also a little apart from a fundamentally unsympathetic world, and could have been attracted by Niemeyer's picture of a small, close knit community held together by love of life, acceptance of death and the presence of a great spirit.[25] Nathanael's music as he comes bearing the Teacher's Message is one of Schubert's unmistakable Beethoven-impressions,[26] audibly influenced by the start of the closing scene in *Fidelio* with its bouncing multiple-upbeats. Don Fernando is also the bearer of good news.

In March 1820 Schubert spent a night at the police station after the police had descended on a gathering of his circle at a friend's house, and he had given them what might nowadays be classed as 'verbal'. He had been at work on *Lazarus* since February and it was due to be performed on Easter Sunday, which that year fell on 2 April. No charges were laid against Schubert, who was in custody no time at all and got away with a black eye and a caution, unlike his good friend Senn, who was banished to the Tirol and saw his legal career in ruins, but it was an upsetting experience and quite out of keeping with Niemeyer's other-worldliness. There is sense in Christopher Gibbs' recent suggestion that Schubert's involvement in a quite serious police matter made him unable to do truly creative work for a while.[27] A set of six antiphons for Palm Sunday, which that year fell on 26 March, is not a major counter-argument, for they are slight and according to McKay he wrote them in half an hour. Certainly the Deutsch catalogue has virtually nothing to offer between an unspecified time in March and September, only one set of Ecossaises (D. 697) written in May. Even

---

[25] The hero of Walter Pater's long-forgotten but once eminently fashionable novel *Marius the Epicurean* comes across a small community of early Christians and is converted. The chapters in question could interest anyone fascinated by *Lazarus*.

[26] Another can be found in much of the music of the ballad *Der Sänger*, where there was obviously room for an identification between the idealised great composer and Goethe's selfless minstrel.

[27] *The Life of Schubert*.

the A♭ Mass may have hung in abeyance, given the likely chronology of its first three movements.

Had Schubert returned to *Lazarus*, its high moral tone could have wearied him; the rejoicing at the end of Niemeyer's third act might have been enough to put him off.[28] And was he even capable of 'composing a resurrection' in 1820, before his own descent into a deeper darkness than that of a police cell? The Raising of Lazarus is only reported by Martha, but Schubert would still have needed to surpass even what he had written for Jemina. Perhaps he wondered too. Act 3 with the resurrection seems never to have been begun, and *Lazarus*' true continuation could be sought rather in the Unfinished Symphony. That begins (or 'resumes') in precisely the key reached at the end of Act 1, after the hero's death, B minor;[29] is it too fanciful to hear in the symphony's monumental, searching music Lazarus' journey, Gerontius-like, into the hereafter?

The intended performance at Alt-Lerchenfeld Church obviously could not happen. *Lazarus* was replaced by Haydn's 'Nelson' Mass, which Ferdinand let his brother conduct – 'with such enthusiasm and with such energy and attention to detail[30] that a better production can scarcely be imagined'.

Otto Erich Deutsch's documentary biography contains not one contemporary reference to *Lazarus*. Schubert usually shared his new compositions freely with the friends he knew would appreciate them,[31] but not even Ferdinand saw the score of this one until it turned up in his brother's papers after his death. With hindsight, it emerges as a link unwittingly forged between two kinds of musical work from different stages in the development of the art, and between two seemingly separate worlds – Viennese classical chamber music, late-nineteenth-century music-drama. It has the spirit of the one and at times the air of the other. For an intense evocation of an intimate personal world, cantata and oratorio can offer nothing comparable until Elgar's *The Dream of Gerontius*; set alongside it, even the tenderness of the best of the Brahms *German Requiem* has the air of a statement of public policy. And if any work ever argued for the thesis that there is a guiding pattern in the development of European music, that in some obscure way great minds do indeed think alike, that work is *Lazarus*. Yet

[28] Manuela Jahrmärker's suggestion, *Schubert Handbuch*.

[29] The two works were combined in concert, at my suggestion, by the BBC Northern Symphony Orchestra (now the BBC Philharmonic) during the 1978 sesquicentennial celebrations; an interval before the symphony obscured the musical link, which was restored when the recorded concert was broadcast, the two then running *segue*. There is one problem about this idea – *Lazarus* calls for a small orchestra whereas apart from performances by 'period' orchestras the symphony is likely to be performed by larger ones. That need not necessarily be a disadvantage from the point of view of symbolism.

[30] See Ernst Hilmar, 'Ferdinand Schuberts Skizze zu einer Autobiographie', in *Schubert-Studien: Festgabe der Österreichischen Akademie der Wissenschaften zum Schubert-Jahr 1978*, Vienna, 1978. The Grimm brothers' etymological dictionary of the German language gives no example of the word 'Preciosität', which Ferdinand used. It could be taken to mean 'preciosity' rather than 'precision', but it was clearly meant as a compliment.

[31] See Walburga Litschauer, 'Ein vereintes Streben nach dem Schönsten', *SSF*.

its prime claim to attention lies elsewhere. Above all, it enshrines something of the numinous Schubert. Years before he had cause to think his own life might be drastically shortened, his genius was set working by the picture of a man who has loved the world, who knows he must leave it, and who firmly believes there is life everlasting.

4

Grace under Pressure
Schubert's conflicts between 1821 and 1824

A period of fateful recognition of a miserable reality, which I endeavour to beautify as far as possible by my imagination, thank God.

Schubert, letter to Ferdinand, 17 July 1824

Im Walde (Schlegel); Abendstern; Der Unglückliche; Versunken; Grenzen der Menschheit; Suleika I; Gesang der Geister über den Wassern (D. 714); Symphony in B minor (Unfinished); Wanderer Fantasy; Moment Musical no. 6; Lied (Des Lebens Tag); 36 Originaltänze (D. 365); 16 Deutsche and 2 Ecossaises (D. 783); 12 Deutsche Tänze (D. 790); Valses nobles (D. 969); Funeral March for Tsar Alexander I; 2 Characteristic Marches

---

The full complexity of Schubert's 'right and true devotion' emerges as one reaches 1823 and the time of his illness. Wonder and awe have always been two faces of the same coin, for, as traditional Roman Catholic theology puts it, the 'fascinating' (fascinans) and the 'terrifying' (tremendum) are complementary elements of natural, non-rational religious experience.[1] Rilke has the measure of this in lines from his first Duino Elegy:

Denn das Schöne ist nichts
Als des Schrecklichen Anfang, den wir noch grade ertragen.

For the beautiful is nothing else
Than the onset of the terrible, which we can still just endure.

We left Schubert at work on his Mass, and with *Lazarus* abandoned, early in 1820. Around the turn of the next year his mind was again at its most active. It turned, in the powerful and prophetic Schlegel setting *Im Walde* (D. 708, December, see 'Schubert in Love?'), to a poem where the 'divine afflatus' is indistinguishable from the creative urge. Near its end there is a most unconventional chord to send a shiver down the spine. This acts like a dominant seventh with an extra dissonance, but as laid out it consists of

---

[1] Otto's classic study sets out that, and much more, in intriguingly convincing detail.

fourths piled one on top of another, which make a very strange impression, gaunt and a little frightening. Many decades later Skryabin was to base much of his harmony on chords built out of fourths, though unlike this one of Schubert's they were expected to make their impact precisely because they were not underpinned by a 'root'. In the passage in *Im Walde* there seems to be a shudder of awe at something mysterious and dangerous. A similar chord subtly conveys alienation in the 1824 Mayrhofer song *Abendstern* (D. 806, fourteenth complete bar, at 'Ich bin der Liebe treuer Stern' (I am Love's faithful star)), though the next words are necessary to make the alienation clear: the star's companions stand aloof from it (Sie halten sich der Liebe fern; also bar 28). The stormy Quartet Movement in C minor (D. 703), from the same month as *Im Walde*, also conveys an almost alarming excitement, especially through the tremolo at its opening.

That eruption of creativity from December 1820 onwards may or may not have owed something to a final surge of emotion over Therese Grob. Any such experience would have laid a firm foundation for Schubert's creative reaction, eight years later, on coming across a Heine poem where the poet has to endure the sight of 'myself when young' – the poem he turned into *Der Doppelgänger* (see 'Pride of Performance'). Several fine songs from early 1821 turn to texts that cover a range of emotion, 'profane' rather than 'sacred' and some of it reflecting unhappy love. The ambitious *Der Unglückliche* (D. 713) does full justice to its theme of a vision realised then snatched away to leave the lover's 'last state worst than his first'. It is also a curiosity, since for a change Schubert took an idea for a song from one of his own instrumental pieces rather than doing the opposite, as he so memorably did in song-based works from the 'Trout' Quintet to the late Violin Fantasy. The opening of *Der Unglückliche* (Ex. 22b) looks back, especially in its sixth bar, to the slow movement of the A major piano sonata from 1819 (Ex. 22a). That is a lyrical, mostly light-hearted work, but its slow movement probes deeper.

Ex. 22a Piano Sonata in A, D. 664, 2nd movement

Ex. 22b *Der Unglückliche*

Versunken (D. 715, February 1821) is his most successful sensual love-song,[2] to a late Goethe poem about a head of irresistible, rippling hair. Its perpetual-motion piano part, when played, should meet Mozart's criterion of 'flowing like oil'. The song is a worldly counterpart to the ecstatic *Rastlose Liebe* (D. 138) from six years earlier. Schubert, one of seventy musicians to be inspired to song by the latter Goethe poem, set it in a state of excitement that surprised even himself; he is more likely to have smiled a smile of quiet creative satisfaction after penning the totally hedonistic music of *Versunken*.

The following month saw the composition of the two great *Suleika* songs, to poems later revealed as by 'the youthful love of Goethe's old age', Marianne von Willemer, and two settings of genuine Goethe poems, *Geheimes* (D. 719) and *Grenzen der Menschheit* (Mankind's Limitations, D. 716). The latter is in tessitura a 'basso cantante' song, immensely effective delivered by a singer with the right voice and legato. That, however, does justice to only one side of it, and not the one most personal to its composer. The grandeur and

---

[2] His least successful sensual song dates from only two months earlier. In *Der zürnenden Diana* (To the angry Diana, Dec. 1820, D. 707) he struggled to find an erotic, masochistic vein matching the poem's central image. Actaeon the hunter is convulsed with joy at the sight of the naked goddess of the chase and of chastity, even then raising her bow to despatch him. (Mayrhofer shied away from the legend's original version, in which Actaeon, already transformed into a stag, was torn to pieces by his own hounds, and preferred to see him off with one clean, clinical arrow.) To the ancient Greeks, the naked human body in its prime was something else mysterious and dangerous, 'a source of energy and light, a *corps éclatant* . . . Powerful attributes played over its surface like a kind of aurora corporalis' (Book review by James Davidson, *London Review of Books*, 18 June 1998, quoting the French classicist Jean-Pierre Vernant). As a classical scholar, Mayrhofer must have known something of that, but it finds no musical correlative in the music, such as is often present to match even things Schubert would not have experienced; a striking example is the sea wind screaming through the rigging in *Schiffers Scheidelied*.

unattainability of Goethe's 'Gods' are powerfully conveyed, less so Schubert's reaction, which follows the poet in accepting the limitations of being human. 'Man can reach for the stars, but then his feet lose touch with Mother Earth and he is blown about by fate. Or else he can stand four-square and rooted, but the oak and the vine can do as much.' This song puts the idea of Schubert's inborn submissiveness and natural piety to the acid test, for no poem was better designed to bring it out, if there.

Any composer may set any poem to music, so we must remember (not for the first time) that what speaks to the musician is the music's sound. If that is boring and mediocre, the greatest text in the world will not make it less so. Indeed, such a piece will say less than does the poem on its own, which is reason enough to make a great writer cautious about unknowns' attempts to improve on him by adding music. The poems set by musicians Goethe favoured tended to be his strophic rhyming lyrics suitable for singing with the same melody used for each strophe; the grand blank verse and irregular strophes of *Grenzen der Menschheit* seem beyond the scope of any contemporary save Schubert. Later composers were more likely to set it as a cantata, Hugo Wolf dared to challenge comparison with Schubert in a *Lied*, and from not so long after Schubert's time there is one by Ferdinand Hiller (Op. 63 No. 3).

To realise Schubert's full intentions in setting the poem, a lyrical talent is also needed, with in all likelihood a bass-baritone rather than a pure bass voice, even if one nonetheless able to incorporate the many low notes; upper-octave ossias[3] making the line easier to sing also distort it and make nonsense of Schubert's characteristic curves.

Before the voice enters, Schubert shows a measured response to the poem's opening. Both here and in the companion poem *Prometheus* Goethe sets out from the image of a thunderstorm: in the one case, Zeus is vainly exerting his powers, 'like a little boy beheading thistles', in the other he 'sows over the earth his blessings of lightning' (rather than the refreshing rain greeted by the shepherd in the finale of Beethoven's Pastoral Symphony). The other composer to set both poems was Hugo Wolf, who in composing *Prometheus* could not resist the chance to write a whole introductory page of piano music matching Zeus the Thunderer; both composers, however, noted Goethe's philosophical response to the thunder and lightning in *Grenzen der Menschheit*. Schubert in fact begins the more vigorously of the two, setting out with a rising figure in the piano (b to c, as upbeat to a ringing major chord, which resolves on to its quieter dominant). This rising conjunct interval, as minor or major second, will pervade the song's accompaniment and is too general to interpret in any obvious hermeneutic way – for it would have to represent equally the Gods' determination to use their power and man's acceptance of that. And yet it clearly is a major element in Schubert's inspiration when composing the song, like a hand in the small of the back, impelling him ever onwards. The only trace

---

[3] Alternative version (from Italian, 'o sia', 'or let it be') of a musical passage, often though by no means always simplified to make performance easier.

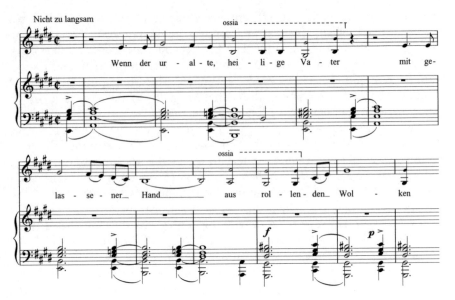

Ex. 23 *Grenzen der Menschheit*

of it in the voice part is an inversion at 'Uns hebt die Welle, verschlingt die Welle' (the wave lifts us up, the wave swallows us up); this initiates the final extraordinary transition discussed below. At the opening, one is briefly left wondering what key the music will be in, for after five bars it could as well be making for C or G major as for the song's overall E major. (As the song's tonic, this shows yet another side of Schubert in a key often associated in his music with happiness,[4] though here with unapproachable grandeur.)

The first stanza follows calmly in the 'right' key (Ex. 23), with the resolute rising semitone become a dignified rising whole tone; the temptation to imagine this accompanied by Wagner tubas is part and parcel of a 'basso' conception of the song. There is a brief VDB from 'Hand' to 'Wolken'.

Once the text reaches the contrasts between Gods and men, the tonal calm is disturbed; that opening C/G major reappears, leading to a strophe-end in F. The opening vocal line was not so far removed from the 'form-out-of-chaos' shape that Schubert found in Haydn's *The Creation* and turned to good account in works from second *Salve Regina* to Great C Major Symphony (see 'Harvest' and

---

[4] Schubert shows an engaging tendency to use some particular key over and over again for music that shares a basic mood. In the spring and summer of 1816 this produced a cluster of pieces in a happy-sounding E major – *Trinklied im Mai, Minnelied, Die frühe Liebe, Blumenlied, Seligkeit, Erntelied* (all composed in May), *Das grosse Hallelujah, Schlachtlied, Gott im Frühlinge, Der gute Hirte,* and the Five Piano Pieces ('Sonata', first and last pieces in E, D. 459, August), then finally *Ferne von der grossen Stadt* (September). This association of E major with a carefree mood throws an interesting light on his incomparably poignant use of it for the String Quintet's slow movement. *Grenzen der Menschheit*, the final song of *Die schöne Müllerin* and the slow movement of the *Arpeggione* Sonata come somewhere in-between in mood.

Ex. 34). Now, as Goethe tells of man played with by clouds and winds, the curve reappears in more like its original form in Haydn; to press the point, Schubert sets the line in an impressive VDB.

Ex. 24 *Grenzen der Menschheit*

One of *Grenzen der Menschheit*'s most fascinating features lies in two utterly original transitions between strophes. They are very quiet and seem designed to drive home the littleness of man. That between the stanza just discussed and the one about 'standing four-square on Mother Earth' treats its dissonant notes in a way that challenges the rules of harmony, for a dissonance was supposed to start as a consonance, become 'dissonant' as the texture around it changed, then 'resolve' to become consonant again. In the second complete bar of the next example the e shamelessly appears on the strong beat, followed in bar 3 by a weird chord seemingly made up of superimposed fourths (see the December 1820 *Im Walde*), which resolves only onto the not-totally consonant dominant seventh. And an e♯ two bars later is eminently mysterious: it could be simply there to 'fill in' the interval between e (upper part just before) and f♯ (bass of ensuing chord), but coming in unaccompanied in the bass it is liable to send a shiver down the spine.

Ex. 25

The transition from this strophe to the final reappearance of the first's music is less complex – merely an accented dominant–minor-ninth chord – but still a wonderful sign of man cringing in his little corner, confessedly a mere creature. The resolute opening b – c reappears as a sign of something very far from resolve, and instead of leading away from home it helps to set up the return of the tonic. The final very low vocal line again uses VDB, prompted by the idea of endless generations subsumed in the timeless grandeur of the Gods.

There were precedents for some of *Grenzen der Menschheit*'s more surprising features: the growling left-hand trill leading into 'Denn mit Göttern soll sich nicht messen' (For no man shall measure himself against the Gods) occurs as early as 1815 in the piano's postludes within another Goethe song, *Der Schatzgräber* (The Treasure-Hunter); in both cases the figure conveys resolve of one kind or another. The vocal line at 'nirgends haften dann Die unsicher'n Sohlen' (Then his uncertain soles find no support) explores the interval of the minor ninth, which is found in pure culture in *Freiwilliges Versinken* (Voluntary Extinction, D. 700, September 1820); one of Mayrhofer's finer flights there has the great golden sun itself 'submitting', as each evening it sinks down behind the mountains. Only then can those lesser luminaries, the moon and stars, make themselves apparent. (The same song also shows at its opening the same resolute trills in the piano part, and its final four bars are another of Schubert's postludes shedding new light, here a quietly aspiring line that turns the song's minor mode into the major. Instead of alarm and terror as the sun disappears, there is now a sovereign calm and benevolence.)

Another Goethe setting, already mentioned, broke new ground, the *Gesang der Geister über den Wassern* – Song of the Spirits Over the Waters (D. 714). Schubert's choice of violas, celli and double-bass to partner the voices suggests that the 'Chaos' Prelude was not the only passage in Haydn's *The Creation* to impress him deeply. This rich low-string texture resembles the one accompanying God's injunction to the birds and beasts, 'seid fruchtbar, wachset, mehret euch – be fruitful, grow, multiply'. In Schubert's own output, the lower-string sound takes one back a year to the opening of *Lazarus*, but also half a decade forward to the introduction to the Great C Major Symphony's first movement (bars 17–28), and then three years further on, to the chromatically harmonised deep textures in parts of the String Quintet. The 'ecclesiastical' fourth resolving down to the third in bars 9, 11 and 14 is especially prophetic of the strange graveyard 'trio' section in the quintet's third movement.

Gesang der Geister was not one of Schubert's public successes. It was performed (who knows how?!) at a concert in March 1821, prompting a diarist's[5] pun that 'it didn't come over, it went under'. The Viennese *Allgemeine Musikalische Zeitung* wrote it off as 'an accumulation of every sort of senseless, disordered and purposeless musical modulation and side-tracking': so at least the critic noticed the strangeness of its picture of the soul blown about by the

---

[5] Josef Karl Rosenbaum, 7 March 1821 (Deutsch, *A Documentary Biography*, henceforth referred to as *Doc.*, p. 165).

winds of fate. The poem touches on the 'creature-feeling', the sense of nothingness in face of infinity and eternity, and it is no surprise that Schubert's setting develops at least one idea from *Lazarus*, the end of its second strophe matching closely the descending sequential modulations at the heart of the B minor chorus after Lazarus' death.

The end of the third looks forward rather than back. By this stage of the poem the water is subsiding after its stormy passage over a cliff, to flow peacefully through the meadows. Schubert does not simply pass from one strophe to the next; he brings about a magical transition through a restless instrumental bass line winding its way upward, quite like the piano's introduction to *Suleika I* two months later. That opens with a flurry of movement deep down in the pianist's left hand, in keeping with Marianne's image of dust blown about by the east wind. At the end of his life Schubert leaves this most mysterious fingerprint yet again in the slow movement of the string quintet; a series of arabesques deep in the bass is added as further accompaniment to the reprise of the main melody.

One musical link between *Suleika I* and the Unfinished Symphony is that the latter work likewise opens with a mysterious line deep in the bass.

Ex. 26 B minor ('Unfinished') Symphony, opening of 1st movement

One might suppose that the purpose of these ideas was simply to set up the melody that follows. That is so in the song, but not, as we shall see, in the symphony.

The crucial works from autumn 1822 – B minor Unfinished Symphony, Wanderer Fantasy – can scarcely be over-valued. The symphony was well advanced by September, when Schubert promised it 'soon' to the Styrian Music Society that had made him its honorary member, and its title page is dated 30 October 1822. He fell ill during the ensuing weeks, but that tells us nothing about what he composed, only about what he didn't compose to complete it. Nor can one reliably relate the amazing moods in the Wanderer Fantasy, from even nearer the crucial time, to anything specific in his life, even if one believes in trying to do so.

Before the Unfinished Symphony's mysteries it would be best to stand like the fool Parsifal before Amfortas, unable to ask 'Father, what ails thee?' Its unique mixture of amiability, visionary beauty and terror is impossible to rationalise in words (and certainly not those of a Chinese commentator named Chau Hau in 1974, quoted by Reininghaus: 'the Unfinished Symphony reflects class feelings of depression, hopelessness and disappointment, flight from reality, dreams of freedom: that is its social content'. Goldschmidt taught for a year in China during the 1930s, and had something to answer for). Was there ever such a symphonic first movement, on its so-deliberate way (but where?), with its gaunt first phrase growling in the deepest bass? That line for the cellos and basses will play a very substantial role in the movement, whereas the 'first subject' that follows is a haunting melody destined to appear only here and, slightly extended, at the corresponding point in the recapitulation. So let us enjoy it while we have it. Both in itself and even more through its accompaniment it takes up the mood of *Suleika I*'s first half, composed in the same measure and same key of B minor, and virtually the same tempo; in actual contour the two melodies' differences exactly balance their similarities.

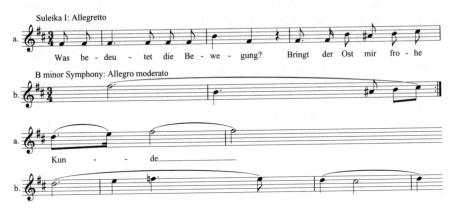

Ex. 27 *Suleika I* and B minor ('Unfinished') Symphony

The famous slow-waltz second subject was linked at the height of a wave of American political correctness (American Musicological Society Congress, 1991) with a phrase in *Erlkönig* – 'Ich liebe dich, mich reizt deine schöne Gestalt' (I love you, your beautiful form provokes me) – as evidence of sexual abuse in Schubert's childhood. The great twenty-first-century Schubert conductor has yet to appear and convince us of this when we hear the symphony. It is heard, broken off, developed and brought to a close; then the substantial development section returns to, and carries to unheard-of heights and depths, that mysterious introductory line, dark successor of Schubert's earlier unconventional 'ways into the work'. This development's opening hints at unheard-of things, with its imitative entry of the opening figure stretching out its arms towards the upper octave, only for its reach to exceed its grasp and fall short at the most dissonant note just below (a high b in the first violins, over a low c in the cellos and basses). Such a passage of toil and trouble could put one in mind of a new arrival in the Great Beyond, say Newman's and Elgar's Gerontius, at last facing his Maker, blinded by such splendour and forced to turn his face away in terror. (In 'Harvest' we shall see how recent thinking has developed the idea of a hidden programme for a symphony.) If Schubert was drawn to Niemeyer's libretto, then after Lazarus' death at the end of Act 1, with its attendant B minor, he could have been far more in sympathy with the hero and what awaited him than with the exceptionally tiresome Sadducee and his yammering. And if in the longer run he was left with a sense of having failed to rise to the occasion by abandoning *Lazarus*, this symphony could have been his creative response, his attempt to make amends to himself. Ironically, it too was to remain unfinished, so a major problem in applying the 'Lazarus' idea to it as a whole would be that it is not a whole: impossible to 'read' its later stages when the scherzo is incomplete, and so much less inspired[6] as to be a write-off, for all the attempts to complete it down the years.

Nor has a finale come down to us. The B minor Entr'acte from *Rosamunde* (considered in 'Hard Sayings') has been suggested as solution. To put it crudely, either it was meant as the finale or it wasn't and nobody can prove it either way, but in various ways it fails to fit the bill for either a conventional finale or a very unconventional one matching a resurrection. Its well-nigh hysterical ending would be particularly unsuitable; the most that can be advanced in its favour is a certain affinity of mood between the moment in the symphony we have just reached, the start of the development section, and passages in the Entr'acte.

To return to the first movement, after a mere sixteen bars it is back at a point[7] from which Schubert could without more ado have launched into his recapitulation: but he has an appointment elsewhere. The entire section shows a new Schubert, dark and threatening, and nowhere more so than in the six bars of minatory full-orchestral unison (170–5) that soon follow. A prophetic tone to choral unison passages in the Masses has been noted; this is still more intimidating. Now there are repeated attempts, if not at the lyrical second subject then at least at what went with it – 'four bars of accompaniment in search of a melody'; but the intensity is ratcheted up to the sticking-point, with the introduction's theme marching in the bass, and above it furious violin figuration, like a demonic parody of the running accompaniments in the masses. This is of an earnestness to suggest Last Things. In layout and atmosphere it is comparable with the music in the *Gloria* of the A♭ Mass from 'quoniam' onwards, which built over a pedal-point until it broke into the unison 'triumphal march' and the fugal 'Cum sancto Spiritu' with its running violins. That was a passage of riveting seriousness – but Schubert has moved on, and nothing as sombre as the development sections of the Unfinished Symphony will be found in his liturgical music until the anguished 'Domine Deus, Agnus Dei' of the late E♭ Mass.

After all that, it is not really surprising that the 'introduction' figure is left out of the recapitulation: one has heard little else for several minutes. (In due course, the two bars that preface the Andante con moto second movement will also prove to be far more than an introduction.) But after a reasonably literal reprise Schubert ends the movement by squeezing yet more out of his introductory line. He echoes the start of the development in a more resigned

---

[6] The B minor minuet-and-trio of the G major piano sonata (D. 894, 1826) would, if orchestrated, make a more fitting continuation but the finale problem would remain.
[7] On the dominant of B minor.

way, and from bar 336 onwards there is a hint of an imitative duet; something similar appears both in an outstanding number in *Fierrabras* (No. 19), and at the end (bar 357ff.) of the slow movement of the Great C Major Symphony.

The similarity of development-technique between the Unfinished Symphony's two movements is a virtue or a weakness, depending on one's analytic criteria and, especially, one's views on literal repetition. First and foremost, they share at times the fevered note described above, which in view of its final appearance in the E♭ Mass one could call Schubert's 'Domine Deus . . . Miserere nobis' mood. But unity extends further; both are in a quite leisurely triple time, both have second-subject melodies with syncopated accompaniments, and the latter are in both cases used briefly on their own. And there is a common tendency to revert to widely spaced outer parts with, seemingly, an emotional void between. The first movement does that most memorably at the opening of the development, with a less anguished echo at the start of the brief codetta, the second as early as bar 25.

The second movement, in Schubert's 'bliss' key of E major, might suggest Lazarus' spirit moved on and acclimatised, though still being put to the test. It too has its introduction – three chords (tonic, dominant, tonic) whose top notes trace not a minor third, as at the opening of the first movement, but its major version (bracketed at the start of Ex. 28a); the bass-line falls in pizzicato on double-basses alone, where the rising-and-falling line in the first movement, intended to be heard as a melody, was doubled by the cellos. The main melody picks up the rising scale in the most natural way.

Ex. 28a B minor ('Unfinished') Symphony, opening of 2nd movement

Ex. 28b B minor ('Unfinished') Symphony, coda of 2nd movement

Much of the second movement's seductive quality comes precisely from its succession of minuscule figures, one generating the next. The generative process carries us irresistibly but gently along: this is the 'arabesque' technique favoured by painters of the time (see 'Harvest'), and it gives the music a wonderful feeling of improvisation.[8]

The three-chord figure is not technically part of the opening melody, but is ever-present. Schubert again works with a complex 'idea', as at the opening of *Lazarus*; all its components are necessary if it is to make its full effect. At the climax of the melody (bar 14) the second chord (a dominant seventh) appears to marvellous effect on a different degree of the scale and provides a quintessentially Schubertian touch of colour.

The serenity is clouded as something of the first-movement-development's life-and-death struggle reappears. There is confidence in the processional that begins after the main melody (bar 33 onwards), but after the 'episode' turmoil develops (bar 96 on). Once again the celebratory running strings from the masses turn into avenging angels, as the main figure of the episode's melody runs its ineluctable course in the bass.

Schubert later repeats this section's pattern literally (175 ff.), with the transpositions necessary to end in the right key,[9] so his single exception comes as all the more of a master-stroke. In the second hearing of the episode the leisurely lead-back (bars 111–41) does not reappear, which is a shame given its beauty – but the movement is now headed elsewhere, not into a rehearing but into a coda, and something different is needed. Schubert comes up with a six-semiquaver figure from the end of his main melody, which he briefly spins out in preparation for a return of the melody itself, then he surpasses expectation with an idea of the greatest beauty (Ex. 28b). Instead of the opening melody yet again, its introductory figure is at last set free to fulfil itself, in a soaring phrase with a dying fall. 'The last shall be first.'

Schubert does not cease to delight and amaze us even at this closing stage. His main melody makes not one final appearance but two, first in the mediant (in E major, Ab) and then back on the tonic. His skill in doing recondite things with harmony is one of his music's most original and often disturbing features; in particular, a quick ride round the cycle of descending thirds (mostly major) can

---

[8] Hans Keller said of Schubert's Austrian successor Franz Schmidt that he owes much of his originality and effectiveness to a sense of constantly finding something new and improvisatory.

[9] The 'right keys' for the reappearance of the episode are, as so often in Schubert, not quite as one might expect; a second subject first heard in the relative minor (c♯ in E) returns in the subdominant minor (a). Schubert has covered himself, since the episode, after its lengthy spell in the relative minor, went nowhere else at all permanent, but modulated back to the tonic for the second appearance of the main theme; so he is under no tonal obligation when he repeats the episode, save that he wants, once more, to return home to E at the end. The key to which he unconventionally moved for the opening movement's immortal second subject melody was the submediant, and that is a relatively 'submissive' move at a point where a sonata-form movement tends to assert the 'sharp side'. The melody's recapitulation is in the mediant, i.e. the tonic-minor's relative major – not the conventional fifth lower (as might have been expected, given sonata-form's long-range scheme of tonic – dominant [or, from the minor, tonic – relative major], tonic – tonic), but a fifth higher, and in any case not where one would have most expected it, namely in the tonic. Schubert has his own way with sonata-form, and it is no-one else's! Hence the age-old misunderstanding of what is in fact a highly sophisticated approach.

be used to alarm us and wring our withers, as in the *Sanctus* of the E♭ Mass (see *Pride of Performance*). This passage, however, is a thing of pure wide-eyed wonder. The successive harmonic areas are used not to re-harmonise the melody but merely to bring it into view from a new angle. The first-violin line that guides us through it all was first heard linking the main section to the episode. Its expansion here is the final, logical step, the ultimate thinning-down after the bare two-part textures earlier. The entire passage is another reminder that for Schubert music itself, with its unlimited possibilities, was chief among the objects of wonder.

Not the least amazing thing about the Unfinished Symphony is that it shows so little relationship to anything else of Schubert's apart from *Suleika I* and the *Rosamunde* Entr'acte. By a lovely creative irony, the nearest parallel for the winning six-semiquaver figure mentioned above lies in the 1816 song *Seligkeit* (Bliss, D. 433, likewise in E major and 3/8 but in a trippingly happy tempo ('lustig'). The quality one could read into the most unclouded music in this movement can scarcely be better summed up than with that same word, *Seligkeit*.

The Unfinished Symphony and Wanderer Fantasy stand like two contrasting Pillars of Hercules through which one enters a new land. The Fantasy must be one of his most-discussed works, for one feature after another astonishes and points the way forward. Liszt was so fascinated by its formal innovativeness, with linked and thematically interrelated movements, that he made a version of it as a piano concerto. Schönberg's blend of four-movement form with continuous sonata structure is also anticipated, since the first section constitutes the entire work's exposition and development, while the recapitulation, with its total insistence on the tonic key, is delayed until the finale.[10]

One can read a wealth of comment on the Wanderer Fantasy and yet be denied the basic information that it was inspired not by one song but by two (see 'Lyric Intermezzo'). The melancholy of the famous *Der Wanderer* underlies only the Adagio second section, but foreground thematicism, to borrow a term from Hans Keller's Functional Analysis, is an all-too-potent lure to those concerned with deep structure. Elsewhere, the demonic energy of the obscure *Fels auf Felsen* is indisputably more apparent, yet the song's crucial role in the Fantasy goes unnoticed.

That Adagio, which interrupts the unfolding of the Wanderer Fantasy's super-sonata-form, 'stands apart from its surrounding movements'[11] – except in the extraordinary cadenza-like passage where it breaks loose from its melodious melancholy and goes on a rampage. Here Schubert seems to go mad at the piano. It is like a wild exaggeration of the vigorous writing in most of the first and last movements. The same kind of exordium reappears in another slow movement for piano, that of the late Sonata in A (D. 959), and

10 Newbould, *SMM*.
11 Ibid.

pretty terrifying it is. Who knows what got into Schubert? Almost certainly more than (Newbould, *SMM*) the wish 'to vanquish Hummel', who had taught the Fantasy's landowner dedicatee the piano. Here, for the first time since the 'Et iterum venturus est' in the first Mass eight years earlier, we find the primal shudder before the 'Tremendum' – unless one senses that the Unfinished Symphony's darkest moments say similar things in a more controlled way. Something 'inartistic' about these outbursts recalls a taunt by Schubert's Leipzig reviewer that one of his turns of phrase was 'a neat little cobbler's patch and may confidently be recommended to pianoforte tuners to test purity of intonation'[12] – and yet just that sense of being on the very edge extends his expressive range.

Any straight-line, one-dimensional thinking about a figure like Schubert would be a great mistake, as the closing weeks of 1822 clearly show. During that time he also found it in him to set to music the dancing Goethe of *Der Musensohn* (D. 764), most famous of a whole group of Goethe settings; they cover a wide range of moods from the serenity of *Über allen Gipfeln ist Ruh* (*Wanderers Nachtlied*, D. 768) or *Am Flusse* (D. 766), through the wistfulness of *An die Entfernte* (D. 765) to the youthful exuberance of *Willkommen und Abschied* (D. 767).

Schwestergruss (D. 762, November 1822) reflects a real-life tragedy in music that places it among Schubert's great songs. An hour-long lecture could be devoted to its harmonies alone. In 1820 his old school-acquaintance Franz Seraph Ritter von Bruchmann had lost a dear sister, Sybille, to consumption, and two years later Schubert set to music his poem in which she appears to him by night, telling him, 'turn to God while there is still time, or you will never know the bliss that I have earned'. Bruchmann's wife also died not long after, at which point he did in fact renounce the world and turn to God, eventually becoming a priest. You can't keep a good man down, though, and in his new life he became very influential (see 'The Complete Voice').

The November 1822 song *Schatzgräbers Begehr* bears the Deutsch number 761, which makes it the Fantasy's immediate successor. Its text by Schober could be significant, given the connection anthropology makes between digging and sexual activity. Schober, self-centred as ever, muses on a 'treasure hidden deep in the earth', which he will continue to search for even if it means digging his own grave. *Absit omen*; for the moment Schubert turned the poem into a song of wondrous warmth, with one of his most consolatory changes from minor to major in its second half.

Whatever brought about his syphilis at the end of 1822 scarcely had to do with love or the Anima:[13] nothing whatever is known about the circumstances,

---

[12] *Leipzig Allgemeine musikalische Zeitung*, 24 June 1824, review probably by G.W. Fink, for all its adjudicator-tone not totally unperceptive, if only (as Hans Keller used to say) 'the evaluation were stood on its head'. See 'Schubert, The Complete Voice'.

[13] A comment from the great Viennese writer Heimito von Doderer: 'It may be that we deviate out of our life-situation into a sexual situation; but most people seem to bring about situations through their sexuality' (1 Sept. 1948). That Schubert certainly did, with a vengeance, in 1822.

so it is best to leave it at the known fact that some sexual episode left him chronically ill.[14]

Moving into the initial phase of that illness, we meet a strong shudder of some kind in the A minor Piano Sonata from February 1823 (D. 784). I grew up ignorant of Schubert's life-story, and this work's gaunt textures and tremoli made me think of it as his 'Sibelius' sonata. It was therefore intriguing to read half a century later that a perceptive and super-practical musician, Gordon Jacob, had summed it up in the same way.[15] One feature amounts to another of Schubert's 'red threads' – the first movement's insistence on a series of thrice-repeated figures (here falling thirds, which reappear in Florinda's aria, No. 13 of *Fierrabras*, mid-1823, becoming four straight repeated notes in the finale of the Great C Major Symphony and the *Agnus Dei* of the E♭ Mass.)

Mysterious incursions of something like bird-song in the middle movement seem to find an echo in the *Arpeggione* Sonata eighteen months later,[16] while in D. 784's finale one is left deeply uneasy by the alternation of nebulous, swirling figuration and a melody in the major but tinted by the darkness of the minor sixth. The last of the six *Moments Musicaux* (D. 780) can leave a similar impression. The pieces were not published as a set until 1828 but date at least in part from 1823. Meticulous musical analysis by the American scholar Edward Cone[17] led him to diagnose from the final one in A♭, published late in 1824 under the picturesque but all-too-fitting title *Plaintes d'un Troubadour*, Schubert's horror at realising his illness' full implications. Purely as music it evokes a feeling perfectly hit off in Rilke's lines about beauty and terror already quoted.

Cone sees the 6th *Moment Musical* as relentlessly teasing out the ever-wider implications of a single apparently innocent note – e (or f♭) within the key of A♭ major, where it is not by nature at home, but where Schubert's easy way with harmony effortlessly accommodates it:

[14] For all Schubert's devotion to Schober, and his willingness to regard him as a fully worthy artistic collaborator (as witness the libretto for *Alfonso and Estrella*), the testimony of other friends and of Kupelwieser's drawing of him strongly suggests that he was, in an immortal phrase of Kingsley Amis's Lucky Jim, a 'Byronic tail-chaser'. Schwind certainly thought so when in his famous picture of a Schubertiad at Spaun's, painted from memory decades later, he showed him flirting with Justina von Bruchmann instead of listening. Rita Steblin's 'The Schober family's "tiefe sittliche Verdorbenheit" as revealed in spy reports from about 1810 about Ludovica and her Mother' (*Brille*, June 2002) shows that an adventurous strain ran in the family: his elder sister Ludovica had numerous affairs before her premature, accidental death, while at the same time his mother was in a relationship of some kind with a bishop. Schubert's prudish friend Kenner wrote of the family's 'profound moral degeneracy', but that in no way entitles one to jump to the (in itself tempting) conclusion that Schober had a hand in whatever incident, whether isolated *à la* Adrian Leverkühn–Nietzsche or part of a continuing pattern, led to Schubert's falling ill; on such circumstantial evidence no jury in the world would convict.

[15] Newbould, *SMM*.

[16] See Leo Black, 'Schubert's Ugly Duckling; the Arpeggione Sonata', *Musical Times*, Nov. 1997.

[17] 'Schubert's Promissory Note', *Nineteenth-Century Music*, V, Spring 1982.

[the piece] dramatizes the injection of a strange, unsettling element into an otherwise peaceful situation. At first ignored or suppressed, that element persistently returns. It not only makes itself at home but even takes over the direction of events in order to reveal unsuspected possibilities. When the normal state of affairs eventually returns [i.e. at the start of the varied da capo at the end of the main section], the originally foreign element seems to have been completely assimilated. But that appearance is deceptive. The element has not been tamed; it bursts out with even greater force, revealing itself as basically inimical to its surroundings, which it proceeds to demolish.

Medicine calls such a pattern anaphylaxis, and very deadly it is. In Cone's view, this piano piece can be taken as a model of the effect of vice on a sensitive personality, and as summing up the sense of desolation, even dread, that pervades much of Schubert's work after late 1822. A problem about this analysis is the 6th Moment Musical's overall form, a simple A–B–A; it is as if the protagonist went through the whole process again, repeating it verbatim after a trio that 'tries to forget the catastrophe – just as one might try to comfort oneself in the enjoyment of art, or natural beauty, or the company of friends'. Cone takes account of that, regarding the *da capo* as 'the memory of the original course of events'; it could, however, be sounder psychology to imagine morbid thoughts resuming where they left off, and leading into ever-deeper water. The second piece of the same set manifests some such pattern, but not this final one.

The musician all-too-familiar with Schubert's harmonic ways may also find that too much is made of a mere minor submediant, and wonder what the 'method' could make of the far more drastic harmonic deviations at the end of songs such as *Das Heimweh* (see 'Harvest'). All the same, the image of something deadly gradually establishing itself, so that its host is at its mercy, tallies uncomfortably with more than one pianist's intuitive way of playing the last Moment Musical, and also with the ominous phrase in Schubert's March 1824 letter to Kupelwieser about 'a man who instead of making things better makes them steadily worse'. That could at best refer to his self-medication with alcohol.[18] Even so did Tannhäuser, his salvation finally ruled out by the Pope, retrace his steps towards the Venusberg.

Once a man knows himself objectively and physically tainted and at risk, it is hard if not impossible to distinguish in his black moments between awareness of all that and the inborn religious 'creature-feeling', the sense of utter unworthiness in face of God. The Kupelwieser letter is the outburst of a man tried beyond endurance and writing things he might not care to be held to later. And yet, even there, Schubert still bears in mind the path that will 'pave the way towards a grand symphony', namely the composition of instrumental works such as 'two quartets . . . and an Octet'.[19] And he immediately conjures up the magic name,

---

[18] Gibbs' interpretation in *The Life of Schubert*.
[19] Gibbs (ibid.) gives more examples of this tendency to complain first and end more optimistically.

Beethoven, whose forthcoming concert of his own music he wishes to emulate. All of that was to happen in the fullness of time.

Nor would it be any easier, in the music from 1823–4, to tell moments of relief, hope or even euphoria from moments of wonder at a numinous Deity. Instrumental works, without a text to offer even the hint of a clue, must be the most inscrutable of all. What one does hear is Schubert in an unparalleled state of flux. The despairing text and musical progression from light to dark in the May 1823 Schiller setting *Der Pilgrim*[20] are, on the face of it, as good a summing-up of his situation as one could wish: the pilgrim who set out so confidently is being carried ever further adrift on an endless stretch of water. But only a week or two after the Kupelwieser letter he produced the Stolberg setting (*Lied*, D. 788, April 1823) known as *Die Mutter Erde*, Mother Earth. Its poem begins 'Des Lebens Tag ist schwer und schwül, Des Todes Atem leicht und kühl' (Life is a heavy, sultry day, Death breathes upon us lightly and coolly), ending on a note of heavenly reassurance: 'could we but look Mother Earth in the eye, we should see nothing to fear'. Schubert takes this as cue for one of his sublime songs of resignation and reconciliation, with wonderfully expressive melodic curves. It is rounded off by another eloquent postlude for the piano, clearly quoting from his 'safe haven' Beethoven, in a reference to the serene slow movement of the Violin Concerto. From there, it is no great step to the 'lullaby of the brook' that ends *Die schöne Müllerin* on a note of total submission to the inevitable.

Even Schubert's dances are at times ambiguous. Great composers' treatment of 'set' forms tends to manifest an all-important element of what Hans Keller called 'composition against the background of . . .'; high art never lets things be what they seem, and what Bach could make of an allemande or jig has to be heard to be disbelieved. In a less well-known passage from Mendelssohn's famous letter to his wife's relative Souchay about music's 'meaning', he wrote that one cannot even draw a clear distinction, as the 'content' of, say, a Song Without Words, between 'the love of God' and 'a formal hunting-party', since for a certain type of person the latter could be the ideal expression of the former! (He might also have invoked the not-uncommon type for whom the physical movement of dancing is the highest good;[21] Schubert's dances, even without

---

[20] The Goethe–Schiller duality is nicely underlined by the fact that if one seeks a counterpart to *Der Pilgrim*'s downward curve, one need look no further than the climb from disgruntlement into happy idealism in the Goethe setting *Der Schatzgräber*, already cited in the context of *Grenzen der Menschheit*'s trills. The songs are in fact separated in time by eight years – *Der Schatzgräber* 1815, *Der Pilgrim* 1823 – but their technique of composition in both cases relies on juxtaposition of two contrasting yet related blocks, in the earlier case linked by a mode-change from minor to major, in the later song from major to minor with a new melody.

[21] Letter to Marc-André Souchay, 15 October 1842. A further refinement, or degradation, of the idea would be the man for whom the conquest of woman is the be-all-and-end-all: in the Schubert circle, Schober was of that mind, and there is enough in Friedrich Schlegel's then-fashionable novel *Lucinde* masquerading as 'love of womanhood', to show how little times have changed. A fairly random sample:

Under even the deepest heap of ashes some sparks still glow. To awaken these sparks, to clean up the ashes of prejudice, and, where the flames already burn brightly, to feed them

their shadow side, make it crystal clear that he was not that kind of person.) As a composer of dances, Schubert is often prolific rather than inspired, but there too one finds occasional puzzles.

That is already true before 1823, in sets of short pieces based on music very like the improvisations with which he would accompany dancing at the Schubertiads. A collection of no fewer than thirty-six *Originaltänze* (D. 365) composed between 1816 and 1821 follows up twenty-one mostly facile pieces with a strange twenty-second ringing the changes, moment by moment, on major and minor. It is written in 'variants of B major'; the very first harmony heard is the tonic minor, the first half oscillates between the modes in the kind of instant transition most memorably found in the 1826 G major string quartet, and the second half is entirely in the relative minor (G♯ minor), never returning 'home' at all. Having made his point ('do you know any jolly music? I don't' may or may not be an authentic remark of Schubert's), he reverts to yodelling, thigh-slapping mode for a few dances more, then settles into an urbane sensitivity of the kind later immortalised by Schumann in parts of *Papillons*. The dances were published as Schubert's Op. 9, and he was at pains to provide an original ending, quieter than most of the other music, with a concluding dance that brings us near to the world of the strange 6th Moment Musical. Here, as there, the flattened sixth offers a disturbing challenge to the established tonal order. This concluding piece is dated 8 March 1821, the month in which he composed *Grenzen der Menschheit* and *Suleika I* (possibly also *II*), not to mention the intriguing little Goethe song *Geheimes* (D. 719). The mysterious twenty-second dance cannot be dated, the manuscript having disappeared.

Sets published later offer still more impressive surprises and shadows. A set composed at various times between early 1823 and Schubert's 1824 return to Zseliz (16 Deutsche plus two Ecossaises, D. 783), again has moments that hardly reflect the bonhomie and physical vigour of an evening's dancing, while in twelve German Dances (D. 790) precisely assignable to May 1823 he seems to leave the real world entirely. They are a pure reflection on the idea of the dance, having little more to do with its actuality than have Degas' figures of dancers relaxing or suffering. In both cases a deep tenderness settles over the worldly idea of physical movement. D. 790 begins as it means to continue – *piano legato*, and despite an immediate contrast in No. 2, with some super-virile piano-writing, it turns constantly back to its reflective mood. No. 5, with the extraordinary marking *ppp*, is a scarcely moving paragraph in B minor, key

with a modest sacrifice – such would be the highest goal of my manly ambition. Let me confess it: I don't love you only, I love womanhood itself. And I don't merely love it, I worship it; because I worship humanity, and because the flower is the apex of the plant, the apex of its natural beauty and form. The religion I have returned to is the oldest, the most childlike and simple. I worship fire as the best symbol of the Godhead – and where is there a lovelier fire than the one nature has locked deeply into the soft breast of woman? Ordain me priest, not that I may idly gaze at the fire, but that I may liberate it, awaken it and purify it; wherever it is pure, it sustains itself, with no need for vestal virgins to watch over it.

of the Unfinished Symphony, while the G♯ minor No. 6, the other strident piece in the set, clearly anticipates the grim Scherzo of the D minor String Quartet (D. 810, *Death and the Maiden*), which Schubert began to compose in 1824. No dancer in their senses would try to dance to a good performance of D. 790, because no good pianist in their senses would play the music in a way that let them! By the end of the very quiet final dance, Schubert is in a cocoon of sound of his own weaving – and where else but in his 'bliss' key of E major? Something deeper is in the background, receding even beyond the world of folk music and of what Adorno was to term 'dialect' (see 'The Complete Voice'). What that 'something' may be, remains to be seen. These twelve tiny pieces are the crown jewels in Schubert's output of dances.

Exceptionally sonorous piano writing characterises the late set D. 969, published early in 1827 under the title (not Schubert's) *Valses nobles*; right from its opening, where each hand plays *forte* in octaves, there is often a vigour and fullness that one would associate rather with the piano sonatas. The final dance in C major contains a brief passage in B♭ hinting at the Scherzo of the great sonata in that key (D. 960, September 1828).

There is a comparable variety to his many marches for piano duet. With his abstracted, unaggressive nature and dislike of violence, Schubert had little reason to value the march for itself – but there are marches to suit all occasions, notably funeral marches, and the one composed in 1825 on the death of the Russian Tsar Alexander I (a great ally of the Austrian Emperor) is much more than a mere 'occasional piece'. As is its companion for the coronation of Nicholas I, and other marches, notably the ones in G minor and E♭ minor (Nos 2 and 5) from the set of *Six Grand Marches* (D. 819). Those were probably written in Zseliz; scholars are uncertain whether it was on his 1824 visit or the one in 1818 that produced the enormously famous *Marche Militaire* in D (first of three, D. 733); but the sombre nature of some of the music could point to the later date.

What D. 790 had done for the dance-sequence, two 'Characteristic Marches' (D. 886, later renumbered 968B, research having failed to establish when they were written) do for the march, namely break the mould and throw it away. Both are in a quick 6/8 tempo, and in C major with a more sedate trio in A minor, and they are more like tarantellas of the most ethereal kind. There is at times the sense of feeling the earth's movement in space, which will occur in the Great C Major Symphony (see 'Harvest'), at others a sunnier version of the relentless onward drive found in the 6/8 finales of the D minor and G major string quartets. They seem, on such 'internal evidence' to count among the pieces that show Schubert emerged, not unscathed but wiser, from the traumas of autumn 1822–4.

Those years were a very rough ride for him. Venereal illness added an immense load of physical suffering and mental stress to an already mercurial temperament amounting to a degree of a hereditary syndrome, cyclothymia.[22]

---

[22] McKay's chapter 7, 'Fight against Illness', offers a detailed account of them.

Not that one need be a Schubert to feel tied to a seasonal pattern, and at the mercy of a 'summer depression' connected with obvious things like temperature, atmospheric pressure and the tendency for social circles to disperse. There is all the more danger of that in a land-locked city like Vienna, where the summer heat and humidity can become intolerable. It would be risky to assert too positively that for most of his creative career Schubert produced little if anything of interest in the high summer, since precise dates cannot be assigned to particular parts of major works that occupied him over a long period. It is, all the same, striking how seldom the word 'August' features in Deutsch's thematic catalogue. But 1823 became such a disturbed year that it could have been a case of 'one nail driving out another, even if four nails make a cross'[23] – of Schubert's desperately seizing any opportunity to compose, even when consigned to Vienna's General Hospital. As already mentioned, it counts as a great year of fighting back against self-imposed misfortune; it took well-nigh super-human self-control and detachment to produce *Die schöne Müllerin*, the best of *Fierrabras* and the *Rosamunde* music under such circumstances, not to mention songs like *Auf dem Wasser zu singen* and the Rückert settings, happy in such a variety of ways: *Greisengesang*, the song of an old man still young in heart and warmed by his memories, beauty and love unmistakably present in *Dass sie hier gewesen*, love's cylic moods reflected in *Lachen und Weinen*, and peace found in the loved one in *Du bist die Ruh'*.

All of that should warn us against begging an enormous question: 'may one assume that circumstances condition a creator's output?'[24] It could be that when times are worst, the haven of a differently organised, reliable inner world beckons, positively inciting him to reassert lasting values. The ups-and-downs of everyday life are insignificant in comparison. By the same token, art may mean most to people in less-affluent and more onerously governed societies. Certainly there is a remarkable divorce of 'art' from 'reality' in Schubert's 1823 song-production.

A classic expression of his wonder may or may not date from the same time – the Friedrich Schlegel setting *Abendröthe*,[25] one of two strikingly beautiful, very different evocations of sunset, the other being the solemn *Im Abendrot* (D. 799). *Abendröthe* is crucial to an understanding of this side of Schubert (see 'The Complete Voice').

In 1824 the production of great chamber works and piano duets edged out song-composition, apart from a final Mayrhofer group, in which the extraordinary textures and surging waves of *Auflösung* lend credence to the suggestion that one relaxation in the Schubert circle was to pass round a hookah loaded with opium and enjoy the supposedly harmless illumination the

---

[23] Cesare Pavese, diaries *This Business of Living* (*Il mestiere di vivere*).

[24] 'Music is something that comes from the depths of one's experience and one's feelings. I never wrote anything on the moment of an event, this could never happen to me. Music went from a depth independent of the moment's experience.' Hans Gal, unpublished interview with Leo Black, in BBC Archives.

[25] See Leo Black, 'Wort oder Ton?', *Musical Times*, March 1997.

drug provided.[26] And of specifically religious music there was hardly a trace – interestingly, the sole liturgical piece was yet one more *Salve Regina*, a male-voice quartet, Brown's high opinion of which has been quoted. A prayer, *Gebet* (D. 815), for vocal quartet and piano, was written in a single day at the request of Countess Esterhazy, for her musical family and their guest Baron Schönstein to perform during Schubert's second stay at Zseliz. Its text reflects the wartime experience of Baron Friedrich de la Motte Fouqué, who says 'Thy will be done, whether in battle or in peace at home'. Given its domestic purpose it is no surprise that this sizeable and well-constructed piece stays charmingly on the surface, encompassing its various moods but with not a ripple of the 'Tremendum' or the 'Mirum' such as is met in the most remarkable passages of the first five Masses. Far profounder music in sympathy with a military man's apprehensions is found in the Rellstab setting *Kriegers Ahnung* (1828). Nor does this Ab major work compare for profundity with the finest passages in the piano-duet variations (D. 813) from the same year and in the same key.

Stupefying moments become commoner, as in the predominantly convivial Octet (D. 803, 1824), above all in the introduction to the finale, with its bass tremoli and flat-side minor harmonies. They reappear, with an additional rising violin line that explodes upward like a flare telling of grave danger. That introduction has been cited by David Cairns[27] as conveying 'the spectre of annihilation which returns to cast its shadow . . . and which beckons again with menacing gestures at the height of the revels'. Any musically sensitive listener senses something of the kind, the writer has described it most perceptively, so how is another writer with a different 'angle' to say whether 'annihilation' means premature death following syphilis, or the annihilation of the self inherent in an underlying experience of the numinous?

All one can say is that for someone who knows the shudder before the numinous, terrible things happening in the world may strongly reinforce the feeling, as a resonator reinforces a vibrating string. And the fact that the shudder waited so long, then broke out so forcefully, might argue the influence of worldly disaster, as against natural religious experience. But there is enough in the Masses and the Unfinished Symphony to make one think twice about that.

So when at the end of the D minor quartet's first movement the music finds itself rooted to the spot by a terrifyingly ambiguous, heavily doubled chord that

---

[26] After performing *Auflösung* for the BBC the leading accompanist Martin Isepp said to me, 'He must have been on something when he wrote that!' For 'when' I would substitute 'before'; performance is not heightened (at least not in classical music, whatever the different disciplines of other music may throw up) by such substances. That is one of the few enlightening points made by the ex-DDR writer Peter Hacks while arguing, in the most vitriolic manner, that the entire output of German Romantic literature (including poets set by Schubert, such as the Schlegels) was the second-rate product of opium addiction, not to mention its having been written to the instructions of the British Secret Service (*Zur Romantik*, Konkret Literatur Verlag, 2001). No such commission has so far been discovered as the source of Schubert's music, but someone's probably working on it.

[27] Cairns, 'Responses'.

is not its tonic triad, only to shake itself loose into alarmingly rambling harmonies that make the earth seem to move under one's feet, there is no point in asking what precisely the music 'reflects'. One simply waits for the hairs to die down on the back of one's neck. The 'Death and the Maiden' quartet is as full of turmoil as the A minor of song, by turns lyrical and wistful. Two years later the G major quartet will pull the two strands together, leaving nothing unsaid. But that already takes us into a later and comparably great productive period.

5

Harvest
The Great C Major Symphony and other music of Schubert's fullest maturity

> The symphony, like the novel, and most other works of art on any great scale, must present us with a complete view of life and whatever conception of its before and after the artist may command.
>
> Samuel Langford

String Quartet in B♭ (D. 112); Symphony No. 3; An den Mond (D. 296); Symphony No. 6; Auf der Riesenkoppe; Der blinde Knabe; Des Sängers Habe; Totengräbers Heimweh; Ellens dritter Gesang (Ave Maria); Piano Sonatas in C (D. 840), D; So lasst mich scheinen (D. 877 No. 3); Das Heimweh; Die Allmacht; Symphony in C ('Great C Major'); Abendlied für die Entfernte; Auf der Bruck; Nachthelle; Piano Sonata in G

Schubert's second visit to Hungary in the summer of 1824 was something of a watershed. Though a let-down after 1818's idyll, it brought a vital new element into his life, a relationship of spiritual depth with Countess Caroline Esterhazy. Once back in Vienna in the autumn, he had reason to take stock, and did so in the first music written on his return, the curious *Arpeggione* Sonata. It hovers between euphoria and apprehension,[1] casting a glance back to the time of his illness, but also seeming to look ahead to *Winterreise* and its piano-writing.

With his professional routine re-established he worked through the mornings to produce songs of the calibre of *Nacht und Träume* or *Die junge Nonne* (the epitome of 'all passion spent', with its final quiet 'Alleluia' ideally evoking '. . . a nun Breathless with adoration'[2]), and two reminders of his total identification with the art of music. Both are in B♭ – *Der blinde Knabe* (D. 833), considered below, and *Des Sängers Habe* (D. 832), which looks ahead three years to the great piano trio in the same key. Some of the minstrel's confidence in his art ('my zither is all I need, even if life is hard to me') may have rubbed off on to

---

[1] For a fullish account of the *Arpeggione* Sonata, see 'Schubert's Ugly Duckling'.
[2] Wordsworth, *It is a beauteous evening.*

that great work, one of the rare ones where, to quote Hans Gal, the 'hero' or opening theme proves himself by his actions, i.e. shows his mettle by developing thematic possibilities, that being the principle behind sonata- or symphonic form's vital tension as found in Beethoven. It is one to which Schubert rarely adhered.[3]

He was caught up in the vogue for Sir Walter Scott's historicising romanticism. Scott settings in a variety of German translations date from 1825; of the three to lyrics from *The Lady Of The Lake* (April), the first (*Ellens erster Gesang*, D. 837) is a masterpiece of construction,[4] and the second (*Ellens zweiter Gesang*, D. 838) a charmingly mysterious evocation of horns faintly heard. The third (*Ellens dritter Gesang*, D. 839) is the enormously famous '*Ave Maria*', simple and satisfying, with an eminently singable melody heard three times over to an accompaniment that at no point aspires to do more than accompany; even in the interludes between the strophes it adds nothing new, save an expressive arch of the same broken chords it has played from the outset. Offering such delight unblurred by complication, *Ellens dritter Gesang* went down especially well with his listeners; the 1825 'right and true devotion' letter includes the sentence, 'they wondered greatly at my piety, which I expressed in a Hymn to the Holy Virgin and which, it appears, grips every soul and turns it to devotion'. *Ellen III* counts as a *locus classicus* for Schubert the pure melodist as for Schubert the man of occasional devotional impulses.

In *Der blinde Knabe* he was inspired by a poem saying that the inner life, the life of the imagination, is all, the outside world illusion. This is his most poignant evocation of the great artist's vulnerability and insight, with a sublime submissiveness about its floating music for the blind boy who taps his way along with his stick, but a leap of the heart as he finally proclaims 'Ich bin so glücklich, bin so reich/ Mit dem was Gott mir gab' (I am so fortunate, so rich, with what God gave me). That crucial passage is more Craigher, the translator, than Colley Cibber, the original English poem's author, for the latter wrote at this point 'Then let not what I can not have/ My Chear of Mind destroy'. The self-concerned melancholy of *Der Wanderer* is thus stood on its head; if the happy world is where one is not ('Dort wo du nicht bist, dort ist das Glück'), then conversely happiness is where the world is superfluous. The blind boy no longer needs the light, any more than the composer, sure of his inner world, needs the 'miserable reality' of the world outside. In the words of a medieval mystic, Arnold Gueulincx, 'where you count for nothing, you need demand nothing' (Ubi nihil vales, nihil velis).

Such 'two-world' views of the function of art have been criticised, notably in the interesting work of the German musicologist Hans Heinrich Eggebrecht,[5]

---

[3] My paraphrase of part of p. 111 of *Schubert and the Essence of Melody*. See also 'The Complete Voice' for a fuller consideration of the differences between Beethoven and Schubert.

[4] See 'Oaks and Osmosis'.

[5] Notably in his 'twelve questions', serviceable enough both to open a Graz symposium on Schubert and folk music (*DOE*) and be addressed to another in Ettlingen on Schubert's songs to texts by writers from his circle (*Schuberts Lieder nach Gedichten aus seinem literarischen*

but even he is obliged to acknowledge a basically religious attitude behind them. If 'art as other world' is, as he says, obsolete and a throwback to nineteenth-century ways of thinking, it is less than easy to place a viable alternative, except in music so banal as to fit without more ado into the world as it is.[6]

The more sombre *Totengräbers Heimweh* (Gravedigger's Homesickness, D. 842, April 1825) epitomises world-weariness and recourse to prayer. A figure in octaves in the piano's interlude between its two main sections has much in common with one in the first movement codetta of the next piano sonata (A minor, D. 845), composed a month later.

In the Deutsch catalogue a different piano sonata, the one in C major (D. 840), immediately follows *Ellens dritter Gesang*. The summer's eruption was clearly beginning to rumble as Schubert wrote it, while still in Vienna in April, for it contains unusually grand, assertive music, particularly in the majestic opening movement. He had not written a piano sonata since the strange one in A minor at the time of his illness two years earlier, and now he achieved in this movement one of his truly impressive extended structures. A second was completed and the final two were on their way to becoming comparably elaborate, but there he seems to have lost the thread, wandered ever further from his main line of thought, and eventually given up. There have been various attempts to complete this work, which is often referred to as his *Reliquie* sonata.[7]

One of its striking features is the frequent use of massive repeated chords in the piano's middle or upper register, very like those found from time to time in song-accompaniments when there is a reference to mountains. The outstanding examples are the Pyrker settings *Das Heimweh* and *Die Allmacht* from a few months later, and such chords also appear in the D major piano sonata from the same month as those songs. Four years earlier, a different text about mountains had prompted not-dissimilar writing in the accompaniment to *Fels auf Felsen hingewälzet*; we have seen how that went on to colour the important Wanderer Fantasy for piano solo.

An impressive moment in the opening movement of the C major piano sonata comes when at the transition from recapitulation to coda the bass slowly falls away from the seemingly conclusive tonic. As one window closes another opens on to a new panorama. The feeling is a little like that at the same point in

---

Freundeskreis, Schubert's songs to poems by members of his literary circle, Bern, 1999, henceforth referred to as SLGLF), also in his 1997 book *Die Musik und das Schöne*, especially the essay 'Zwei Welten und Eine', where he quotes an intriguing example of 'co-existing worlds', a sustained major scale within music in the minor, from Bach's Cantata no. 12, *Weinen, Klagen*.

[6] According to Hanns Eisler, Bertolt Brecht's ideal of music (which he preferred to call 'Misuk') in a world that 'needed changing' was something that 'recalled, perhaps, the singing of working women in back courtyards on Sunday afternoons' (*Brecht as They Knew Him*, ed. Hubert Witt, London, 1974).

[7] Newbould (*SMM*) is, as ever, eminently sound in his analysis of this sonata's strong points. Its opening idea seems still to have been in Schubert's mind as he sketched yet another D major symphony (D. 936a) in 1828; that has a super-confident opening, with an unmistakable reference to the sonata's first full bar.

the first movement of Beethoven's *Eroica* Symphony, and will recur at a similar point in the Great C Major.

Here is yet another reminder of priorities. This craggiest Schubert piano sonata puts one automatically in mind of Alpine grandeur, but his holiday did not begin until a month after he composed it. No mountains, however grand, could have prompted whatever music the Alps 'inspired' in Schubert during his 1825 holiday, had not that music been waiting to get out, as Beethoven's was when he came to set Schiller in the Choral Symphony.

In the third week of May Schubert was off to a rendezvous with Vogl in Steyr. So began a time when his creative powers went into overdrive. Its major product was at least a considerable portion of the Great C Major Symphony, but first came the A minor piano sonata, completed by the end of May. Like its immediate predecessor it sets out in bare octaves. A comment by Paul Hamburger on this musical device is apposite here; 'narrowing is traditionally "down", whereas in terms of musical effect it can rather be "up", enhancing'.[8] By the same token, the German word *Einsamkeit* means loneliness, a negative thing, but also solitude, which can be one of the most positive, as Schubert's remarkable song with that title from his 1818 Zseliz visit makes clear. The octave openings of three Schubert piano sonatas point each in their own direction. The A minor D. 784 is as if stripped right down, falling and falling, whereas the C major seems confident in its two-bar-by-two-bar alternation of octaves and harmony, and its line that sails down, hovers, then works its way up again in stages. The A minor D. 845 sets out like the C major but with less confidence, for we are in the minor and the melody interrupts itself and doubles back. With hindsight, this sonata could be thought a retrograde step, showing the moodiness and irritability of the Wanderer Fantasy and the previous A minor sonata rather than anticipating the summer's euphoria, but it is a major work in its own right, if without the elemental shudder of the outburst in the Fantasy.

A British conductor's contribution to better understanding of the Great C Major Symphony has been to dub it Schubert's '*Sommerreise*'[9] – a sympathetic and plausible fancy, since the work was conceived and much of it written in summer, and because it complements the exploration of the depths in his winter song-cycle. The symphony stands for a whole yes-saying side of Schubert, as does a song such as *Auf der Bruck* from about the same time. And yet there is in this music something of autumn, of ultimate ripeness and 'harvest', a sense of long-delayed affirmation and achievement. So much that he had sowed and nurtured here comes to fruition.

---

[8] Private communication.

[9] Sir Roger Norrington, *inter alia* in a Radio 3 interview before conducting the symphony at a Henry Wood Promenade Concert, 23 July 2001. Should one look to divide Schubert's life into periods, the three long-established as a classic format for composers could be profitably replaced by a division into spring (1797–c.1820), summer (c.1821–summer 1824), autumn (late 1824–early 1827) and winter (to November 1828). Hans Gal proposed a similar division in the case of Brahms (*Johannes Brahms, Werk und Persönlichkeit*, Frankfurt-Main, 1975).

Schubert's 1825 holiday was by no means his first exposure to sub-Alpine scenery, but it proved by far the most extended and impressive. He wrote a long vivid letter to Ferdinand about the stages from Steyr to the valley of the Salzach above Salzburg; the mountains and lakes near Gmunden inspired his reproof about an attachment to 'puny human life'. The letter took him so long to write that he finally decided to hand it to Ferdinand once back in Vienna, then tell him about the most spectacular stage, from Bad Gastein onwards.

Such scenery would have reawakened early memories. Around 1800 the city of Vienna extended only just to the parish where Schubert was born, from where there was an uninterrupted view of the woods. The heights of the Wienerwald beyond the easily accessible vineyard areas such as Grinzing still had a slightly forbidding air, as of the 'horrid mountains' viewed by the eighteenth century, and were only just beginning to be places where one would go for pleasure.[10] Anyone who spent formative years within sight of a range of hills knows how much bigger they seemed than they turned out to be when revisited in maturity, so that view of the Wienerwald would have imprinted on the young Franz Peter's mind a template for later reactions to natural grandeur. It would have complemented the memories passed on by his mother – who

> doubtless told . . . stories of the countryside she had known and of her own early life, thus unconsciously sowing in the mind of her youngest son the seeds of passion for mountains, rivers, streams and lakes, which were to germinate and blossom through the Romantic climate of his youth, and then inspire some of his most beautiful songs.[11]

In the summer of 1825 Schubert's music was more strongly affected by visual impressions from Nature than at any other time. His reactions were nothing unusual, for artists in every field had begun to sense an element of the Divine in Nature's beauty, power and splendour. Such insights were easier to express pictorially or verbally than in music, but there was the unforgettable example of Beethoven's Pastoral Symphony, which we have already seen reflected in Schubert's early F major Mass.

A close contemporary parallel with Schubert in the summer of 1825 can be found in the Bolton-born painter Thomas Cole (1801–1848), who took to his new homeland of America ideas from English Romantic thought and became a dominant figure. The school of painters he founded depicted the Hudson River valley's still-virgin wilderness. Cole painted his first American landscape pictures after a trek up the Hudson to the Catskill mountains that began in

---

[10] Schubert's painter friend Schwind left a series of pictures of the Schubertians on a trip to one of the highest hills, the Leopoldsberg (see Eva Badura-Skoda's Introduction to *SSF*). Doderer's novel *Die Dämonen* contains an account of a typically light-hearted trip to the 'woods' in the late 1920s. The villages along the Danube at the foot of the hills, such as Nussdorf, Kahlenbergerdorf and Klosterneuburg, figure in the documentation of the Schubert circle (see Carl Nödl, 'Die Entdeckung von zwei Schubertstätten in Wien XIX', *SSF*).

[11] McKay, *Franz Schubert*, p. 11.

the autumn of 1825, weeks after Schubert's five-month tour through Austria
had ended. His first great series of wilderness paintings dates from 1826
onwards. Cole set out from the 'belief that nature manifested to man the
mind of the Creator as much as did revealed religion';[12] and in 1826 he also
wrote a poem, *The Wild*, which included the lines

> those wild blue mountains
> That rear their summits near the Hudson's wave;
> Though not the loftiest that begirt the land,
> They yet sublimely rise, upon their heights
> Your soul may have a sweet foretaste of Heaven.

All of which, apart from the blueness of the mountains, could be applied
verbatim to the sub-Alpine splendours experienced by Schubert in 1825. A
pictorial equivalent for his 'sacred intoxication' (to adapt a phrase of
Hölderlin's) is best looked for in Cole's contemporary wilderness pictures,
which for all their dazzling colour are composed with an eye to carefully
controlled design.

Cole soon began to find Nature's greatness less an absolute value than a
pathway to moral rectitude, a view which Pyrker, as a leading churchman, was
also bound to hold. Cole was, moreover, one of the first prominent figures to
realise the danger to Nature as the much-vaunted 'spread of American
civilization' began, even so early, to tame and spoil the wilderness.

The American writer in whom such wild virgin grandeur first became vividly
manifest was Fenimore Cooper. Like Scott, he enjoyed a vogue in German-
speaking countries during the 1820s, as translations by various writers became
available. Schubert took to Cooper straight away. On 12 November 1828
Schober received his very last letter, asking from his sickbed for any more
Cooper that was available. He had already devoured *The Last of the Mohicans*,
The Spy, *The Pilot* and *The Pioneers*. Over the ensuing century and more,
America was to become a never-never land for European artists – the land of
milk and honey, or, as for Brecht, the irresistibly fascinating realisation of their
worst nightmares – and it is intriguing to find in Schubert one of the first great
European minds to succumb to the spell of the 'American Dream'.

It may seem odd to see similarities to Schubert in an American painter rather
than in his own artist friends, but, loyalties apart, Schwind and Kupelwieser
were not on his level, even though Schwind became one of the most celebrated
nineteenth-century illustrators and was thought worthy of a centennial
symposium in Karlsruhe in 1971. One could look to the work of the greatest
German Romantic painter, Caspar David Friedrich, whose landscapes and
religious canvases alike proclaim a highly developed 'right and true devotion'.
A strong kinship has been argued between Friedrich, who was criticised for his
deliberate distortions of perspective, and Schubert, reproved for his apparently
wilful excess of 'modulation'. The idea of 'planes' of harmony in Schubert,

---

[12] Matthew Baigell, *Thomas Cole*, New York, 1981.

juxtaposed rather than connected by recognisable modulations, offers a technical basis for comparison, its counterpart in Friedrich being the use of multiple viewpoints. But a specific comparison, say between one of Friedrich's Riesengebirge paintings and Schubert's song *Auf der Riesenkoppe* (D. 611, 1818), inspired by a Körner poem about standing on top of just such a 'giant mountain', reveals sizeable differences as well as similarities.

The 'Riesengebirge' or giant mountains are a range running from south-east of Dresden into the former German province of Silesia, so are nowadays mostly in the Czech Republic, with their northernmost area in Poland. Their highest peak, at 1,260 metres (5,266 feet), is Snezka (the Schneekoppe) in Bohemia. Friedrich lived in Dresden from 1798 onward (he died in 1840) and painted many pictures of the Riesengebirge. *Auf der Riesenkoppe*, like *Geheimnis* two years before, falls into two distinct sections separated by rests, which delay a striking if less extreme change of key. Here one just could sense two unrelated 'harmonic planes'. Comparably puzzling harmonic changes occur (without the rests to soften their effect) even in a light-hearted piece like the *Zwillingsbrüder* overture from 1819 (D. 647), where they may have been modelled on those at the same point in the finale of Mozart's G minor 40th Symphony (beginning of the development). And yet on closer examination the change in *Auf der Riesenkoppe* amounts to little more than a conventional 'interrupted cadence'; it would be hard to find many Schubert passages truly impossible to explain in terms of the functional harmony codified ever since Rameau's time. That is, indeed, one of the strongest cards in his hand, and (to pursue the card-playing analogy) when he plays his joker, as in *Geheimnis*, he does so for a very special reason.

Friedrich's most deeply satisfying landscapes, of the Elbe valley in Saxony and Bohemia, have truly Schubertian qualities of peace and luminosity, though the side of him most appreciated in recent years has been his conscious and powerful tendency to use distortion as an indication of depth, darkness, the unnameable. The harmonic adventurousness of the A♭ Mass's *Sanctus* springs to mind as an obvious counterpart in Schubert. But Friedrich's distortions also point a religious moral as remedy for his own deep spiritual unease, and that could make a parallel with Schubert less than totally convincing. A musical kindred spirit might well be sought rather in Schumann, with his frequent awareness of impending mental unrest, or even Bruckner. In his more dramatic pictures Friedrich's glowing distances and illuminated skies are a considered attempt to convey hope in another, better world. Until then, only figurative painting had been thought amenable to allegory, and Friedrich's outspoken critic Ramdohr declared categorically that 'no well-composed landscape picture will ever lend itself to allegorising' – but that was Friedrich's intent and achievement. In *Auf der Riesenkoppe* Schubert was inspired rather by the sheer warmth of Körner's joy at the sight of a panorama and the distant prospect of a homeland where he has lived and loved. The landscape is emphatically of this world, the music shimmers with a euphoria far removed from any hopeless longing for the greener grass on the other side of the fence. Sentiments of that kind are familiar enough elsewhere in his work, unforgettably conveyed in songs to texts such as that of the Schmidt von Lübeck *Der Wanderer*, while Schober's *An die Musik* gets the best of both worlds: times are bad, but music really can take us somewhere better.

In Romantic thought there was a triangle of ideas, with the Divine at its apex and Nature and Art at the other corners. Art was an enclave of its own, with its apex at one of the base-line points of the higher triangle. A leader of the Romantic movement in Germany, Friedrich Schlegel, dreamed of 'universal poetry' and 'universal art', all poems one poem, all art the same art, and one divine breath running through all creation. Such ideas were the more infectious in Vienna after Schlegel went to live there in 1808; we have already come across them in his text for *Die Gebüsche*. Wagner's concept of a 'total art work' (Gesamtkunstwerk) would take up that tradition, but with power politics and economics to the fore.

The productive figures in the Schubert circle duly tried their hand at each other's arts, though despite a few occasional ventures on his part into creative writing it was mostly one-way traffic.[13] Schwind played the piano, wrote music, and much later in life 'composed' a quartet of pictures entitled *Die Symphonie*. He also sketched but never executed an entire room devoted to his interpretations of Schubert songs. Music's dominating position gave cause to hope that the other arts might take on some of what the 'General Secretary of the Romantic Unity Party', Ludwig Tieck (he of the *Magelone-Lieder*) called 'this extraordinary music Heaven writes nowadays'.[14]

One specific concept spanning the arts was arabesque, an organic, branching network of related figures.[15] The north-German painter Philipp Otto Runge used it to link separate engravings (*Die Vier Zeiten*, The Times of Day), and conceived but never completed a full-scale version (four paintings) – 'an abstract, painterly-fantastic musical poem with choirs, a composition for all *three* arts together, since architecture should come up with a suitable building'. In Schwind's work, arabesque is the link between the world of real life and the abstractions of natural philosophy and mythology. Musical arabesque has lately come under scrutiny (for example by Andreas Krause), as an intermediate stage between motive and variation. It contributes to the Great C Major Symphony's enormous effectiveness, and places Schubert in a line that was to become ever more reticulated in the course of the nineteenth century. That line found its fulfilment in Art Nouveau, and was then rejected by figures such as Schönberg and the architect Adolf Loos, for whom 'ornament' was Public Enemy Number 1.

In the summer of 1825 the Great C major Symphony was already begun, but a work of such magnitude took time to complete, and the next milestone is yet another piano sonata, in D major (D. 850, August). It is in many ways a

---

[13] The ensuing owes much to Helga de la Motte, *Musik und bildende Kunst*, 1990.

[14] In *Franz Sternbalds Wanderungen*.

[15] This and more is illuminatingly pointed out by Andreas Krause in 'Arabeske, Subthematik und öffentlicher Raum' (*SSF*).

metamorphosis of the glowing nature-mysticism in the 'Pleni sunt coeli' of the A♭ Mass half a decade before. Where April's A minor sonata stopped and started, seeming in constant argument with itself, this one surges irresistibly on like a force of nature. The rolling piano figuration takes up an idea found in the 1819 *Abendbilder*, with much use of the euphonious interval of the sixth.

The D major sonata's second movement shows a great composer producing endless variety and nuance with very simple material. Following its course, we could be passing through some woodland scene above Gastein, with the sun's rays piercing the foliage and showing the trees in an ever-changing light. Its principal rhythm is shared with a major song from a few months later, one of four (D. 877) to Mignon's lyrics from Goethe's *Wilhelm Meister*. Mignon's songs had fascinated Schubert for years; at eighteen he had set one of the most famous, *Nur wer die Sehnsucht kennt* (D. 310, October 1815), and just a year later he followed it up with *Kennst du das Land?* He set the other two, now-less-familiar, Mignon poems in April 1821 (even earlier, a fragmentary setting of one, *So lasst mich scheinen*, D. 469, survives from 1816), and he returned to them for the middle two songs of D. 877. *So lasst mich scheinen* (D. 877 No. 3) is sung by Mignon after a children's party where she has been dressed up as an angel; she refuses to take off her costume, saying 'Let me still seem to be what I soon shall be!' Like the slow movement of the D major sonata, the song has an opening melody firmly founded on a static bass, which seems reluctant to 'get off the spot'. The tempo in the sonata is Con moto, and in the song, with its ambiguous moods, Not too slow (Nicht zu langsam). The rhythm of Goethe's first, second and fourth lines dictates to Schubert precisely the rhythmic pattern he had used in the sonata, except that some of the many feminine endings come at different points.

Ex. 29

For his earlier settings of the poem Schubert had found a different musical prosody. The strong contrast between the closeted misery of Goethe's persecuted character and the sonata's euphoria and *al fresco* is another reminder that Schubert's 'self-quotations' are seldom a simple matter. The firmly founded theme within the frame of an inventively repetitive sonata movement seems to say 'I like it here, this is where I'm glad to stay'; Mignon is no more anxious to change her momentary state, though she foresees a very different future. In both pieces Schubert suggests stasis of that kind by working wonders with the subtlety of his harmonic movement over a series of pedal-points in the piano's left hand. In the course of the song, Mignon's future transformation and past sufferings are simply conjured up – by a minor chord in the second verse that replaces a major one from the first, by the slightest extension of a phrase, and by a piano postlude. The hermeneutic aspects of the sonata movement – as distinct from its 'dialect' features listed below – lie in its evident and impressive reflection of mountains in the middle section, and, as a complement, the apparent water-symbolism of much of the first movement's most excitable writing.

The sonata's repeated chords are hinted at straight away, begin to obtrude in the development of the first movement, and become a major feature of the slow movement's episodes. There they eventually figure in one of Schubert's most memorable 'dying falls'. Now and again in his music one meets an 'invaded reprise', where it seems that an idea from the preceding section is too powerful to be altogether banished, even though the section is over. This tends to happen in slow movements; an early piano sonata in E (D. 157, 1815) offers a striking example, the second and final return of the main subject in the D major sonata another, and there is just a hint of it at the first return of the main subject in the C minor (D. 958, 1828). As we shall see, the examples in the Great C Major Symphony are in a class of their own, and come in the outer movements. On the first return of the main melody in the D major sonata's slow movement, it is charmingly accompanied by bird-song, but after the enormous pile-up at the climax of the episode second time round, the mountains continue to cast their shadow on the final music. Schubert used all his craft to ensure that the episode ended differently on its second appearance, yet kept the two passages virtually the same length. For six bars (179–84) it even seems that the mountains' presence is becoming too much, and that Schubert is about to have one of his panic attacks. That averted, the sonata goes safely on to its immensely vigorous scherzo and finale. The mountains are there again in the scherzo's quiet trio, but transfigured, as if seen in a painting (though, if one is being sensible, not by Cole!).

Features of the D major sonata make very clear the occasional element of 'dialect' in Schubert.[16] It has yodelling themes and 'horn-fifths', sustained sounds over a drone-like bass, accents on the second beat of a bar, and in a 'faded-down passage' in the second movement 'the sounds of nature seem

---

[16] The ensuing catalogue of features leans totally on Dieter Schnebel's 'Schuberts Ländler' (*DOE*). To Schnebel, the 'Dialectale' is even a component of the D major sonata's entire form, it being composed as a 'protracted diminuendo: the first movement ends *fortissimo*, the second and third *piano*, the finale *pianissimo*. Precisely what is 'dialectal' about that is unclear to me, but the observations are acute.

distant and as if under a spell – and with the tone of dialect into the bargain'. There is also 'the folk-music-like waltz that in bars 49ff. of the third movement quietens the storm of the opening'. This sympathy for a different, more demotic speech shows again Schubert's openness to everything good and potentially beautiful in the world, and there is the purest logic in its appearance within a work so obviously inspired by Nature's splendour. Yet a sense (see 'The Complete Voice') that musical dialect has been bypassed, turned into something purely musical and elemental, illuminates in particular this sonata's often-childlike finale. It is as if his identification with Nature had carried Schubert into a world where impressions from very early indeed began to bear in on him.

The two great Pyrker settings *Das Heimweh* (Homesickness, D. 851) and *Die Allmacht* (Omnipotence, D. 852) more than repaid any debt to a great churchman for patronage down the years. They tell of intense participation in Nature, felt within the soul, and are worthy successors to the A♭ Mass. *Das Heimweh*, the D major sonata's immediate neighbour in the Deutsch catalogue and likewise from August 1825, spells out a possible, purely emotional background to that work's 'invaded recapitulation': in its middle section a man exiled from his native mountains has an aural hallucination of his homeland, which gradually fades like the mighty chords near the end of the sonata's slow movement. (Here there is no overlap of ideas between successive sections.) Powerful repeated chords in the companion song, *Die Allmacht*, serve from the outset to impress on us that the grandeur of mountains, as of all Nature, is inseparable from that of the Creator.

Das Heimweh has many remarkable features, with Schubert's nature-impressions at their most bizarre when the benighted man from the Alps, on his suburban tump, seems to hear cows. A listener familiar with the A♭ Mass may feel they are mooing the word 'Osanna'![17] The piano's weary opening octaves are yet another version of the 'unison' beginnings to piano sonatas, and the end shows Schubert reaching out effortlessly to the most distant harmonic area within his home key, then snapping back just as easily. That is a feature of a number of great songs[18] from late in his career, and is something inherited from Haydn, who could with a flick of his pen switch from, say, G major into the farthest-distant C♯ minor, so that even the performers hardly knew what was happening.[19]

This song also helps dispel the idea that Schubert never needed to revise a piece. Its original version lacks the extensive reprise and development of the

---

[17] The poet's yodelling 'Tirolese girl's song' (das Lied der Sennerin) is suggested in the piano's right hand, but these cows moo in the left, where the crickets set up shop in *Der Einsame*; God's creatures, too, are a kind of authoritative voice, though there is no doubling by the vocal line to bring about an actual VDB.

[18] As early as the 1821 *Sei mir gegrüsst* a g♯ – b – d – f♯ chord is effortlessly reached within a home key of Bb, where only one note of the chord in question (d) is diatonic. Tonality is, immediately restored but the passage leaves behind a sense of extreme strangeness (Stupor).

[19] 34th–20th bars from the end of the slow movement of the String Quartet in C major, Op. 74 No. 1.

opening minor-key music, which help to make it one of his most overwhelming constructions: the opening is quoted only briefly, the hallucinatory middle section is longer.

Die Allmacht offers the clearest 'text for the day: Gross ist Jehovah der Herr' (The Lord Yahweh is great). It sets lines from Pyrker's epic poem based on the Old Testament, *Perlen der heiligen Vorzeit,* which had appeared in 1821, the year after his appointment as Patriarch of Venice. The prophet Elisha or Eliezer was Elijah's successor; he disappears from Kings II 1–8 with no account given of his end. Pyrker's lines, paraphrasing no obvious Biblical model, have him declaring, first, that God's omnipotence is manifest in the whole of creation, and then, as would befit a good son of the Church, that His voice is heard clearest of all in the heart of the true believer. Schubert the melodist is at his peak in this song's vocal line, and Schubert the nature-mystic in its powerful chordal accompaniment. Its clear C major recurs in the symphony (D. 944)[20] that he began to compose that summer.

Schumann compared that work, the 'Great C Major Symphony', to a four-volume novel, perhaps by Jean Paul,[21] an analogy lately given a new lease of life by the Swedish scholar Klaes-Göran Jernhake. The late twentieth century produced a variety of academic disciplines aiming to show how much more there is in a work of art than its creator was aware of, and Jernhake is conversant with philosophical and technical ideas in hermeneutics developed by the French philosopher Ricoeur. In a full-length study of the symphony[22] he sees it as the musical equivalent not merely of a novel but of a *Bildungsroman,* the 'novel of maturing' fashionable in Schubert's time and found at its highest in Goethe's *Wilhelm Meister.* The claim is not that this or any other musical work is autobiographical, for a novel and an autobiography are or should be two quite different things, rather that the symphony, heard rightly, reveals a progression of ideas that can be summarised in words, so contradicting Mendelssohn's famous dictum about music's 'untranslatability' in the letter to Souchay. Erwin Ratz's remarks on music's appeal to the ordinary music-lover quoted earlier were in fact made in the context of a hermeneutic approach to Beethoven, and under strict control such a discipline can throw light on music as few others can. (As against Jernhake's hermeneutics I would call my examination of the Great C Major exegesis.) Summarising, Jernhake says the work's aesthetic intention is 'to express the presence of the Eternal in life and shape an individual's moral maturity in an exemplary way'.

Before examining the idea of a hermeneutic approach to the Great C Major, we should look briefly at something more limited but still important, the

---

[20] The symphony acquired its misleadingly late Deutsch number while it was still thought to have been composed in 1828.

[21] *Neue Zeitschrift für Musik,* XII, 1840, pp. 81–3. Schumann's much-misquoted expression 'heavenly lengths' is often invoked in faint praise of Schubert, but is in fact singular and enthusiastic, 'die himmlische Länge'; he applied it specifically to this symphony.

[22] *Schuberts 'stora C-dursymfoni' – Kommunikationen med ett musikalisk Konstverk,* Studia Musicologica Uppsaliensis, Uppsala University Library, 1999.

musical shape known as 'sonata form'. Found primarily in the individual movements of sonatas and symphonies, especially the outer ones, it has been variously interpreted. The questing reader desiring insight, in whatever field, is liable to find himself reading sociology – not what things are but merely where they came from – and there is a consensus (surely more appropriate in the case of the concerto?) that sonata form represents a 'struggle' between, or collaboration of, opposing forces: contrasted themes and keys, and the contrasting processes of exposition and development. Ernst Hermann Meyer[23] pinpointed its origins in the 'bourgeois world of thought and feeling at the end of the 18th century, which struggled to achieve an ever free-er form and expression'. In keeping with that, he saw its content as the 'expression of a basically positive, life-affirming, combative view of the world'. Wilfrid Mellers too related the growth of sonata to an incipient transfer of power from the feudal aristocracy to new 'bourgeois forces in the Age of Enlightenment . . . who knew the future was with them'.[24] Given the enormous range the form covered over a century and a half, he wisely preferred to speak of a 'sonata principle'. Webster's comprehensive article in *Grove* acknowledges Sir Donald Tovey's view of 'sonata style, i.e. the articulation of events in 'dramatic' or 'psychological' fashion',[25] and he adds the rider, 'the meaning of each event depends both on its function in the structure and its dramatic context'. A movement's 'true form [thus] becomes clear only on close analysis in terms of its effect in actual performance'.

Sonata form consists of exposition of themes that move away from home, their development and transformation in 'foreign' keys, their return home and confirmation there, and in its full maturity a further degree of development leading to a new level. So complex a structure is clearly more than a mere pattern for composers to cut their cloth by, but not even Carl Gustav Jung seems to have looked at it as a possible paradigm for human life itself. A good deal of which must pass before certain things are brought home and become axiomatic: as Keats said, 'axioms in philosophy are not axioms until they are proved upon our pulses'.[26] To a Jungian, sonata form could be virtually a symbol of individuation.

Jernhake's proposal is a bold further step, but once one is determined to discover a great composer's view of the world and spiritual attitude, one should surely look for it in a major work long foreseen and carried through over an extended period. So George Bernard Shaw was all the wider of the mark in calling the Great C Major 'the most exasperatingly brainless composition ever put on paper'.[27] All due respect to the owner of one of the most engagingly argumentative brains there has been, and to a man with his own supremely

---

[23] *Musik im Zeitgeschehen*, Berlin (DDR) 1952, p. 71.

[24] *The Sonata Principle*, Ch. 1.

[25] *Music Essays from the Encyclopedia Britannica*, London, 1945.

[26] Letter to J.H. Reynolds, 3 May 1818.

[27] *The Star*, London, 23 March 1892, review ('Joachim and Schubert') of Crystal Palace concert on 12 March. One prime use for Shaw's brain was to help bring about world socialism – with which we once again find ourselves beset by Chapter 1's twin monsters, politics and economics.

articulate view of what that organ is there to bring about, but in this case he wrote nonsense. The symphony's ideas are presented with great sophistication: for example, when its first movement recapitulates the events from the start of its main section, it does so in a new light, falling into a breathless *pianissimo* that persists for all of fifty bars, before the music is allowed to resume the original confident *forte*. The slow movement moves from amiability to terror and only some of the way back; the finale sounds alarm bells at the same point as the first movement. Schubert's brain, as well as every other centre, was engaged in all that.

In the Great C Major he yet again seems intensely involved with other music. His unparalleled degree of 'cathexis', of creative attachment to his own work, has been mentioned, and the symphony's self-echoes, together with its echoes of Haydn, are as illuminating as any thoughts of pantheistic ecstasy in summer.

The action begins with the first notes of the 'introduction' to the first movement. The horns'[28] initial fragment of scale rising through a third in each of the first two bars might be thought too frequent a feature of Schubert to be singled out, even though in bar 2 it has precisely the rhythm it has at the opening of *Lazarus* (see Ex. 20, p. 88). Its ascent to e is reproduced in every movement of the symphony, whether in C major or A minor.

Ex. 30 Opening motives of the Great C Major Symphony's four movements

By bar 4 we find an echo of the *Credo* in the 1816 C major Mass. That set out with a strikingly angular theme in unison expressing belief in One God; the curve of the horns' melody in the symphony's fourth and fifth bars is very similar. (See Ex. 31.)

Schubert had reason to look back with nostalgia on 1816 and its 'sense of impending release and freedom',[29] reflected in his diary entries from mid-June of that year onwards. He had been hoping for a proper job, which he perhaps thought might pave the way for marriage to Therese, Goethe had been approached on his behalf, and he had for the first time composed for money.

---

[28] Not a solo horn ('the horns of elfland faintly blowing' as in Weber's *Oberon* Overture) but two playing quietly in unison, as some form of summons, however gentle. In 1815 Schubert had opened the overture to his Singspiel *Der vierjährige Posten* with two horns playing alone, but in parallel thirds and to quite different effect.

[29] McKay, p. 61.

Franz Schubert

Ex. 31 *Credo* of C Major Mass, Introduction to Great C Major Symphony's 1st
movement

(A cantata, *Prometheus* (D. 451), which vanished long ago, was commissioned
to mark the 60th birthday of a well-loved law teacher, Heinrich Joseph
Watteroth, by pupils who included many of the Schubert circle, such as
Spaun, Mayrhofer, Grillparzer, Schlechta, Sonnleithner, Stadler, Witteczek
and the poet Castelli.)

As the music fills out, the melody's continuation on lower strings sounds
strikingly similar to the 'be fruitful, grow, multiply' passage in Haydn's *The
Creation*, memorable in any case but all the more relevant to Schubert during
those few months of the one year in his life when a 'normal married life' could
have appeared a distinct possibility. We have already seen, apropos the second
Salve Regina, the importance to him of a different idea from *The Creation*; that
too will recur to striking effect in the Great C Major Symphony.

It has, for that matter, to some extent already recurred. Life brings moments
of awe: a grown man may feel a flutter of apprehension when his mind engages
with the concept of death, sensed as an endless nothingness in which one is not
even there to be aware of nothing, or when he is faced with the vastness of
endless space (hence the fascination of astronomy for so many of us, young and
old). An immensely sensitive schoolboy will be even more struck by such things,
so the impact on Schubert of hearing the first few minutes of *The Creation* can
be profitably imagined. (The Wiener Tonkünstlersozietät, founded in 1772,
gave the first performance of *The Creation* in 1799, and presented Haydn's
oratorios every year at concerts in Vienna that raised a good deal of money to
help retired performers and their families. Schubert thus had ample opportunity
to hear those great works during his formative years.)

In the *Representation of Chaos* Prelude a brief rising-scale figure (A, B in Ex.
32) is the first modest impulse towards organisation within primeval nothingness. By the time it is taken up in the first recitative, there has been progress –
God has created the world out of chaos, but it is a world 'without form and
void', hence the long downward slide after the brief, productive rising scale
(Ex. 32, C). That Janus-faced figure particularly haunted Schubert. As early as
September 1812 the rising scale-fragment appeared strikingly in the orchestral
introduction to a D minor *Kyrie* (D. 31), and nowhere else in the piece (any
more than the Chaos prelude would reappear in Haydn's oratorio).

The first movement's main section (Allegro ma non troppo) takes us back a
little further, to the spring of 1815 and his D major 3rd Symphony (D. 200). The

Ex. 32 Haydn, *The Creation*, Prelude

principal section of that work's opening movement set out with a melody made up of two elements. A two-bar figure, floating up and down the tonic chord and almost yodelling, alternated with a flutter of activity on the violins. In 1825 Schubert hit on the same idea again, but in the Allegro of the Great C Major Symphony the opening bars stamped rather than floating as they had in the earlier symphony. He later took his penknife to the score and gave his theme the less obsessive, more dancing form we now know. Here the answering 'flutter of activity' is a block of repeated chords that ends with an assertive rising third[30] on the woodwind. That interval will play an ever-increasing part in the entire symphony.

Ex. 33a 3rd Symphony, 1st movement

Ex. 33b Great C Major Symphony, 1st movement (simplified)

Schubert is not one of the composers who seem always to be trying to write the same work, and nobody would or should make out that everything in the Great C Major is compiled from earlier music by himself[31] or anyone else. Its

[30] Hans Gal (*Schubert and the Essence of Melody*) pointed out that the rising third is often inaudible, not because conductors fail in their work but because Schubert never had a chance to hear his symphony and did not realise that at this point its scoring needed improving.

[31] A briefly notorious symphony 'rediscovered' in the 1970s, a veritable palimpsest of self-quotations, was thought by one or two true Schubertians (among them Harry Goldschmidt, who declared it a 'defectively and arbitrarily restored picture, but by a master') to be genuine, and progressed as far as a recording by a fine American symphony orchestra. By now the majority view is that it is a quite inexplicable piece of extensive pastiche whose motivation is hard to fathom, except that the 1978 celebrations were on the way and an 'accredited' new Schubert symphony would have had enormous commercial potential.

'self-references' do, all the same, show the underlying continuity within a startling process of development.

The second subject's initial E minor confirms a hint thrown out in bars 22–6 of the introduction. In both the movement's main subjects the great melodist Schubert equips himself with 'pools of rhythmic cells'[32] rather than lines of outstanding melodic interest. Rhythm and continuity are the great impulses in this enormous work; but, even so, its themes also engrave themselves on our minds.

By the time the second subject is well under way, the listener may (depending on the conductor!) have begun to share the strangest sense of mingled stillness and impulsion. An old saying runs, 'We are all in God's hand', and so we are here, but it is not a hand at rest, rather that of someone moving irresistibly and very fast. Even so, were one but aware of it,[33] is one borne through space by the earth's movement. A sense of automatic motion is attainable of one's own accord, if one is prepared to work: marathon runners know it, and even walkers who after many arduous miles suddenly find themselves on an 'automatic pilot' which carries them much further without their needing to do more than let it. The memoirs (*The First Four Minutes*) of Sir Roger Bannister contain a wonderful account of its first happening to him as a boy – his expression is 'rapturous running'. By the start of the third millennium A.D. the connotations of 'expanded consciousness', like those of 'submission', have been corrupted to imply almost exclusively intervention from outside, the use of some 'substance' ingested for its mind-expanding effects. Dire need may lie behind that, but it still substitutes for a man's own two feet someone else's limousine, or dust-cart, or in the extremest cases hearse. True expansion of consciousness is the essence of heightened experience (be it physical, artistic or religious) achieved through work: one becomes aware of more, of everything even.

Which can be wonderful, or terrible, and the one can change into the other without warning. Towards the end of the first movement's exposition section (bars 199–217), after typically discursive statements and restatements of the second subject, the trombones break in with what sounds like an admonition, a reminder of things overlooked. It is the fragment of rising scale from bar 2 of the introduction, and, for the moment, no more than that. Trombones were rarely used as melody-bearing instruments. Their sound had solemn overtones through their frequent use at the more impressive moments in church music, and near the end of Act 1 of *Lazarus* Schubert made them intervene to memorable effect between the other characters' reactions to the protagonist's death. At this point in the symphony their intervention is, to put it mildly, sobering, and what ensues far more so, but its full significance will only emerge once their figure has been expanded in the course of the development.

This makes play with first- and second-subject figures in counterpoint one

---

[32] Newbould's formulation (*SMM*).

[33] As one can indeed to some extent be, for example when standing at a great height overlooking a panorama.

with another, and slowly builds towards a climax. That (bar 516ff.) is where the trombones again sound their warning, far more urgently than before, and though the music briefly continues to build, there is soon an abrupt change. In a memorable passage of quiet music the trombones' scale figure is taken up by other instruments, as if the prophet at last found honour in his own country. It is answered by one going in the opposite direction. Schubert is methodical; only after this juxtaposition and combination of upward and downward movement does he take the final, logical step of quoting and extending the entire Haydn line, which contained both. (As early as the 1814 *Salve Regina* it seemed to be reflected in a striking figure associated with the 'earthly vale of tears' – Ex. 34a; see also Ex. 32.) The reflection in the Great C Major (Ex. 34b) stays still closer to Haydn before turning upward again at the end.

Ex. 34a *Salve Regina*, D. 106

Ex. 34b Great C Major Symphony, 1st movement

Given Schubert's propensity for VDB when bowing to the voice of authority, it is no great surprise that at this point in the symphony the phrase enlarging on Haydn and a 'formless void' comes not in the melody-bearing treble register but in the weight-bearing bass.

This passage marks the start of the wonderfully wistful transition to the recapitulation. It sets up and appears to trigger off that section's amazing quiet start, with its new light on what was a *forte* exposition. Any man might well go quiet when 'panic and emptiness'[34] threatened to engulf a well-ordered life, and Schubert had by now discovered what it meant to 'fall into the hands of the living God'.[35]

A musical model for this transformed recapitulation can be found in Beethoven. Schubert had cast his 1819–22 Mass, so complementary to Beethoven's *Missa Solemnis* from the same period, in the most distant possible key; here he could have had at the back of his mind a high point in the 'Great D Minor' – that is to say, the older man's Choral Symphony – but have been careful to avoid mere duplication. (The Choral Symphony had had its first two performances as recently as 1824.) Schubert took the precaution of reversing one of the model's essential features. Beethoven's first movement opens in an emptiness like that of primal chaos, without form and void, but by the time that

---

[34] E.M. Forster, *Howard's End* (1911).
[35] Hebrews 10,13.

opening returns it has taken on such momentum as to blazon the same music forth, turned from *pp* to *ff*, and from minor to a major,[36] which, so far from reassuring, intimidates by its feeling that there is yet farther to go. Both outer movements of the Great C Major reflect this in their different ways: in the first, Schubert retains the major mode but carries out the exact reverse of Beethoven's intensification of dynamics.

Schubert's first movement finally throws off its shadows to end positively, discovering new possibilities in one particular continuation of the first subject; previously little 'developed', it now leads in no hurry at all to a grand build-up that runs its leisurely course not once but twice, allowing itself even more time when it is repeated.

Nor is that all, for the final thirty-six bars recreate the feeling of the sun unexpectedly coming out that transfigured the 'Amen' of the Ab Mass's *Gloria*. Final sudden euphorias occur in Schubert as from the 1817 D major Italian Overture (D. 590) and 1820 *Zauberharfe* Overture (D. 644), where they come more unexpectedly than the one here. That Italian Overture (there are two) was the first piece of Schubert's performed in public, apart from those given in church. Its *Allegro vivace* coda contains no fewer than three figures that recur at the same point in the first movement of the Great C Major – a dotted rhythm like that of the first subject, the sixfold, quickly repeated chords, and a motive that rises through the notes of the tonic triad. The six-bar grouping so frequent in the symphony is also found. The end of the Italian Overture, with its totally unexpected switch into 'Great C Major mode', confronts us with another of the occasional time-faults or trap-doors in Schubert's output. It is as if he caught sight for a moment of something that had been beyond him, but didn't yet know quite what to do with it. There is in this a touch of Seuse's 'for I know not truly what it may be'. The leap from the end of the Ab Mass's 'Pleni sunt coeli' to *Der Lindenbaum* is through just such a trap-door.

In a symphony of the period one would not expect to re-encounter an introductory theme at this point, but here, to set the crown on the rejoicing, we are given the introduction's opening melody again. Another sign of Schubert's total command of his craft is that he wrote the movement in such a way as to obviate the need to change the beat between 'slow' introduction and 'quick' main movement; if continuity of pulse has been maintained, the opening melody seems absolutely logical as it returns to round things off.[37]

Analysis of the Great C Major's second movement is likely to concentrate on its two melodies or groups of melodic figures, and on the amazing eruption when the first-subject group is repeated. But here again there is an introduction,

---

[36] The tonic major harmony in first inversion.

[37] Conductors great and small often settle deliberately or unthinkingly for two different tempi, and the less dogmatic among us are free to enjoy it either way, just as one can enjoy a landscape in a multitude of different lights, or even with salient features hidden by cloud. The symphony suffers greatly in performance when conductors let the abstract principle of constant pulse override their concrete sense (if any) of musical character.

a tune on the cellos and basses (see Ex. 30, first six bars) accompanied by chords on the upper strings. It is minimal compared with the one before the main body of the first movement, taking about ten seconds to play, yet it contains the nucleus of much that follows. The dotted rhythm in its fourth bar, and then its final two as, are especially full of possibilities. As early as the third bar of the ensuing melody that pair of identical notes establishes itself as a basic element in the drama.

The 2/4 'walking' rhythm here just might be inspired by the obsessive slow movement of Beethoven's 7th Symphony. Schubert's works contain many themes in A minor, but few are much like this movement's main melody, which begins on the fifth; the others that do so mostly start on an 'upbeat', this one on the main beat. So does the one that opens the 1824 A minor string quartet, but there the rhythm and motion are different, floating rather than marching. The theme of the Beethoven slow movement also opens on the fifth, and that could contribute to any resemblance between it and Schubert's slow movement; it continues quite differently, and on a larger scale the two movements are dissimilar. Beethoven composes against the background of theme-and-variation form, and even his contrasted section in the major mode adheres to the movement's basic tonality of A (minor). There is a thoughtful and energetic fugal development before his major section is repeated, but it feels studied and well under control, compared to the near-catastrophe in Schubert's slow movement.

Schubert's other source, Haydn, is still 'in the frame'. The *Benedictus* of his 'Nelson' Mass is strikingly similar to this Schubert movement. The key there is D minor, next stop down the line from Schubert's A minor, and from the point of view of rhythm the two pieces have much in common, especially a prevalence of dotted rhythms (dotted semiquaver + demisemiquaver). Schubert profited from the experience of singing the 'Nelson' Mass as a chorister, and even conducted it in 1820, as we saw in connection with *Lazarus*. Another very early liturgical piece, a second D minor *Kyrie* (D. 49, dated 15 April 1813), had been strongly influenced by the opening of the same Haydn Mass.

The first section of the slow movement has in fact three tunes. The one quoted above loses no time in expanding the introduction's two repeated notes into four. In its sixth and seventh bars it presents a motive in dotted rhythm four times, continuing with four straight e-s in its eighth and ninth. It is repeated with two bars fewer, ending with those four e-s at twice the original speed.

There follows one of the great examples of Schubert's instant mode-change, here from minor to major. The briefest snatch of rising major scale dispels any clouds over the opening melody. This is, however, only the half of it, for there is a further member of the cast, like a cousin of the first one; they share a dotted rhythm and a pair of repeated notes, but this third idea is more bracing and determined to move things along. Here is the pushy character who will throw the movement into disarray.

It all unfolds at a leisurely pace, with the three elements repeated and varied.

Curiously, the first two are heard exclusively on the wind instruments, with only the more forceful third one heard on the strings.

The other main section is in F, and is made so much of as to constitute a second subject. As so often in Schubert's sonata-form movements, it is developed even as it is stated. Here at last the violins are allowed to sing a tune, the seconds beginning it and the firsts taking it up. It reverses the upward scale movement from the consolatory middle member of the first-subject group, in a downward scale that takes us back once more to 1816 and the C major Mass; this long descending line is almost identical with one, also in F major, to which Schubert set the text 'propter magnam Gloriam' (for Thy great Glory).[38] It was given to the soloists, so again Therese's voice had the melody.

Prop - ter   mag - nam   Glo - ri - am__   Tu - am

Ex. 35a C Major Mass, *Gloria*

Ex. 35b Great C Major Symphony, 2nd movement, 2nd subject

The symphonic melody spans almost the same range as in another movement of the C major Mass, the *Benedictus* (which figured prominently in an earlier consideration of Schubert's feelings for Therese Grob). The Mass movement (see Ex. 7, p. 47) used surprisingly wide intervals; here the melody is sinuous but smooth, and though both movements show odd phrase-lengths the one in the symphony makes by far the more natural impression. Schubert's art has deepened immeasurably over ten years, and if Therese's spirit walks here, she is seen with 'emotion recollected in tranquillity'.

The interplay of wind choir and strings is at the heart of this movement's music; the wind soon add their colours to the unfolding of the melody, and the sound of eleven woodwind and brass instruments delivering yet another version of it is memorable (even the bass trombone is allowed to join the choir). By way of answer, the high strings at bars 116–20 offer a hauntingly spare texture in three 'real parts' that could be out of one of the more rarefied moments in *Lazarus*.

A further melody in D minor is once again given to the woodwind. For a few moments, three 'choirs' answer one another – high woodwind, strings, and very

---

[38] Newbould (*SandSy*) detects here a phrase in the slow movement of Mozart's E♭ major violin sonata K. 380; that Schubert, as a violinist, could well have had in mind in the early summer of 1816, composing the Mass and writing ecstatically about Mozart (see p. 146, note 50).

quiet trombones – leaving the horns free to seize their moment, which comes at the transition from middle section to repeat of first section. In one of the most haunting passages in all Schubert, repeated horn notes (both horns, as at the opening of the symphony) alternate with changing chords on the strings: these, as the dominant sevenths of, respectively, the key we are leaving and the one we are approaching, also alter the horn notes' harmonic meaning. The relationship between this and its terrifying negative in the slow movement of the G major string quartet (see 'Hard Sayings') lays a measure to two of the extreme opposites in Schubert's make-up. In *Abendbilder* the evening bell sounded thirty-two times to summon the faithful; the horns here have nine repetitions of their g before its unforgettable dying fall.

As the main melody reappears it is the first trumpet's turn to offer striking brief interjections. They look back to a couple of brief but curious trumpet-and-horn entries at the end of the first movement's introduction, and further back to the trumphet's enigmatic contribution to the A♭ Mass's 'Pleni sunt coeli'. An ultimate source could again be the 'Nelson' Mass' *Benedictus* and its trumpet figures. The first violins pick up the trumpets' comments, while the trumpets themselves mutter away through the consolatory afterthought in the major, like a cat talking to itself.

The sergeant-like third figure duly reappears (with more chuntering down below, from the celli and basses), and this time sets off an appalling chain reaction. First time round, the soft answer – a couple of meek woodwind chords after two stern ones for the full orchestra – turned away wrath, but now Schubert finds himself stuck. Some full-scale confrontation has developed, and the four insistent statements of the same note trigger off a crisis.

The four-note figure's repercussions in the finale will be shattering, but even here it starts something that threatens to bring the house crashing about one's ears. The strings insist on three-bar phrases, the wind echo each other in pairs of bars, and, like a clash of tectonic plates deep under the earth, it triggers off an earthquake.[39] The trumpets and horns play a crucial role, for their calls drive the music staggering on to the very edge of the cliff. These brassy insistent strangers make up another 'foreign body' to place beside the one in the 6th Moment Musical; still a third will be found in the slow movement of the G major string quartet. In the Great C Major their influence proves controllable, for after relishing their role in the disturbance the trumpets participate in only the most token way for the rest of the movement.

The moment when the music breaks off after the loudest chord of all is yet again reminiscent of Beethoven, in this case his *Hammerklavier* piano sonata

---

[39] Hugh Macdonald's metaphor ('Schubert's Volcanic Temper', *Musical Times*, November 1978, elaborated in 'Schubert's Pendulum', *Brille*, June 1998) is of an explosion of 'volcanic' nature, not uncommon in Schubert's music though seldom 'capped' as it is here and in the slow movement of the G major string quartet. He puts the disturbance down not to a clash of metres but to 'the superimposition of matching rhythms which generates the mechanical phenomenon of resonance, when two superimposed identical vibrations lead to a combined vibration of infinite amplitude (the reason why soldiers must break step when they cross a bridge)'.

(Op. 106 in B♭ major), whose first-movement recapitulation in that key is violently broken into by B minor, a key Beethoven designated as 'black'.[40] The stunned silence after his 'chord of pain' is matched by Schubert. After something like the final twitch of a dying body, the music gathers itself together to offer a new, infinitely wistful version of the first melody's opening. Much of that quality comes from the fact that the tune now appears on the flattened second degree of the scale, in what is known as a 'Neapolitan' relationship. The cellos are given this expressive line, the first oboe adding a brief counterpoint. A second statement returns us to A, and its major mode, for the repeat of the 'episode'.

After so colossal a variation of his first section, Schubert adheres in every detail to the original layout as he repeats the second, transposed in true sonata-form fashion from the mediant, F, to the tonic major, A. And yet his 'literal repeat' is felt as a miraculous expansion, for it is one of the most beautiful sustained examples of embellished repetition in all music. This time the strings are not entrusted with the melody, but what they have as consolation prize makes that more than worth while. The inner string parts sing a new flowing secondary-line, such as transformed a dry opening into something of endless charm at points of repetition such as 'qui propter nos homines' in the *Credo* of the G major Mass, or 'confiteor' in the one in A♭. The frightful crisis at the end of the preceding section left one badly in need of comfort. With this enrichment of what was already a divinely consolatory stretch of music, Schubert once more proves equal to every challenge.

There is a further, extraordinarily refined embellishment in the first violins. In the slow movement of the D minor (*Death and the Maiden*) string quartet, the first variation makes the leader comment on the theme, almost entirely off the beat, as if breathing in but never out; this catch in the breath or sobbing, conceived as a single violinist's contribution to a quartet,[41] is now demanded of the entire first-violin section, and quite disturbing it is. After the high-point of the section the first violins again play on the beat, but finally fall into pizzicato before the very last return of the great tune, which is distinctly subdued.

The final transition is shorter by four bars, without the dying fall, and the horns' questioning notes are now given to the clarinets. That suggests a loss of magic, but Schubert knows what he is doing; a man can give out just so much energy and no more. The final appearance of the main theme will be very short, and the compression is already beginning.

In fact the reappearance of the first melody is the merest summary, as if the memory of that painful upheaval were still all too present. But the missing magic now materialises, with the music dwelling on the theme's dotted-note figure for all of ten bars. That prompts the melody to give a further, more self-

---

[40] In a sketch for the D major cello sonata Op. 102 No. 2. 'He did not have to invent a plot in order to represent tragedy: a single chord of B minor is all that is necessary to characterise all the pain of existence' (Ratz, 'Analysis and Hermeneutics').

[41] An observation of Hans Keller's, recalled from a never-transmitted 1970 BBC2 programme on Schubert.

respecting account of itself, and Schubert's wealth of invention provides still one more idea, one more variant of the first melody, indeed of its element in the major. That is now put into the minor – 'pleasure will be paid, one time or another', as Feste says to Duke Orsino in *Twelfth Night*. The variation process produces a brief rising figure with flute and oboe in imitation; some such feeling is familiar from the end of the Unfinished Symphony's first movement, with the sad duet for Charlemagne and his lovelorn daughter in *Fierrabras* as missing link. The duet's blend of sternness and tenderness will appear yet again, memorably, in the revised *Benedictus* for the C major Mass. As ever, Schubert's second or third thoughts are on a higher level, for in this passage from the Great C Major there is not only the double resource of further variation and imitative duet, but also a yearningly expressive counterpointing line on the cellos.

The scherzo's superhuman dance takes us further back than anything else in the symphony. In 1814 one of Schubert's many youthful string quartets written for family music-making (in B♭, D. 112) ended with a 3/4 Presto finale. Apart from the fact that its opening (start of Ex. 36a) anticipated his charming way of sliding into a piece (*Geheimnis*, 5th Symphony), the movement as it developed came to be dominated by its second subject, a four-bar pattern (bars 58–61) derived from the first (e.g. 11–22). This eventually took on a form (92ff.) more or less identical with the symphonic scherzo's opening (Ex. 36b) – but, as ever, that does it better, the repeated note providing a far greater impetus (as did Schubert's late correction to his opening theme in the first movement).

Ex. 36a D. 112, 4th movement

Ex. 36b Great C Major Symphony, 3rd movement

It was not the first time his mind had returned to a similar idea, for his 1821 D major symphony (D. 708A, sketched but never completed) contains a lively scherzo built from a continuously developed 3/4 six-quaver figure of the same kind.

The 'hymn of praise' in the scherzo's trio is a special case. It is in A major and in triple time with a dotted rhythm. So is the hallucinatory central section of *Das Heimweh*, but there any resemblance ends. The symphonic Trio has no trace of the benighted mountain-dweller's 'anxious listening', rather a gigantic confidence and manifest well-being that brings to mind the same section of Beethoven's 7th Symphony.[42] The slow movement came through a crisis that questioned someone's entire existence: now it is time to say "Thank you". The Trio's opening phrase reappears in his 1828 Mass in E♭, whose *Gloria* contains, at 'agimus tibi gratias', not quite a quotation but something fascinatingly similar (see 'Pride of Performance'). The feeling that this music is an outpouring of gratitude is strengthened when one hears a cadence from another number in *Fierrabras*, a trio (No. 6d); at one of the opera's most touching moments a pair of eloping lovers say a grateful farewell to the hero, who could have stood in their way but has chosen not to – the text runs 'Leb' wohl, mög dich der Himmel Schutz bewahren' (farewell, may Heaven protect you.)

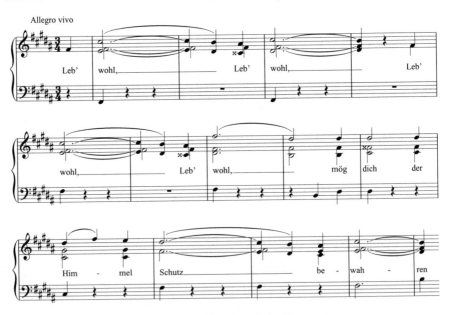

Ex. 37a *Fierrabras*, No. 6d

[42] See Nicholas Temperley, 'Schubert and Beethoven's 8/6 Chord', *Nineteenth-Century Music*, vol. 2, Fall 1981. Temperley stresses the appearance at many significant points in Schubert's music of a version of the tonic chord derived from that Beethoven movement. Following time-honoured figured-bass practice, he designates it as the 8/6 chord, also tracing Schubert's innumerable dactylic rhythms back to the slow movement of the same Beethoven symphony.

Ex. 37b Great C Major Symphony, Trio of 3rd movement

The finale sets out with yet another major third rising to e,[43] this time *fortissimo* on the full orchestra. Another version of it will appear a year later, as a deadly parody of itself, in the slow movement of the great string quartet in G major (D. 887; see 'Hard Sayings', Ex. 42c). Here there is a quiet answer on the stringed instruments in unison. That is a mere curlicue, four notes long, going down and up the tonic chord,

Ex. 38

but, both in its original form and turned upside down, it becomes a driving force and pervades the violin and viola parts to such a degree that for many years few orchestras were willing to perform the symphony. Schubert worked within a Viennese tradition that made the string players in Masses carry out such taxing menial work.

The finale's second subject with its four equal notes is one of Schubert's most dynamic inventions. We have already come across the four-equal-note figure; it is important in Schubert's work at least as early as the 'Dona nobis pacem' of the A♭ Mass, and strikingly present in the 1823 A minor piano sonata, though there it takes the form of falling thirds rather than single notes.[44] In the Great C Major the repeated notes generate enormous energy as the finale progresses.

What follows them as the main body of the subject, its real 'melodic' element, is yet another of the waves identified by Tenhaef.

---

[43] No wonder Jernhake interprets this interval as some kind of cicerone or implicit composer guiding the course of the entire 'symphonic novel of maturing'.

[44] For an example during the intervening time, see 'Schubert and the Composition of *Fierrabras*'.

Ex. 39 Great C Major Symphony, 4th movement, 2nd subject

The subject with its two components develops into a mighty paragraph; near the end, the wave-figure takes on a descending form that rounds the section off very fittingly.

As the development begins, that closing version is lengthened and given an upward tilt, which lends it a surface resemblance to Beethoven's 'Ode to Joy' theme in the finale of the Choral Symphony.[45] Schubert makes a symmetrical 48-bar paragraph out of it all, then the music begins to disintegrate. The sky clouds over, the closing figure, now in the minor, is taken up in close imitation on the violins and violas, with held notes chiming in on the woodwind. That is a constellation very like the one in the opening idea of *Lazarus*, but the other way up. The gradually growing apprehension here is like that before the storm in Beethoven's Pastoral Symphony.

The ever-growing wave breaks on the hard rock of those four massive equal notes, which reappear after an absence of over a hundred bars. From here to the start of the recapitulation is a clear if extended run-in, much of it over a dominant pedal. It builds up a great deal of tension with its gradual series of changing harmonies over an unchanging bass. Schubert had already achieved this effect on a smaller scale in yet another number from *Fierrabras*, a quintet (No. 10) in which anger and thoughts of revenge are dispelled by a sudden ray of hope ('Doch eine Hoffnung lacht').

The apparent straightforwardness of this passage in the symphony makes its final surprise all the greater. If there was hope here, it now suffers a blow, at the start of Schubert's most drastic 'invaded recapitulation'. The four-note figure has seen us home, now it should bow out until it is due to come round yet again as part of the second subject. But it is going to do no such thing: it is stuck on E♭ major (in fact on an 8/6 chord in that key, to match the 8/6 in the Trio) and will not give way. The first subject has to yield and reappear in that key too. Even more than Beethoven's change from subdued minor to raging major, or the crushed quietness in Schubert's first movement, this interrupted cadence calls in question the whole harmonic basis of sonata structure. No gain without pain.

Eventually C major is restored, the second subject reappears transposed as tradition would dictate, and we seem to be nearing the end. But after so much striving, so much strife, and with fulfilment seemingly achieved, there is yet

---

[45] Newbould (*SMM*) takes this as a tribute, which would certainly not have been out of character. For that matter, the music immediately after the double bar in the Scherzo's trio could be taken as echoing bars 76–81 in the opening movement of the same Beethoven symphony.

again the slide into doubt and alarm. The opening of the finale's coda is like the corresponding point in the first movement of Beethoven's 'Eroica' Symphony, the bass-line sinking to the submediant (a). Schubert again reverses Beethoven's dynamics; instead of an irresistible surge forward with fortissimo chords for the full orchestra, Schubert's crucial downward move at the end of a forty-four-bar *diminuendo* is made on the cellos unsupported even by the double-basses, *pianissimo*.

Well might the composer ask of his destiny, as Ariel of Prospero, 'Is there more toil?' Once again the music is off in a new direction. A-major as dominant of D soon proves merely the starting-point of a laborious climb, semitone by semitone, with each step lasting a dozen bars. One important harmonic area after another is passed through without a sidelong glance ('been there, done that!'), until the music can heave itself up on to the tonic. This gradual climb up the well has things in common, technically speaking, with the 'torment' harmonies in *Gruppe aus dem Tartarus*, yet one is not reminded of the song hearing the symphony. Even Schubert's fingerprints are superhuman: they change over the course of his life.

With C major finally and irrevocably achieved, the four repeated notes take over.[46] Even here, in the most four-square juxtaposition of four-bar chunks imaginable, Schubert is subtly asymmetrical: twice-four unison c-s are answered by twice-four chords, an A♭ triad followed by a diminished 7th on f♯ – but a second time round, the chords come in the opposite order. Only once all that is out of the way can the final 'sprint to the finish' (Newbould, *SMM*) provide much-needed confirmation of tonic-and-dominant. And that's that, apart from a small question-mark over Schubert's final dynamic indication, one of those hairpin-shaped signs that could mean 'get softer' but here probably means 'hit it with an accent, it's the final chord'.[47]

In the Great C Major Symphony there is a complex train of thought, a whole series of vicissitudes (what Greek drama called *peripeteia*) running from beginning to end, and Schubert's many self-quotations suggest that he was still engaged on the kind of review identifiable in the *Arpeggione* Sonata. But now he looks down from the mountain top with new self-confidence, rather than up from the humble working-desk of the still-young composer home from meeting his new Anima image and yet with his problems unsolved. As the

---

[46] The great conductor Hans Knappertsbusch used to make what was felt to be a much-exaggerated slowing-down at that point, which one can still experience on his recording of the work with the Vienna Philharmonic Orchestra (e.g. DGG 435–328–2); given the passage's significance within the symphony as a whole, he could well have been right, and have been on to something vast and monolithic in Schubert's nature so often missed in performance. Newbould (*SMM*) characterises these notes as 'hammer-blows that call the finale's accumulated hyper-activity to account'. Given the different ways in which this chapter's pseudo-hermeneutics interprets them, it is no surprise that different conductors take the passage in different ways.

[47] Newbould (*SMM*) and David Montgomery ('Performance and Criteria for Franz Schubert's Great Symphony in C major D. 944', *Brille*, Jan. 2000) agree that the final marking is an accent, since a decrescendo at that point would be neither logical nor practical.

symphony's 'analyst', Jernhake holds that the music constructs a narrative, played out in 'God's theatre', with a purely imaginary protagonist guided by an imaginary 'narrator', who is likewise not the composer in real life but an imagined composer, a 'producer on a world scale'. That producer's voice, we are told, is heard from time to time in the all-important rising third.

In Jernhake's 'plot', worked out with the aid of the most modern hermeneutics, the implied composer leads the hero to become ever deeply aware of the 'gentle law that governs relations between Man, Nature and the Eternal' [a formulation drawn from a great Austrian successor to Schubert, the writer Adalbert Stifter]; 'thus, through Providence, the Wanderer discovers the element of necessity within freedom'. Anyone doubting their ability to absorb that kind of information from a piece of music may be curious to survey the Great C Major's self-references in search of a tip from the horse's mouth, showing what the train of thought, if any, in this particular 'novel of maturing' might rather be. So, for that matter, may those inclined to reflect that a clever-enough mind could as well make out a case for *Wilhelm Meister* as covert symphony.

There are two possible approaches: to take the quotations in the order of their appearance in the symphony, to-ing and fro-ing between stages of Schubert's life, or to follow the quotations' own chronology. Since not all are from his own music, that is the less logical course of the two, but worth examining. He was a long time completing the Great C Major, he made at least one utterly crucial late amendment to its themes when he altered the opening movement's 3rd Symphony quotation, and if there is any 'plot' to this work, whether it involves an 'implicit' composer/ narrator, an actual composer/narrator, or such a person's created 'hero', it could have taken shape at the back of Schubert's mind in any order. What the different approaches produce can be tabulated as follows.

Symphonic order
I **Introduction:** C major Mass, *Credo*
'Seid fruchtbar' (Haydn *The Creation*)
1st subject 3rd Symphony, I, 1st subject
Exposition codetta: trombones (*Lazarus*)
Development: motives from *The Creation*, 'ohne Form und leer', then entire curve from same (cf. *Salve Regina*, D.106)
Coda: Italian Overture in D, 6th Symphony, *Zauberharfe* Overture
II Haydn 'Nelson' Mass
F **major episode:** C major Mass, *Benedictus*
C major Mass, *Gloria* ('Propter magnam gloriam Tuam')
Coda: *Fierrabras* Duet
III **Scherzo 1st subject:** Finale of 1814 B♭ Quartet D. 112
Trio: Forward to E♭ Mass, 'Gratias agimus tibi'
IV Four repeated notes:
A♭ Mass Dona nobis pacem (1822)
various 1823 passages (A minor sonata D. 784, *Fierrabras*)
Opening idea of *Lazarus*

The 'plot' to match all that would be a flight of ideas running roughly:

'I believed in God, one God, and that the world would go on happily reproducing itself. God was good to the carefree young man with his cheery symphonies and overtures for his friends to perform, and those friends danced as I played, without a care in the world. Then it started to go wrong – I found I was not one of those who pass on the race, only its finest thoughts, I was reminded that despite all intercession the submissive go under, like Lazarus, whose resurrection I never set to music, and that the world can come to seem without form and void: when I should have been carrying earlier achievements to new heights, I was cast down. But it was good to remember how I had loved a voice and its owner, and as I thought of those times my spirit danced, as my friends had danced to my playing: an overwhelming feeling of gratitude came over me, and I knew indeed that one mighty power was at work, one-two-three-four, taking me I knew not where, and saying that though death must come, it is not the end.'

Chronological order
(Haydn *The Creation*: 'without form and void'; 'be fruitful'; Haydn 'Nelson' Mass)
1814 Haydn quotation in *Salve Regina* D. 104 ('ohne Form und leer' = 'Hac lacrimarum valle')
D. 112 String Quartet in Bb, Finale
1815 D. 200 3rd Symphony, 1st movement, 1st subject
1816 D. 452 C major Mass – *Gloria* ('Propter magnam Gloriam tuam'), *Credo*, *Benedictus* ('Benedictus qui venit in Nomine Domini')
1817–18 Italian Overture in D, 6th Symphony
1820 D. 689 *Lazarus*
1822? D. 678 Ab Mass 'Dona nobis pacem', four-equal-note figure
1823 D. 784 Piano Sonata in A minor, I, fourfold repetition
D. 796 *Fierrabras* Act 2 No. 13

The 'plot' is now a flight of ideas roughly like this:

'In the beginning was *The Creation*, once heard, never forgotten; some of the things it told a sensitive boy were disturbing, others comforting and inspiring, even if in the longest run they had a "not-for-me" quality. Should life prove a vale of tears, there was always the goodness of Woman to intercede, and the joy of movement, and of trying to compose something of stature. I was happy to affirm that I believed in one God, happy beyond measure to have found whole hidden sides of myself seemingly made real in the singing voice of a dear friend. It could not stay so – I fell into doubtful company, bad ways, came to know the fear of death, and all too often had to entreat God to let me know a little calm, a little peace. I was ill, dark thoughts hammered in my brain, one-two-three-four – and yet in spite of it all I was grateful.'

The outcome is similar, apart from the quite other interpretation of the crucial repeated notes, the journey different. In neither case is it very much, and piecemeal compared to Jernhake's polished presentation. It is also simplistic, since it falls into the trap of identifying the music's protagonist with Schubert himself. That is a danger Ricoeur's method sedulously avoids. But insofar as it undeniably reflects thoughts – *musical ideas* – in Schubert's mind over a decade and more, it may not be total invention or foolishness. A 'conflict between resignation and hope' (Jernhake on the second movement) there undoubtedly was in Schubert during his final years: does it really take the philosophical armoury of Ricoeur's hermeneutics to spot that? The mighty dance of the Scherzo, with its Trio suggesting what the text of the later mass makes explicit – gratitude – does indeed point to 'the need to reconcile a longing for the Infinite with a care for the earthly and for a human community', so that 'the Wanderer at the height of his maturity overcomes his fear of death'. And that the 'destructive powers in his inmost soul are held in check by a creativity and joy that never dry up' is precisely this book's thesis, though it takes a bold man to analyse it out of a symphonic score.

With which reflection we find ourselves less far from Schubert's 'right and true devotion' than might be imagined. In his time Pantheism, the sense of God manifest throughout Nature, was in the ascendant, whether in the Apollonian Goethe or the Dionysian Romantics. Even nowadays the traveller arriving in Bad Gastein may be much impressed by the waterfall that plunges noisily under the main street, metres from the house where Schubert met Pyrker again in 1825, while the surrounding mountains, valleys and forests make for an elation that in the mind of a sensitive genius could speak volumes about the natural splendour of God's creation. Wildlife, another of Nature's delights that can make one grateful beyond measure, is absent from Schubert's letters home, as from his music, give or take the odd bird and cow, but the 'fruitfulness' quotation so early in the symphony's introduction suggests that nature's burgeoning was not far from his mind. His 'right and true devotion' letter also touched on the duty of a married man, his painter brother Karl, to produce 'works of nature as well as art'. That he curtly dismissed as 'not for me', which makes the Haydn quotation seem distinctly double-edged.

It has become almost a cliché that the Great C Major is a pantheistic outpouring, a 'Hymn to Nature'. Our paragons among scholar-conductors can turn it into a Hymn to Hysteria, which may be not entirely bad (even if the performance in question was), in view of its profound doubt, wrestling and complication, its moments of awe and terror. Jernhake's 'secret programme' could even be a shade too sanguine: one nineteenth-century symphonic finale after another was to emphasise how very far from a solution a composer could find himself at quite a late stage. There is virtue in that, for it heightens the vital tension; the classic case of a great mind wrestling with its doubts and fears and winning, in sporting parlance, the closest of split decisions is the finale of Bruckner's often Schubertian 4th Symphony.

The 1825 holiday was cut short by Vogl's sudden decision to leave Gmunden and prepare for a long visit to Italy. Schubert had meanwhile composed more excellent songs. Friedrich Schlegel's *Fülle der Liebe* (D. 854) at first sight clashes with the holiday mood, for its text scrupulously examines the minutiae of love's suffering and ecstasy. Schubert turns it into one of his obsessed, totally repetitive songs, successor to the remarkable *Du liebst mich nicht* (D. 756) from three years earlier. He never lets up on its single dotted rhythm, and finally plunges into far-distant harmonies just as he had at the end of *Das Heimweh*. If it is of the essence of religious art to go to extremes, then this extraordinary song qualifies.

Abendlied für die Entfernte (D. 856) to a poem by the other Schlegel brother, August Wilhelm, could scarcely be more different, a comparable rhythmic continuity apart. Its gently rocking theme is subtly varied as it returns, with major and minor gently fading one into the other. The music wonderfully exemplifies a central thought in the poem, which tallied so well with Schubert's own experience:

Ach, dürften wir mit Träumen nicht	Ah, were we not allowed to interweave
Die Wirklichkeit verweben,	Dreams with reality,
Wie arm an Farbe, Glanz und Licht	How poor in colour, brightness, light,
Wärst dann du Menschenleben!	O life of man, would you not be!

Two settings (D. 857) of songs from a play by Wilhelm von Schütz, *Lacrimas*, also date from September 1825. In *Delphine*, one of Schubert's great love-songs, a woman revels in a young man's devotion. *Fülle der Liebe* wrung from love the last drop of pseudo-religious anguish; the protagonist of *Delphine* is unashamedly self-indulgent, she has earned her desperate feelings and is going to enjoy them, even to the extent of neglecting her plants. As for the young man, the piano's left hand obediently follows every twist of the vocal line, in a unique reversal of the VDB principle. *Florio* is a quieter song of amorous devotion, with a tempo very hard to judge, which may be one reason why it is scarcely ever sung.

A final song, probably from the same period, deserves examination. The poet Ernst Konrad Friedrich Schulze had died of consumption in 1817, aged only twenty-eight. Schubert's settings of him date from 1825 and 1826, and at their most outspoken, as in *Über Wildemann* (D. 884, April 1826)[48] are fierce and sombre in a way that looks forward a year or two to *Winterreise*. An exception in many ways is *Auf der Bruck* (D. 853), probably composed in August 1825, though it could date from as early as March of the same year (another Schulze setting, *Im Walde*, D. 834, is definitely from March and shows the same dynamism). *Auf der Bruck* is on the face of it a love-song, in which a man rides back to a beloved not seen for three whole days, but its incessant onward drive, with eleven hundred rapidly repeated chords in the piano part, makes it a sheer release of vital energy. In that respect it is on a par, not with the strange Overture from 1819 discussed in 'Hard Sayings', but with the strongest moments in the Great C Major Symphony. In this radiant counterpart to *Erlkönig*, the night and its terrors are banished, the day illuminated by a vision. (In *Willkommen und Abschied*, D. 767, from the end of 1822, Schubert had left an even more direct exorcism of *Erlkönig* – text likewise by Goethe, a furious

[48] See 'VDB', *Brille*, Jan. 2001.

night ride but towards a loved one. The night's terrors seem to have returned in the spectral finale of the September 1828 C minor piano sonata.)

This whole divine 'summer madness' of 1825 could mark the start of an enormous coda in the sonata-form of Schubert's life, as a definitive symbol of individuation. Its rich vein of grandeur is still detectable in some of the music he composed over the ensuing year. So, too, his reflective side, in the tenderness of the Seidl *Wiegenlied* (D. 867) and *Das Zügenglöcklein* (D. 871), the reflection on death, decay and reawakening in *Totengräbeweise* (D. 869), the glimpse of panic and emptiness in the Mignon–Harper duet, which opens the set D. 877, or the serene awareness of security through friendship in *Im Freien* (D. 880). But Schulze's melancholic, despairing tones fascinated Schubert more and more, and the songs that resulted hint at his still profounder reaction on discovering further Wilhelm Müller poems.

Schubert went into a deep depression in the late spring of 1826. Once back in the world, he sounded a new and sombre note in the G major String Quartet (D. 887), composed within eleven June days. But in September and October 1826 he produced two more remarkably unwintry masterpieces, one on a small scale, one full-length. *Nachthelle* (Night's Brightness, D. 892), for tenor, male voices and piano, conveys ecstasy bordering on awe, and there is his 'pastoral'[49] Piano Sonata in G Major (D. 894). The calm and balance of its main melodies, the playfulness of its finale, which matches that of the D major in an air of childlike innocence, the Mozartean haven of the 'maggiore'[50] trio within the assertive B minor Menuetto – these may seem far removed from 'Tremendum' and 'Mirum' alike. But one need only remember the end of the 1818 *Einsamkeit* or the 'Pleni sunt coeli' of the Ab Mass to be reminded of the numinous overtones that pastoral carried for Schubert.

There is also something almost unique in the G major sonata's second movement. The serene D major melody gains a special colour from being played for the most part in octaves; its texture, tempo (slowish triple time), outline and rhythm all recall a very beautiful song to an equally beautiful Goethe poem, *An den Mond* (To the Moon, 2nd setting, D. 296, date contentious). That can be taken as communicating a rare moment of detachment, when an ever-active

---

[49] Robert Hatten, 'Schubert's Pastoral Sonata', in *Schubert the Progressive*, Proceedings of 2000 Leeds Symposium, 2001.

[50] Mozart's major-key interludes within movements in the minor are among music's most heart-easing passages (Finale of E minor Violin Sonata, K. 304; of A minor Piano Sonata, K. 310; fourth variation in finale of D minor String Quartet, K. 421; Trio of 3rd movement of G minor 40th Symphony, K. 550). How much Schubert's beloved Mozart ('As from afar the magic notes of Mozart's music haunt me' – diary, 14 June 1816 – etc. etc.) contributed to his own unprecedented fusion of major and minor is something that would bear investigation. And if Schubert knew his Mozart piano sonatas half as well as he knew his Haydn string quartets, then the 3/4 Ab at the heart of the slow movement in the Sonata in C, K. 330 (by a creative irony, a 'maggiore' within a 'minore' episode within a movement cast in the major mode) could have been at the back of his mind as he composed the second setting of *An den Mond*, discussed below.

spirit such as Goethe's briefly stands outside the pattern of compulsions that run his life, and sees clearly. Otto, however,[51] found in its lines

Was dem Menschen unbewusst	What, unknown
Oder nicht gedacht	Or unthought
Durch das Labyrinth der Brust	Makes its night-time way
Wandelt in der Nacht	Through the labyrinth of man's breast

the principle Immanuel Kant called 'aesthetic perception' and granted no less objective validity than any principle derived from logic. At this point in his second setting of the poem Schubert drops into a variant of VDB, as if saying 'yes, I too know those deep inexpressible feelings – but *I* can express them!' The related mood at the piano sonata slow-movement's opening is still concordant with the whole work's 'timeless sense of continuity' (Hatten), its feeling that in this work the pastoral is for Schubert an 'idyllic space'.

Nachthelle for its part is like a seventh *Salve Regina*, but with piano and with the adoration redirected from Mary to God's created world. It hovers on the brink, the borderline between amazement and awe, and the strange line 'die Häuser schaun verwundert drein' (the houses pull wondering faces) prompts yet another of Schubert's end-of-work harmonic excursions. The tenor voice's upper register is used in an inspired way to communicate a peak of inward excitement. A phrase from *Nachthelle* reappears in another not-insubstantial piece from the autumn of 1826, the B Minor Rondo for violin and piano (D. 895). That is an assertive, sprawling work where Schubert has no compunction about repeating all his ventures into one distant harmonic area after another; all the same, it has striking passages and its second subject displays a melodic outline not unlike that found in *Nachthelle* at the words 'in mir ist's hell so wunderbar' (within me it is so wondrously bright).

Schubert's 'mountain chords' had yet to find their apotheosis, and did so as late as November 1827, in the final climax of the slow movement in the E♭ Piano Trio (D. 929). A deep trough lay between 1825's euphoria and such steel-hardened resolve; against the background of inner radiance manifest in songs like *Die Allmacht* or a choral piece such as *Nachthelle*, the 'hard sayings' in Schubert's music stand out all the more starkly. It is time to examine some of them.

---

[51] Otto, *Das Heilige*, p. 177. For those to whom sexual leanings are a signpost indispensable for their orienteering, there is also the question of the role of male friendship in a male genius' life, raised by Goethe's image in *An den Mond* of 'holding a friend [sex unstated, 'Freund': a specifically female friend would have been 'Freundin'] to one's bosom'; this is made much of in Kramer's 1999 book.

Tragic Intermezzo

Hard Sayings

The waste even in a fulfilled life, the isolation even of a life rich
in intimacy, cannot but be felt deeply, and is the central feeling
of tragedy.

> William Empson, *Some Versions of Pastoral*

Overture to Fierrabras; Entr'acte in B minor from music for Rosamunde; String
Quartet in G (D. 887); cycle Schwanengesang; Incomplete D major symphony
from 1828; Piano Sonata in A (D. 959)

Emphasis on Schubert's positive and naturally religious side, so apparent in a
great work like the Mass in Ab, must on no account mean undervaluing the
darker masterpieces that are nowadays more familiar. The aim is a truly
rounded, complete picture, so even a contrarian survey should look, however
briefly, at the things in him that seem to stand at the most 'negative' pole. In fact
they belong in any such survey; as has been made clear, experience of the
numinous opens doors on to incomparable landscapes of euphoria, but can also
arouse awe to the point of terror. The 'Mirum' is sensed in nature and in one's
fellow-creatures; we have seen that with the 'Tremendum' it may be hard to
distinguish between religious awe and feelings that spring from worldly
misfortune and reduced self-worth. Hence, in part, the confusion and one-
sidedness in current popular views of Schubert.

McKay vividly describes Schubert's 'shadow side'; Macdonald identifies his
'volcanic' temper in passages from works widely separated in time (see p. 135,
footnote 39). So biographer and analyst alike detect a 'demonic element' in
Schubert. But the Wanderer Fantasy's outpouring of energy is seen by McKay as
the music of a man 'subjugating his despair with assumed over-confidence,
selfishness, and boasting', whereas Newbould (SMM) detects in it a 'fresh
confidence' and finds that it 'clears the blockage which had hampered his
progress for four years'. Add in the idea of a complex world of natural religious
feeling, where the knowledge of one's shadow side is a powerful stimulus to
repentance, and you end up with something of a jigsaw; may future scholars put
it together to provide a complete picture of Schubert.

An awe-struck moment comes at the start of the Overture to his last completed opera, *Fierrabras,* which he added after completing the dramatic music in the autumn of 1823. This altogether remarkable piece has one of the most stunning openings in all Schubert, a unique reinterpretation of the conventional pattern 'slow introduction before quick main section'. The effect comes partly from an age-old device used at the start, namely strings playing tremolo, partly from the succession of harmonies, and partly

Ex. 40 *Fierrabras* Overture, opening

from the ensuing solemn melody; that is rounded off by a repeat of the dark opening bars.

Schubert's initial tremolo carries us immediately to the Neapolitan sixth, a favourite move of his but seldom so early in a piece, and he darkens the mood with the flattened-supertonic or Neapolitan chord not in its usual major but in the minor. There are second thoughts here, which as so often with Schubert are 'better yet'; the source for the overture's opening is an emotionally ambivalent Act 1 ensemble (No. 4e), where the flat-supertonic chord is in the major. The music up to this point reappears in the main section's allegro tempo just before the recapitulation[1] (bars 209ff.), and again near the end (bars 365ff.) One could well sing to it a heartfelt 'Kyrie Eleison'.

After the tremolo opening Schubert follows the time-honoured operatic practice of quoting a number from the opera, an unaccompanied chorus of imprisoned Frankish knights in Act 2. This in turn looks back to the 1819 song *Himmelsfunken* (Spark from Heaven). As has been argued from the outset, such quotations are the safest pointer to what went on in Schubert's mind: here we find an instinctive reaction to the idea of a 'Fatherland': home, thought of with piety and affection. If one approaches the Overture knowing *Himmelsfunken,* as Schubert did, that is the automatic association, even though the immediate darkening of the harmonies (back to F minor after the wind entry in F major), a brief but threatening unison passage (bars 17–18), prepares one for emotional conflicts to come.

---

[1] See comments on the 1st Symphony in 'The Early Masses'.

And, sure enough, the Allegro turns out to be something of a musical switchback, setting off with a mixture of resolution and hesitation that will be met again, only with a higher proportion of hesitation, in the B minor Entr'acte composed very shortly after for *Rosamunde*.[2]

That Entr'acte is of considerable interest, quite apart from the question whether it was meant as a finale for the Unfinished Symphony. Sir George Grove excepted it from his general view of Schubert as 'the woman to Beethoven's man', finding it 'one of the few places where Schubert compels his hearers with irresistible power'. Outbursts of sheer energy were no new thing with him. An Overture in E Minor (D. 648, 1819) is a curious example, which can reawaken in the listener a sense, hardly felt since his most awkward early orchestral pieces, of a powerful force without real musical content. Probably influenced by Beethoven's *Coriolan* Overture, it is well enough put together, one 32-bar sequence of chromatically rising harmonies coming twice to cap all Schubert's other '*Gruppe aus dem Tartarus*' passages (and producing, unfortunately, another passage of 'piano-tuner' music), but the insistent repetition of really undistinguished scraps of theme puts one in mind of the weakest Bruckner. Too often, an accompaniment seems in search of a melody. Newbould (*SMM*) is happy to leave it that here Schubert was finding his feet in the use of large orchestral resources in E minor, the key in which he shortly afterwards cast an ambitious symphonic project (Symphony in E, D. 729, August 1821, sketched in its entirety but realised only in part). Hans-Joachim Hinrichsen's article on the smaller orchestral pieces (*Schubert Handbuch*) says that this Overture is 'one of the most astonishing formal experiments in Schubert's instrumental music, but its success is questionable'. In dropping its opening subject after it has been stated at length, it anticipates the undoubtedly successful C minor string quartet movement from the end of 1820, but like the finale of the Symphony in E it tries to achieve too much with too little. A matter of days earlier Schubert had done comparable things to magical effect in the overture to *Die Zwillingsbrüder*, 'too serious' or not, it is a little gem, worthy to stand in a long line of comedy overtures from Mozart to Reznicek (*Donna Diana*, 1894) and Busoni (*Lustspielouverture*, 1897). The E Minor overture was played while still relatively new, at a Vienna concert which opened with Beethoven's 7th Symphony, and also in Graz, so becoming the first Schubert work performed outside Vienna. What its listeners thought, even the handsomely enlarged first volume of *Schubert Documents* cannot tell us.

In the B minor 'Rosamunde' Entr'acte Schubert was in a similar mood, but this time he found ample and fascinating inspiration to give it flesh and blood. Grove's 'irresistible power' is a true enough observation, if ironic in view of the constant indecision the music suggests. It sets out resolutely, but within

---

[2] I argue in 'Schubert and the Composition of *Fierrabras*' that this overture could be a symphonic portrait of the opera's troubled hero, in fact his 'finest hour'. Its terrifying first two minutes are part of him.

two bars meets with some obstacle and is held up by a double echo – 'did I
say that? Do I really mean that?'; it has great difficulty settling anywhere, with
a sense of self-doubt which at first encounter feels new and most strange
coming from this of all composers, though it would be understandable in the
aftermath of the 1822–3 medical crisis.[3] The music tries again in the major,
this time managing to cast off its shadows, but (bars 52ff.) an abrupt change
of mood again disturbs the continuity and brings one of the piece's most
Brucknerian moments: repeated unisons (g♯) lead to a plunge into darkness[4]
(Ex. 41a).

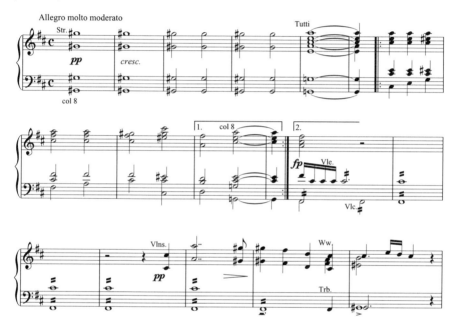

Ex. 41a Incidental music for *Rosamunde*, No. 1: Entr'acte after Act I

[3] Such self-doubts were second nature to, for example, Bruckner, given his upbringing and
education, or lack of.

[4] Technically speaking, the effect is achieved by taking the bass down a semitone, its unison in the
treble up by the same interval, and making the middle parts complete the Neapolitan chord, with
an all-important added seventh in the bass, i.e. the chord as dominant-seventh in its last
inversion. The harmonic progression is I – II♭ 7♭ – 1 – 3 – 5, as in bars 4–5 of Ex. 41a: hearing
this, it is as if the floor gave way beneath one's feet and one was on one's way down to the cellar.
The most overwhelming use of it is in the opening progression of Bruckner's 9th Symphony. But
even without the 'last inversion' the harmonic progression I – II♭ can be awe-inspiring (e.g. A♭
Mass, 'Et incarnatus', bars 8–9), or at the words 'Du hast es gesprochen' (you have said it [that
you do not love me]) in the 1822 *Du liebst mich nicht*.

Ex. 41b

As well as the harmonic progression the rhythm too is important here: two semibreves are followed by four minims. In 'Harvest' it was apparent that this four-repeated-note figure, prominent in the unfinished C major piano sonata and the finale of the Great C Major Symphony, tells of something deep down in Schubert's nature, which appears grandiose and craggy, euphoric or reflective, as his musical genius dictates. Here it is downright threatening. Parts of this Entr'acte can match the C major sonata's first movement for rock-like harshness – hence Grove's perception of it.

The very opening with its doubts was more like Mahler than Bruckner, as is the strange string outcry over a tremolando bass immediately after the modulation to F♯ minor (bars 67 onwards), like an echo of something serious in a Rossini opera. The second Brucknerian pre-echo comes in the later stages of the second-subject group (bars 90–9 and 297–306) – a repeated unison descending figure for almost the full orchestra, the three trombones being called upon at this point (Ex. 41b). Bruckner's craggy unison figures often come at about the same stage in his expositions, as a kind of 'third subject' (3rd, 7th Symphonies). It is typical of Schubert's constructive imagination that each appearance of the 'Brucknerian' unison passage leads to a reappearance of the same melodic fragment in a different key or region.[5] The brief restatement of the first subject follows, rounded off by another 'hard saying' – a four-chord sequence against an upper pedal (bars 144–7), which makes a cliché into something striking.

Though it is tempting to read autobiography into this strange, alienated piece, the text of the play shows that it is, beyond doubt, what the *Fierrabras* overture well may be: a character-study. Fulgentius, the villainous Governor of Cyprus, consumed with lust for his designated successor, the beautiful fifteen-year-old Princess Rosamunde, is determined to marry her or else destroy her,

---

[5] The first is on a G major that proves to be the Neapolitan second degree of the new tonic, F sharp minor: the second is a semitone higher, in G♯ minor (with which G major has b in common), and the passage is longer because the fragment is heard a second time, beginning from the note, b, that it had reached, and so leading through E minor and D major chords to the same tonic.

but between Acts 1 and 2, at the point where the Entr'acte is played as the first music after the Overture, he is at a low point of vacillation. The Entr'acte's opening uses the short rising upbeat scale-figure associated with pomp and circumstance and with Turkish military music; the most famous example is at the opening of Mozart's 'Jupiter' Symphony, and Schubert had laid it on in quantity in *Fierrabras* for both his 'heavies', the Moorish prince Boland and even more decisively the Frankish Emperor Charlemagne. To *Rosamunde*'s audience it would straight away have suggested someone important and dangerous.

It could be argued that the Entr'acte is more curious than satisfying, that something almost incoherent about its phrase-structure suggests a certain haste in composing it; according to the authoress' son, Wilhelm von Chézy, the entire music for the play was written in five days. Or one can argue that precisely these characteristics make it not merely 'interesting'[6] but a 'character document', a remarkable picture of a strong man in two minds. Slight resemblances to some of the music given to Fierrabras, another character pulled two ways, support this idea. Schubert seldom sounds more 'modern' than here.

Seldom, but sometimes. The late G major string quartet (D. 887), written within eleven days during June 1826, shows the full range. In an address on the 1928 centenary of Schubert's death, Franz Schmidt called its first movement 'the seed-corn from which Bruckner's entire life's-work arose!' It has epoch-making features: in the first movement, scarcely remitting tremolo dies away into a beatific calm only at the start of the recapitulation, as if some consuming illness went briefly into remission and the patient were lulled to sleep. Elsewhere and often, major and minor chords fade one into the other as they will, seventy years later, in Mahler's 6th Symphony; and there are the demonic energy and harmonic restlessness of the scherzo and finale.

But there is, above all, something amazing and unique in the slow second movement. The first movement having contained a remission, the second could speak, in its episode, of a relapse. The jerky dotted rhythms from the opening movement break in again. The line to which they do so has a final echo (figure a in Ex. 42a below), which plays a crucial role – an inversion of the falling third in the same rhythm near the start of the work (I, bar 11, Ex. 42b; this is a new version of an even earlier falling second). The music begins to change key in the oddest way, but the rising third seems stuck: first violin and viola insist on it even though the surrounding music has moved on (Ex. 42c). At first making perfect sense as keynote moving to minor third, the interval becomes ever more of a foreign body, explicable only as part of chords which, if actually played, would clash hideously with the one sounding at the time. It is as if something unassimilable had to be faced, or simply allowed to happen without becoming a part of normal life.[7]

---

[6] Sir William Glock, who knew his way around Viennese classical music, was known to say to his underlings in the BBC's Music Division, 'Don't talk to me about *interesting*; is it *any good*!?'

[7] Or (since no analogy applied to sounds can be more than one among many) as if something were being clung to for dear life, or as if an obsessive kept giving the same answer regardless of the

Ex. 42a String Quartet in G major, D. 887, 2nd movement

Ex. 42b

Ex. 42c

Cone's analysis of the 6th *Moment Musical* suggested the idea of a foreign body coming to dominate and demolish its host. In this passage from the quartet there is juxtaposition without connection, a pattern that would exemplify Budde's idea of harmonic planes. Here is the most jagged, brusque music Schubert ever wrote, and by a supreme creative irony the intrusive figure that brings it all about by its obstinacy is the aspiring rising third that in a song such as *Suleika I* helps convey a faithful lover's attachment during separation; a variant in the major has meanwhile pervaded the Great C Major Symphony's hymn of praise. The quartet-passage indeed seems to parody one of the symphony's greatest moments, the slow movement's lead-back from episode to main subject with its dying-fall horn notes against hovering, changing string harmonies. It does not do to grade music according to 'how far ahead of its time' it seems, for, in Robert Musil's words, 'the genius isn't a hundred years ahead of his time, the man-in-the-street is a hundred years behind it';[8] all the

question, as in the various jokes ending 'How on earth can that make you think about God/food/women?' – 'Everything makes me think about God/food/women'. A frequent reaction to this passage is to feel that matters of life and death are involved, something that could find support in the first movement's fading from major to minor and back; the frenzy with which that happens in the final bars makes the hindsighted listener think of the existential terror evoked by the same procedure in the Mahler symphony just mentioned. Certainly Roger Scruton, in *Aesthetics of Music*, is in no doubt that here Schubert was facing terror at the prospect of extinction.

[8] *Tagebücher, Aphorismen, Essays und Reden*, p. 567.

same, this passage shows Schubert near to the world of Bartòk,[9] for the whole section with its dotted rhythms and jagged rising figures is oddly like the march that forms the first movement proper of that composer's 6th String Quartet composed in 1939. More generally, its implication that part of a musical texture can be in one key and the rest effectively in another looks forward to the first half of the twentieth century and its essays in polytonality.

And yet this same quartet's likewise-demonic scherzo has a trio rightly canonised by Schnebel[10] as 'other-worldly, seeming to make its way the far side of time, the more so as the ethereal melody (sound having this tendency to dissolve into its airy substance) is as if evaporated into the infinite'.

The Presto finale carries an often dark, tortured work to a suitably sombre conclusion, like a bitter parody of a Rossini tarantella. Its mood reappears in the finale of the C minor piano sonata.

At times the quartet's finale carries Schubert's 'fingerprint' procedures to an extreme. It shows from the outset the opening movement's uncertainty as to which mode, major or minor, it is to be in, and it has his most extended and bewildering excursion round the cycle of thirds. At various points in the movement he treats in sequence a rising scale figure first heard in bars 51–9, where it sets out from B♭ minor and returns to the tonic G.

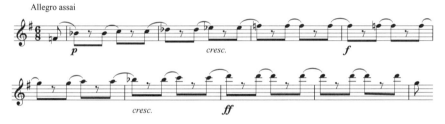

Ex. 43 String Quartet in G, D. 887, 4th movement

Bars 381–91 go through the same simple sequence, but the passage is soon repeated a minor second lower, and this time the crucial four-bar scale is heard not twice but four times (416–31). Since the transposition is here not through a major but through a minor third, this would bring Schubert out in the E minor where he started, only he turns to advantage the fact that the last of his four statements here has been in G minor: that is his cue to bring back a principal subject in the movement's tonic, G major.

At this point the movement has still a long way to run. When more than two hundred bars later (653–81) the main tarantella-like melody has been set out yet again, there is the last and longest of the sequential developments of the scale figure. And here Schubert seems to go mad. He spirals and spirals through his descending cycle of minor thirds, overshooting the point he started from while

---

[9] Bartòk was a great Schubertian: the pianist Andor Foldes used to tell how at their first meeting the great man played not his own music but Schubert's piano-duet Fantasy.

[10] 'Auf der Suche nach der befreiten Zeit'.

shortening his stride from four to three bars, managing to settle into his home key only after six attempts in different harmonic areas, followed by nine whole bars on a dominant pedal trying to decide whether the scheduled G is to be major or minor. If this is not a picture of a mind near to collapse, who wishes to see or hear one? That is all the more so, in that the rising scale passage has ever since its first appearance moved against a bass that fell away. So 'things fall apart; the centre cannot hold',[11] with some of the same feeling produced by the 'Brucknerian' I–IIb 7b progression in the B minor *Rosamunde* Entr'acte (start of Ex. 41a above).

Interpreting such music, it is hard to disentangle inborn apprehensions from acquired 'dread and desolation'. The same goes for all Schubert's dark moments from 1823 onwards. The B minor slow movement of the D major symphony (D. 936a) sketched during his final months suggests in its gauntness a man worn down and gazing into an abyss. The Heine texts Schubert chose for the most impressive songs in the late collection posthumously published as *Schwanenge-sang* (Swan Song) mostly treat themes of lost love and danger, which bring out in him an unparalleled vein of dark beauty. The slow movement of the late A major piano sonata (D. 959) contains another frantic outburst of panic like the one in the Wanderer Fantasy. A readiness to let you hear him giving in before the relentless pressures of reality, which Beethoven at all times kept at bay, is part of Schubert's immense humanity, and one in which he led the way.[12] Other jet-black moments such as the Trio of the String Quintet's scherzo would also belong in the present chapter, but the point has been made.

There are, on the other hand, supreme moments of light in the music from 1828 – mostly a gentle, subdued light rather than a harsh brilliance. There is the turn to the major after the knotty fugato of the F minor piano-duet Fantasy (D. 940, May), which anticipates many an 'O Altitudo' in Brahms; to use Gülke's words about *Im Abendrot* and *Wanderers Nachtlied*, the music seems to be prayed rather than performed. And in the finale of the String Quintet a codetta between the second subject and the return of the first spins a long serene melody for the two cellos against a floating background of moving chords; this glimpse of transfiguration could be Schubert's exhaustive re-casting, in several stages culminating in a 28-bar-long crescendo, of a moment from his beloved Haydn, bars 94–105 in the finale of the String Quartet in G major, Op. 76 no.1.

For the first few months of 1828 the world was very much with Schubert: his mind turned again to religious music only in the latter part of the year, but then he produced a last clutch of liturgical works, which bear examination to find what finally became of his 'right and true devotion'.

---

[11] W.B. Yeats, *The Second Coming*.

[12] This tendency of Schubert's is teased out with wondrous patience in Gülke's *Franz Schubert und seine Zeit*, especially chapter 12.

6

Pride of Performance (the late religious music)

> Verstehst du nicht deine Kunst,
> ist alle Müh umsunst.
>
> Understand your art
> Or it all falls apart.
>
> Abraham a Sancta Clara
>
> What I produce is due to my understanding of music and to
> my sorrows; that which sorrow alone has produced seems to
> give least pleasure to the world.
>
> Schubert's lost 1824 notebook

Das stille Lied; Hymnus an den Heiligen Geist; Mass in E♭; Der Doppelgänger;
Glaube, Hoffnung und Liebe (settings for voice and piano, chorus); New
Benedictus for C major Mass; Tantum Ergo (D. 962); Intende Voci

---

In Schubert's music from March 1827 to October 1828 – 'the richest and most
productive period in our music history'[1] – religious works reappear after five
years' virtual absence. A 'German Mass' (Deutsche Messe, D. 872) from mid-
1827 has no direct connection with the liturgy but sets for use at school services[2]
a variety of improving German texts that are hardly even paraphrases. Spiritual
thoughts were, all the same, in his mind; so much is apparent from an
insidiously beautiful male-voice part-song, Das stille Lied (D. 916), composed
in May 1827. For a long time only a sketch for it was known; a complete score
came to light in time for publication as part of the 1978 Schubert celebrations.
The quietest text is by 'Gottwalt', pseudonym of Johann Georg Seegemund,
born in Stettin in 1794. He interrupted his theology studies to fight, like Körner,
in the 1812–13 war of liberation, in which he too was seriously wounded, but
survived to become a Pastor, working in Silesia, Saxony and Poland. He
published a small number of poems in periodicals between 1814 and 1819,
and sermons and other religious writings later in life.

---

[1] Benjamin Britten, 'On receiving the First Aspen Award', on 31 July 1964, when the Great C
Major Symphony was still thought to date from 1828.

[2] The Deutsche Messe is discussed in detail by Erich Benedikt (Brille, June 2001).

Das stille Lied seems to come from a closed, intact world, conveyed in a triple invocation like the sequence at the Creation: silence, breathing, blossoming. Schubert responds to the poem's will-less deep perception and participation by rising far above male-voice heartiness, despite a texture of the simplest (unbroken homophony arguing strongly for single voices). The musical strophe (heard thrice) is grouped as follows:

4, 4, 3 + 1 (a 'loud echo'), 5 + 2 (echo),
2, 4 + 1 (echo), 2 + 2 ('loud echo')

and is 'sealed off', its end echoing its opening. The group of four semiquavers that helps do so (figure a in Ex. 44) produces a kinship with the *Notturno* for piano trio (D. 897, supposedly from 1828, Ex. 44c) and the slow movement of the C minor piano sonata (D. 958, September of that year, Ex. 44d). The two-bar conjunct continuation (Ex. 44b) harks back ten years to the *Andante* second movement of the final piano sonata of the 1817 group, in B major (D. 575, Ex. 44e), and forward to the late B♭ sonata from the final weeks of Schubert's life a year and a half later: there it is faintly suggested by the end of the opening movement's first musical 'sentence' (Ex. 44f) and more clearly in the episode of the slow movement (Ex. 44g).

Schubert has further musical symbols for the timelessness and directionlessness of the mystical state:[3] the continuation just mentioned (Ex. 44b) occurs first as what German terminology calls a 'consequent' (the answer to a question), only to recur straight away (b') as an 'antecedent' (question, bars 9–12) in its own right. At this point the semiquaver group is for the first time on the 'wrong' beat of the bar (11–12, a'). Here is John Donne's 'no noise nor silence, but one equal music . . . no ends nor beginnings, but one equal eternity'.[4]

Das stille Lied, for all its innocence ('a condition of complete simplicity Costing not less than everything'[5]) suggests Schubert's mind yet again tuned up to confront deep spiritual issues. He looks back to the mood of the 1824 *Salve Regina* (the 1826 *Grab und Mond*, D. 893, is a link, also in its use of echo), but this time in music beyond the need for any unction, and 'posthumously'[6]

---

[3] 'The state of mind influenced by the metrical, calculating, sceptical intellect has a counterpart, no less historically demonstrable even if it has moulded our destiny less powerfully: it has been called many things which all boil down to much the same thing – the state of love, of goodness, unworldliness, contemplation, vision, closeness to God, ecstasy, abdication of the will, inscape, and much else appertaining to a basic experience which in the religion, mysticism and ethics of every society in history reappears with a unanimity matching its remarkable omission to develop.' (Robert Musil, 'Ansätze zu einer neuen Ästhetik, Bemerkungen über eine Dramaturgie des Films', 1925, in *Aphorismen, Essays und Reden.*)

[4] John Donne, Sermon in St Paul's Cathedral, London, quoted by Vikram Seth as superscription to his great novel *An Equal Music*.

[5] T.S. Eliot, *East Coker*, Section V.

[6] 'I have an habitual feeling of my real life having past, and that I am leading a posthumous existence' (John Keats, last letter, written from Naples to Charles Brown, 30 November 1820, two months before his death).

Ex. 44 *Das stille Lied* and related figures in Notturno (D. 897), Piano Sonatas in C minor (D. 958), B♭ (D. 960)

simple. The fine flexibility of this E♭ major piece already manifests the concern with variable phrase-length and echo that Schubert would a year later take to great heights in the *Agnus Dei* of the E♭ Mass.

In May 1828 he set a poem by one Alois Schmidl, *Hymnus an den Heiligen Geist*, for male-voice quartet and choir (D. 948; it also exists in a version with wind band). Sketches for it are part of the same convolute of papers that contains the sketches for the E♭ Mass, and for *Miriams Siegesgesang* (D. 942), which was completed by March. It does appear that around the turn of the year 1827–8 Schubert's mind was a veritable treasure-house of ideas waiting their turn.

The wind band's colours and weight lend a Sarastro-like, simple majesty to much of the alternative version of *Hymnus*, as they will to numerous passages in the Mass that follows. The piece's place in a long line of Schubert melodies beginning similarly has been mentioned apropos the A♭ Mass; the cadence of its opening and closing sections plainly anticipates the spine-chilling 'ecclesiastical cadences' in the slow Trio of the String Quintet's Scherzo (September 1828), right down to the prominent exposed fourth at the end. Listening to the piece's truly hymn-like opening, one may be struck by the way it seems to anticipate the *Winterreise* song *Das Wirtshaus*. There are also similarities between that song and the *Deutsche Messe*,[7] but in *Hymnus* a further, fainter echo of the Ab Mass, as if the warm, comforting flesh had faded from the earlier *Kyrie*'s opening to lay bare the skeleton, which proves curiously reassuring, as in *Der Jüngling und der Tod*, rather than terrifying as in *Der Tod und das Mädchen*. A few weeks later the *Kyrie* of the Eb Mass was to strike a note midway between those extremes.

The end of *Hymnus*' principal section, with a solo voice rising above the choir after the invocation 'in unser Herz leg' Himmelsruh' (lay our hearts to heavenly rest) could have interested Mahler[8] when in 1891 it appeared in the first complete Schubert edition, and have been at the back of his mind as he composed a memorable moment in the finale of his 2nd Symphony. The starkly contrapuntal writing of the middle section matches much in the 1821 *Gesang der Geister*; the sequence of counterpoint followed by a warming into 'walking' motion at 'Es leite uns zu dem was recht und gut' (may it lead us to the True and the Good) is like a first adumbration of the events in the Eb Mass's 'Domine Deus', but there the contrast will be much starker. The middle section's ending continues the 'walking' bass movement, and culminates in an inverted domin-ant-seventh reminiscent of the scherzo of the G major string quartet. It thus takes on some of that movement's urgency; but the quartet went through doors the choral piece merely half-opens, only to shut them again. The 'recapitulation' of the initial music is well varied, with a surprising move to the submediant followed by a series of prominent entries for the first oboe, which again have a quality strangely prophetic of Mahler.

The Mass in Eb

By the spring of 1828 it was six years since the completion of the Ab Mass, and three since its revision. Now Schubert began to sketch another, probably to a commission from one of the Musikvereine (Musical Societies) that played an ever more important part in Viennese life from 1800 onwards. There was one in the Alsergrund, next door to his native heath,[9] and the commission would have been for the Church of the Holy Trinity (Dreifaltigkeitskirche), where the society planned to hold its inaugural event in October. The Mass progressed from sketches to the beginnings of a complete score in June. Nobody seems to

---

[7] McKay, 'Einige Querverbindungen zwischen der *Winterreise* und der deutschen Messe', *Brille*, June 1999.

[8] For his leaving examination at the Vienna Conservatoire Mahler included in his recital programme a Schubert piano sonata, probably D. 850 in D major, which finds an echo in the finale of his 4th Symphony.

[9] The name now applies to Vienna's entire 9th district, Himmelpfortgrund included.

know when he completed it, but if it really was meant for an October premiere at Holy Trinity it was not ready. In July he accepted a commission from the cantor of the new Jewish synagogue, Salomon Sulzer, for whose outstanding choir he set the 92nd Psalm in Hebrew; Rellstab and Heine songs took up some of his time in August, while in September he worked on the String Quintet and the final three great piano sonatas.

The A♭ Mass showed affinities with its contemporary *Lazarus*: the one in E♭ likewise shares ideas with other Schubert works. At its opening the *Kyrie* (E♭, 3/4, Andante con moto, quasi allegretto) immediately echoes, at a distance of a whole decade, the Adagio in E for piano (D. 612, 1818, Ex. 45a) and the piano's introduction to *Das Marienbild* (D. 623, 1818, Ex. 45b). It is curiously in keeping that as he set off on his final religious journey Schubert turned the customary appeal for mercy to the (male) Lord into an echo of a tribute to the female principle.

Ex. 45a Adagio, D. 612

Ex. 45b *Das Marienbild*

Ex. 45c *Kyrie* of Mass in E♭

These references bring Schubert's career full circle, since *Das Marienbild*'s atmosphere was already reminiscent of that modest but totally characteristic *Kyrie* in the 1814 F major Mass.

A striking feature almost from the start is the strings' accompanimental figures, beginning after the first choral 'Kyrie eleison'. They become almost subordinate melodies. That is nothing new, for Schubert had long been aware of the problem of what to do with the orchestral strings in major vocal works. They have often to provide an accompaniment, but even the briefest look at the piano parts of his songs should reassure us that here, too, he will show a great master's resource. We have seen him set out from the Viennese convention that the strings in concerted masses did their boring duty by playing endless repeated figures, and that he endangered the success of the Great C Major Symphony by using such string figuration outside liturgical music. But he had long been writing a type of more melodious accompaniment, still subordinate and yet interesting in its own right. The running piano part of the sensual *Versunken* is a prime example in his songs, while an operatic piece such as the Melodrama, No. 15, in *Fierrabras* shows him using the violins similarly, but in the context of a violently dramatic scene. The violin parts at the outset of this *Kyrie* are part of that process, which one finds continued in Mendelssohn (slow movement of 'Scotch' Sympony) and Bruckner.

The rhythm of the bass accompaniment at the opening is a little like that in the second cello at the start of the slow movement of the String Quintet begun a month later, and there could be an influence from the *Christe* of Beethoven's *Missa Solemnis*, despite the different mood. In the course of the work it will emerge that Mozart, too, was in Schubert's mind as he composed his Mass. A highly Mozartean *Tantum Ergo* is discussed later: in this *Kyrie* the up-and-down minor third near the end of the orchestral introduction recalls the one at 'Te decet hymnus' at the start of the *Requiem*, while in the *Benedictus* Schubert appears to sum up a lifetime's devotion to Mozart.

In the A♭ Mass the conjunct melody at 'Kyrie eleison' was followed by a wider-ranging, aspiring one for 'Christe eleison'. In the E♭ the contrast lies in the field of harmony; at 'Christe eleison' a series of striking changes of key area harmonises a simple melodic figure in a way already met in the second subject of the fine, intense piano-duet Allegro (D. 947, often known by the spurious title – *Lebensstürme*, Life's Storms – attached to it on publication) from a month earlier. (See Ex 46a and b.)

Ex. 46a Allegro for piano duet (D. 947)

There is continuing intensity in the strings' repeated triplet-chords, and here, as in the piano duet and at 'Kyrie eleison', insistent bass figures urge the music onwards; the accent on each third beat is tied over to the ensuing first beat to produce a syncopation.

This is taken up in the wind at the lead-back to 'Kyrie eleison', a point that yet again prompts a moment of magic – quiet falling off-beat horn-calls heard against four wind chords, over a dominant-pedal. A comparable and unforgettable transition in the slow movement of the Great C Major Symphony springs to mind. In the recapitulation the 'Christe' music does not reappear, but the horn-calls do, before the voices launch into an immense sustained phrase (fourteen bars over another dominant pedal), sounding again when they have finished, and yet again, with the horn now purged of its dissonance, as the

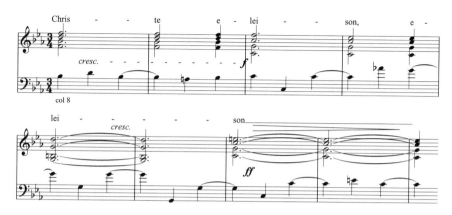

Ex. 46b *Kyrie* of Mass in E♭

movement reaches its quiet conclusion (plagal cadence). It has been entirely choral, a unique case in Schubert's Mass-*Kyries*.

The *Gloria* (B♭, 4/4, Allegro moderato e maestoso) opens strikingly, with a chant-like and slightly modal[10] rising choral phrase broken into by a flashing upward arpeggio on the violins,

Ex. 47 *Gloria* of Mass in E♭

from whose top note the choir continues with the second half of the opening paragraph. That somewhat alarming[11] arpeggio is an integral part of the 'idea', like the sustained top note at the outset of *Lazarus*, recurring a number of times. There is a fascinating interpolation as the opening reappears; 'Adoramus te, Benedicimus te' is intoned twice, but with a typical harmonic subtlety; the first time, Schubert moves 'from F to F' via D♭ major, the second time, with a virtually identical upper line, via D minor. He displayed this kind of punning harmonic virtuosity time and again, notably in the four strophes of the Leitner song *Die Sterne* (D. 939) from earlier the same year. The opening section ends with a codetta in which the rising arpeggio pushes itself to the fore, tacking on a further leap through a third (e♭ – g♭, later expanded to the sixth g♭ – e♭), in a

[10] A♭ in the bass, G major chord in bar 3.
[11] See 'Grace under Pressure' for a comparable figure in the finale of the Octet.

Beethovenian, almost aggressive way.[12] The rising third carries a faint reminiscence of the amazing ones in the middle section of the G major string quartet's slow movement. The wind instruments add what could be a final mute 'adoramus te' and secure the move to the subdominant (E♭) for the next section.

This is continuous, from 'Gratias agimus tibi propter magnam Gloriam Tuam' to 'Domine Jesu Christe, gratias agimus tibi'. As in the A♭ Mass, the first occurrences of 'Domine Deus', which continue 'Rex Coelestis' and 'Pater Omnipotens', are absorbed into music whose character has been established by the text 'Gratias agimus tibi'. The section is unified by a theme largely confined to the orchestra and very like the one in the Trio of the Great C Major Symphony's scherzo. Time-signature and tempo differ but there are crucial similarities in the respective melodies' outline and immediate reharmonisation on the submediant. The powerfully expressive dominant seventh Schubert added to the sixteenth bar of his reprise is replaced in the Mass by a tiny linking three-chord figure for oboes and horn, which joins the two halves of the 'Gratias' melody each time it appears.

The pattern is repeated on the dominant, making four statements of the melody, then recapitulated in its original form (including the repeat on the submediant), but with an added running violin line of the kind familiar from the 'Pleni sunt coeli' of the A♭ Mass, gloriously filling out the texture. The three-subsection form adds to the feeling of being in the middle of a piece such as a symphonic third movement, while the multiple and varied statement of the melody is a procedure he often applied to second subjects in his later sonata-form movements. Each half of the melody is scored differently, first on clarinets and bassoons with the strings pizzicato, as in bars 9–15 at the opening of the symphony, while later the wind fall silent and the cellos have the all-important line. It says something about Schubert's life that in the A♭ Mass his 'Thank You' to the Creator is for music, in the E♭ for euphoria amid Nature's splendour.

Gradually an element of rondo-form emerges; the rising arpeggio quite disperses the serene atmosphere, and 'Gloria in excelsis Deo', in its expanded version with codetta, is recapitulated. Next comes a major change of mood, far more marked than at the same point in the A♭ Mass, for the fourfold 'Domine Deus, Agnus Dei, Domine Deus, Filius Patris', with a change of tempo to 3/4 Andante con moto and a new key, G minor. Of the four comparable subsections (G minor, C minor, D minor, G minor), the final one's sequential repetitions and breathless intensity give it some of the tormented quality of the great snarl-up in the middle of the Great C Major Symphony's second movement: the soul's 'tremor' is made plain. The section is dominated by a four-note motto in even dotted minims, like a passacaglia theme, given out on the trombones and bassoons: against this the choir enters off the beat, much as in *Der Doppelgänger*.

---

[12] *Hammerklavier* Sonata, Op. 106, 1st movement: this becomes more apparent when the same sort of thing returns in the 'Osanna'.

Ex. 48a *Gloria* of Mass in E♭

Ex. 48b *Der Doppelgänger*

Ex. 48c *Agnus Dei* of Mass in E♭

The four-note figure in the six-bar orchestral introduction before the above example turns down through e♭ to d; in the second (Ex. 48a) and third statements it moves to the flattened supertonic, and in the climactic final one the four bars, as so established, are treated in semitonal rising sequence, with the gradually ascending 'torment' harmonies familiar since *Gruppe aus dem Tartarus* again dominating. It does not yet take the form found in *Der Doppelgänger*, with leading-note leaping to upper minor third (Ex. 48b above); that is at the back of Schubert's mind, biding its time until the *Agnus Dei* (Ex. 48c).

The other basic component of the 'Domine Deus' paragraph is the quiet answering 'Miserere, miserere nobis' – tremor followed by self-abasement, with one of the obscurest of all Schubert's self-allusions, to a song in itself obscure, the Schiller setting *Thekla* (D. 595, 1817). This piece of 'internal evidence' could tell us something about Schubert's state of mind in the summer of 1828. He had liked Schiller's poem enough to set it twice, the first setting, D. 73, dating from 1813, but nothing else suggests that it had a special significance for him. It figures in Deutsch's documentary biography only through the announcement (12 Dec. 1827) of its publication as part of his Op. 88, in quite distinguished and mostly more-recent company: *Abendlied für die Entfernte* and *Um Mitternacht* from 1825, and *An die Musik* from March 1817, eight months before *Thekla*. (His friends were devoted to *An die Musik* but it had remained unpublished.) The maturer setting of *Thekla* consists of three identical strophes that ring the changes on minor and major, and begins with a phrase in the minor whose outline is also very much that of the opening theme of the late B♭ major piano sonata (D. 960, September 1828). Rhythm and tempo are identical in song and 'Miserere nobis', the harmonies virtually so, and the actual melodic line of the song's opening appears in the choral bass-line, in the major.

Ex. 49a *Gloria* of Mass in E♭

Ex. 49b *Thekla*

Ex. 49c

Ex. 49d

Ex. 49e Piano Sonata in B♭ (D. 960)

Given Schubert's way of using a melody in the bass as a sign of submissiveness and abdication of the will, this apparently inconsequential detail needs interpretation: why did he choose *Thekla*?

In search of an answer, one could start from the fact that after ten years

Schubert rescued from his bottom drawer this of all unpublished songs, to eke out a set for a publisher. Either his mind had for some reason run back to it, or else he happened upon it and it set him thinking. It is tempting to fall back on the time-worn 'cherchez la femme', but *Thekla* has no known connection with Therese Grob or any other woman in Schubert's life (she was Wallenstein's daughter in Schiller's trilogy of plays about that great general); it came too late to go into 'the Grob Song Album'. At most, the two names begin with the same three letters.

So much for *Thekla*'s resuscitation; what of her re-appearance in a Mass almost a year later? That 'uniquely rich and productive period' including Schubert's creative spell in the second half of 1828 can scarcely have happened without a reassessment of his life – the things he was born with, his successes, his failures, such as the strange spectacle of his younger self obsessed with a voice, and of Frau Bergmann-née-Grob, current and 1815 models. A residual sense of failure over Therese would have been hard to disentangle from the inborn 'creature-feeling' embodied in a text like 'Lord God, have mercy on us'. And if Schubert, against all the odds, found his mind dwelling yet once more on all that in the middle part of 1828, he needed to do something creative about it. (Which suggests that his rediscovery of *Thekla* in the autumn of 1827 was a calmer matter, otherwise he would have done something about it straight away).

He could, for example, build a song-quotation into his Mass at the point where the 'creature-feeling' was intense. There, however, he had to take care. Two things could deter him from quoting any song associated with Therese. Consideration of her feelings forbade him to refer, however distantly, to their 'relationship', however imaginary, in music for a church in the very area where she and her husband lived; and the mores of the time were unbelievably hard on any suggestion of 'improper' approaches, real or imagined, to a married woman.[13] *Thekla* was the one song that could be a reminder of her for Schubert, but for no-one else. The hint of it in the ensuing piano sonata suggests that he became fond of the song, once rediscovered.

But quoting a song was evidently not enough: he needed to write one that would exorcise the ghost. And there the twelfth poem in the *Heimkehr* section of Heine's *Buch der Lieder* would have struck him as supremely relevant. He had known it since at the latest January 1828, perhaps for longer, but only now did he set it to music. The poem is a reminder of the way in which the mind can unexpectedly revert to emotional issues long after they seemed definitively dealt with. Usually nothing world-shaking happens – for a while an old wound aches again, the more-sensitive soul may write a poem, the super-sensitive literary

[13] Theodor Fontane's Berlin novel *Cécile*, written in 1884 with a post-1870 setting, ends with a fatal duel after a man fully acceptable as visitor argues in an over-emphatic manner with a married woman friend, while in George Meredith's *Diana of the Crossways* (1885, set in the early 1830s) a duel almost results from a rash comment on a woman. In recent literature Hermann Kant's classic short story *Der dritte Nagel* (1981), from that 'little Austria in Eastern Germany', contains a splendidly homicidal master-baker.

man will turn his strange mood into a cry of metaphysical anguish, the supreme song-writer will write a supreme song. Hence *Der Doppelgänger*.

The agitated music of 'Domine Deus' found a reflection as Schubert composed the song. There is no way of knowing which was set down on paper first, but the sketches for the Mass go back far enough in the year to show that the raw material for the song existed long before Schubert used it in setting Heine's poem. Various major works were beginning at least to take shape in his mind before he wrote down their definitive versions. That certainly goes for the final three piano sonatas. The sketches also show that the Mass's music came into his mind in an order other than that of the liturgy – for example he sketched the *Kyrie* after most of the other movements, and went from *Sanctus* to *Agnus Dei*, only later sketching the *Benedictus*. And the fugal 'Cum sancto Spiritu' that ends the *Gloria* (following closely on the 'Domine Deus') existed in a well-worked-out form as early as the spring of 1828.[14]

The Rellstab and Heine songs were not begun until August, were composed in who knows what order, and have no definitive performing sequence. (They were published only posthumously, under another of those spurious but irresistibly catchy titles, this time *Schwanengesang*, Swan Song). The difference between the related figures in 'Domine Deus' and *Agnus Dei* might tempt the naive hermeneutically minded analyst to wonder whether the song came between the two, but the sketches for *Gloria* and *Agnus Dei* show both forms clearly present much earlier in the year. This very small instance points to a rule that can be recommended to Schubert researchers, namely that musical similarity is not reliable evidence of closeness in time: his mind buzzed constantly with music, and the only rule of thumb is that whichever version of an idea works best is probably the later.

As remarked, 'Domine Deus, Agnus Dei' gets up a considerable head of steam. Each of the first three subsections follows the same pattern: 11 bars + 'Miserere Nobis' 4 bars. As the section reaches its climax with a fourth statement, upward semitonal sequences bring 4 + 4 + 4 + 5, then 'Miserere Nobis' still at 4, but now in Schubert's ever-striking choral unison, forerunner of an equally striking unison passage in the *Crucifixus*. Like other crucial passages in Schubert, this one faces both ways: despite a different outline it shares the anguished feeling of *Der Doppelgänger*'s 'So manche Nacht in alter Zeit' (so many a night in olden days), but it also sets the coping stone on an enormous internal arch by transforming, not the *Thekla* line (unless some ingenious analyst can show that it does), but the blissful 'Pleni sunt coeli' melody from the A♭ Mass. A further transformation will appear in the ensuing section, at 'Passus et sepultus est'.

---

[14] This was established by the Schubert scholar Ernst Hilmar while librarian of the Vienna City Library. The sketches can be inspected there and are indexed in *Catalogus Musicus*, VIII, Ernst Hilmar, *Verzeichnis der Schubert-Handschriften in der Musiksammlung der Wiener Stadt- und Landesbibliothek*, 1978.

Ex. 50 *Sanctus* of Mass in A♭, *Gloria* of Mass in E♭, *Der Doppelgänger*, *Credo* of Mass in E♭

A one-chord transition restores the tonic key for another 'ritornello' of the 'Gloria' music, the opening paragraph's final version being used this time for 'quoniam Tu solus sanctus/ altissimus/Dominus' (for Thou alone art Holy . . . most High . . . the Lord). In the final 204-bar fugal 'Cum sancto Spiritu' (B♭, Alla breve, Moderato) there is a first attempt at a stretto (at two bars' distance) very early on (bars 310–15). This recourse to a device normally reserved for a point when other contrapuntal artifices have been exhausted could be a sign of either impatience or deficient self-confidence: Schubert was, after all, considering going to the Assistant Court Organist, Simon Sechter, to find out what counterpoint, as understood by Handel, was really and truly about. A curiosity left to analysts to plumb is that in bars 377–80 the bass of a sequential passage yields the famous b [= b♭] – a – c – h [= b] pattern, transposed to begin on d♭. (Anyone anxious to hear all of this must watch what recording he buys; for example, two Viennese conductors, Ferdinand Grossmann with the Wiener Sängerknaben and Erich Leinsdorf in Berlin, made sizeable cuts in this fugue, eliding the three-bar stretto. Taken at a realistic *alla breve*, as by Sawallisch and his Bavarians, it is by no means too long.)

Near the end comes the first clear Mozart-reference of several in this Mass: the chromatic harmonies over a rising bass before the fermata (bars 412–22) hint at a similarly placed passage in the *Gloria* of Mozart's C Minor Mass. The climax is marked by a rising 'Amen' derived from the subject, which brings none of the magical light the same figure and the soloists' unexpected entry added to the conclusion of the *Credo* in the A♭ Mass. In this *Gloria* the five soloists must in a modern performance sit there with nothing to do: if Schubert envisaged their being drawn from the choir, he went on to demand a good deal of the two tenors in his 'Et incarnatus'. The final orchestral B♭ chord dies away, the tonic becoming a dominant that leads on to the next movement.

The *Credo* (E♭, Alla Breve, Moderato) sets out as another tightly knit movement, the music from 'Et resurrexit' onwards reverting to the material of the opening, after a clear switch of mood, pace and degree of elaboration for the grave events at the heart of the Creed. This sets out as one of Schubert's 'walking' pieces: the opening drum-roll is part of the basic idea, so too the wind comment after the first phrase: they will recur. The opening subsection, about the creation, is quiet and homophonic; the mood changes markedly (strings *forte* for the first time, choral texture more imitative) for 'Dominum Jesum Christum'. There is striking use of string pizzicato comments, echoes and answers, while the wind's interjections become briefer after the opening subsection.

For the central 'Et incarnatus . . . Crucifixus' Schubert switches into Rossini-mode: at last the soloists make their entry, and with a vengeance. One is reminded of a melody in the introduction to the *Zauberharfe* (= *Rosamunde*) overture.

Ex. 51a Overture to *Die Zauberharfe*

Ex. 51b *Credo* of Mass in E♭

He spreads himself, the great difference as against the A♭ Mass being that the intense solemnity of that work's 'Et incarnatus' seemed inward and personal. Here Schubert adopts a consciously 'cantabile' style, as if addressing the public. After four bars of cello introduction, three round-like statements of 'Et incarnatus' recall the canonic *Benedictus* sections of the F and G major Masses. Schönstein recorded Schubert's admiration for the supreme tenor Rubini, and here his soloists are not the customary quartet but two tenors, a soprano entering third as an apparent afterthought; a far cry, this, from the days when Therese was automatic first choice, even hogging a second entry in the G major Mass's *Benedictus*.

For 'Crucifixus etiam pro nobis' the choir takes up the running in hushed homophony, with throbbing string-and-wind accompaniment. For once Schubert's tormented minor-second transitions fall rather than rise. His handling of this, here and later, is on a par with the virtuosity of 'Adoramus te, Benedicimus te', or the modulating passage in the G major Quartet slow movement's middle section, though here there is no persistent foreign body. It is also a clear counterpart, but with the direction reversed, of the hysteria at the end of the 'Domine Deus'. The falling 'torment' chromaticisms feel less poignant than the upward ones encountered ever since *Gruppe aus dem Tartarus* eleven years earlier. More choral octaves at 'et sepultus est' (was buried) are doubled in a most Schubertian way, at the third, by the clarinet, and the curve of their line once more brings us close to the anguished ending of *Der Doppelgänger* (see Ex. 50). From an opening in A♭ the section has modulated to F minor. At the climaxes of 'Crucifixus etiam pro nobis' the offbeat accompaniment figures are a reminder of the Unfinished Symphony (1st movement development, bars 148– 72) in their principal rhythm and way of slowly descending.

But now Schubert does something extraordinary: he doubles back on himself after the world-shaking events of the Crucifixion and repeats the beguiling music of 'Et incarnatus'. This is opera run to seed, something the briefest rational reflection on the subject-matter should reprove as anomalous, literally out of order – for as that covert Schubertian Samuel Beckett says in *Murphy*, 'there is no return match between a man and his stars' (not even The Saviour's). It can be rationalised[15] by saying that with this section 'we enter the edifice's central area, where the chronological rule of law hitherto prevailing no longer applies; not once but twice the images of birth, crucifixion and entombment pass before our eyes'. Which is poetic without throwing light on Schubert's motivation: a clue lies (where else?!) in the music, for the 'repeat' of 'Et incarnatus' is in fact an echo. What is heard turns out to be the last of the three round-like entries, the one led off by the soprano: Therese's last-but-one appearance? Here there could be a retrospective glance at life, a confirmation, 'Yes, that was worth looking back at'. A reason now emerges for making the soprano the last of the three original entries; with the use of that voice to lead off the return of 'Et incarnatus' it is as if Schubert turned and headed back towards the start, rather than beginning again. And for the soprano to be the first here, she had originally to come last.

The 'repeat' of 'Crucifixus' is, on the other hand, a genuine intensification. The 'torment' semitone-harmonic-shifts now do again what they always did, moving steadily upwards and for longer; what's to come is likely to be still worse than what has already been.

Schubert's various settings of the words 'et resurrexit' seldom suggest the explosive joy found in that section of, say, Bach's B Minor Mass. Usually he reverts to the movement's opening 'Credo in unum Deum'. In the first two Masses (F and G) the restatement is loud where the opening was soft, as if to match the unparalleled explosion of energy implicit in a Resurrection. In the A♭ it forms a quiet opening to a powerful build-up, elaborating the movement's opening but laying stress on the glory of the risen Christ rather than the unique miracle of His resurrection. The E♭ Mass shows Schubert harking back a decade and a half to those first two Masses, but he has learned a thing or two; rather than simply changing the dynamics and key of the quiet homophonic opening,

15 Jaskulsky.

he reverts to the *forte* imitative texture of 'Credo in Unum Dominum Jesum Christum' (I believe in one Lord Jesus Christ, bars 39ff.)

In no mass after the early F major does 'et iterum venturus est' carry the same charge of existential terror. The E♭ sets it to a new figure, then 'cuius regni non erit finis' (and His kingdom shall have no end) to impressive quiet flat-side harmonies coloured by the solemnity of trombones and an oboe. With this and the ensuing wind interlude Bruckner yet again seems close at hand, and even Franz Schmidt. As if to satisfy, late in the day, any automatic expectation of a literal repeat of the opening for 'Et resurrexit', it reappears for 'Credo in Spiritum sanctum' (I believe in the Holy Ghost), with the wind interludes enhanced by evocative floating figures on oboe, clarinet and later bassoon – a late version of those lifelong sinuous lines at the start of *Geheimnis*, the 5th Symphony and *Abendbilder*, or in the G major Mass. For once the customary textual elision does not yield the strange 'in remissionem peccatorum mortuorum' (in remission of dead sinners – or for that matter dead sins).

The vast fugue for *Et vitam venturi* (224 bars out of 536, so numerically 40 percent of the entire movement: no wonder this, too, has been heavily cut by conductors!) continues in the same tempo, with no division between the sections. Again Schubert reaches almost immediately for stretto.

The *Sanctus* (E♭, 4/4, Adagio; 'Osanna', 2/4, Allegro, ma non troppo; *Benedictus*, A♭, Alla Breve, Andante) has another of Schubert's numinous wandering openings; it moves through the cycle of major thirds to end where it began, but unlike the ones in the F and A♭ Masses it is launched into without orchestral preamble. The descending-third cycle occurs at various salient points in Schubert. The second significant melodic idea in the opening movement of the 1827 E♭ Piano Trio rolls all the way round the cycle from its tonic E♭ through B minor and G minor back to its E♭ home, then sets off again, this time managing to execute the 'required' modulation to the dominant (B♭). A far more stressful, similar passage in the finale of the G Major String Quartet, using not descending major thirds but minor ones, was examined in 'Hard Sayings'. In the E♭ Mass's *Sanctus* much of the effect depends on dynamics, a hushed first entry with the orchestra immediately building to *ff* for the second 'Sanctus' and down again, and so on; within six bars there are three such swellings from *piano* to *fortissimo* and back, and 'Dominus Deus Sabaoth' has the extraordinary markings *fff* with the strings then asked to make a further crescendo! Either healthy awe has since the previous Mass turned to sheer terror, or else 'the lady doth protest too much'.

'Pleni sunt coeli' is set to a falling line (Ex. 52b); this is one of two passages in the Mass that put one in mind of a 'towering cliffs' motive in the 1821 *Gesang der Geister* (Ex. 52a), the other (Ex. 52c) coming in the *Benedictus*.

A fade-out recalls the 'thirds' figure in the *Gloria*, the paragraph concluding with a reflective bar for strings and an 'Amen' formula on the first bassoon, familiar from various Schubert works, not all of them liturgical and most powerfully the Trio of the String Quintet.

Ex. 52a *Gesang der Geister über den Wassern* (D. 714)

Ex. 52b *Sanctus* of Mass in E♭

Ex. 52c *Sanctus* of Mass in E♭

After the momentous detour in the *Credo*, Schubert now makes another, less striking but still a detour, by repeating the *Sanctus* music before he proceeds to the 'Osanna'. This was not something his predecessors had done, nor is it found in his previous masses. The Missa Brevis format of the ones in G, B♭ and C ruled it out anyway, but both earlier 'solemn masses' (F, A♭) follow tradition in proceeding straight through the text. For Haydn, what prompted 'Osanna' was precisely the preceding 'glory in heaven and on earth', while his opening 'Holy, Holy, Holy' tended (with exceptions such as the Little Organ Mass) to be quiet and reflective. Schubert's repeat is in fact a compression, since the first six bars of the original are set at double speed, with only the answering 'Dominus Deus Sabaoth' as before: the regularity of [3 x 2 =] 6 + 2 = 8 thus turns into the asymmetry of [3 x 1 =] 3 + 2 = 5.

The 'Pleni' too is modified, to culminate in a tutti declaration marked *fff*, with the sopranos on top a♭. Like Schubert's multiple repetition of 'Credo' in the A♭ Mass, this over-emphasis seems an excessive attempt to convince himself.[16] In the A♭ Mass there was total rejoicing that 'heaven and earth are

---

[16] Gülke makes this point about the A♭ Mass.

full of Thy Glory'; here the celebration is distinctly muted, tending towards the flat side and its minor-mode harmonies, and the final 'gloriam' is indeed set to a resounding minor chord. Here one might feel nearer the 'miserable reality' of Schubert's 1824 letter to Kupelwieser than to a world resplendent with the Creator's glory, and this text too risks becoming what Imperial & Royal Austrian officialdom used to call a 'Haupt- und Staatsaktion' (a major matter of state).

Or perhaps just one more piece of text – for even the 'Osanna' is a fugue, which quotes the leaping octave – + – third idea from the *Gloria*. As so often in this Mass, musical elaboration seems uppermost in Schubert's mind, where in the A♭ he had rejoiced in the text and its details. To that extent the earlier Mass is the more obviously 'confessional', yet this one's musical integrity, especially at the end of the *Agnus Dei*, unmistakably proclaims its composer.

In the A♭ *Benedictus* (Alla Breve, Andante) Schubert comes nearest the outgoing warmth in so much of the previous Mass, with which it shares its key. It can make one feel 'thank goodness for something we know and love'. The very end of the first main paragraph brings an echo of his song *Harfenspieler II* (D. 479) with its 'und ich werde weiter gehn' (and I shall pass on): this is detectable in bars 10–13 and is spelled out more clearly by the version in the ensuing reprise (bars 15–21).

Ex. 53a *Gesänge des Harfners aus Wilhelm Meister* (D. 478), No. 3, *An die Türen will ich schleichen*

Ex. 53b *Sanctus* of Mass in E♭

We have seen the range of Schubert's reactions to the idea of 'the one who comes in the name of the Lord'; Goethe's old Harper comes as a blessed reminder to everyone else of their good fortune.

After a good deal of music for the soloists[17] the choir enters with a brief but vigorous imitative treatment of it; by now even this text is a serious matter. The

---

[17] With 'good order and discipline' restored, the second tenor from the 'Et incarnatus' has been seen off and the alto has asserted his, her or a Sängerknabe's rights.

choral exposition of a falling figure brings a further reminiscence of 'ragen Klippen' in *Gesang der Geister* (Ex. 52a above). Soon the soloists resume with one of the Eb Mass's magical passages, and its most powerful Mozartean echo. There is first (in the rising soprano sixth: how one soaring vocal motive can lift the heart and open doors!) an echo of the quartet before the ordeals in *Die Zauberflöte* (and when attending that opera, Schubert may have paid more attention than the average member of the audience, then or now, to the text and its 'power of sound'); and, immediately after, an echo of Mozart's last *Benedictus*, the one in the *Requiem* – a downward sequence during that section's *da capo*, at the turn-back from the subdominant towards the home key, and so that movement's moment of greatest tension and release. This passage in the Eb Mass is thus almost a collage, something almost unique in Schubert even where quotations from his own music are concerned, let alone from anyone else's, and a generous tribute, in the nick of time as it turned out, to his beloved Mozart.

After an interlude shared between all the orchestral sections the second half of the section is like the first, and yet unlike (as with the repetition of 'Et incarnatus'). The melody is now given to the violas and celli,[18] the top choral line forming a kind of descant to it; perhaps Schubert was reminding himself of invertible counterpoint before going to Sechter.

The *Agnus Dei* (C minor – Eb, 3/4, Andante con moto: 'Dona nobis pacem' Eb, Alla Breve, Andante) is a towering movement dominated by three crucial features:

(a) The basic four-note phrase in the 'Agnus Dei' section, identical (transposition apart) with the outer lines at the piano's opening of *Der Doppelgänger* (see Ex. 48b, c above), and seeming to resume an inner argument where the bass of 'Domine Deus, Agnus Dei' left off.
(b) Interplay between phrases of four-bar and other lengths.
(c) In the closing 'Dona nobis pacem' an all-pervading four-equal-repeated-note figure, already met in the 'Dona nobis' of the Ab Mass and elsewhere, but above all in the finale of the Great C Major Symphony.

Ex. 54 *Agnus Dei* of Mass in Eb

In view of (a) and (c), the idea of four equal notes dominates the entire movement.

The opening of the *Agnus Dei* feels very like a slow fugal exposition; thrusting

---

[18] Middle-register melodies are a comparative rarity in Schubert; there is a fascinating one in the Florinda–Maragond duet in *Fierrabras* (Act 2, No. 9), and another, equally intriguing, in the piano interludes of *Ellens I. Gesang* (see 'Oaks and Osmosis').

accompaniment figures off the beat in the bass recall the 'Christe'. The first shortening from four bars to three ('peccata', 3 bars, + 4, 'mundi') comes at the first climax, immediately before 'miserere nobis'.

For that further piece of text Schubert creates a strong contrast with the preceding semifugal texture, opening on a choral soprano note doubled only by the first violins, and the choral music that follows is suitably consolatory. This 'miserere nobis' is asymmetrical (seven bars long if one regards the two-bar soprano D as introduction, nine if not). The final bar effectively contains only one beat, the other two being an upbeat to the second 'Agnus Dei . . . miserere nobis' subsection (dominant, G minor), which, double counterpoint apart, goes over the same ground. The exposed opening of 'miserere nobis' is in the bass second time round, and goes down d – c rather than staying put as the sopranos did, in order to ease the next harmonic move, to Eb. For that reason, and despite an identical phrase-structure, this subsection makes a marginally less consolatory effect than its predecessor. (It originally took up on the tonic chord, Eb, after an inconclusive ending on the dominant of C minor; here the first statement is on the latter chord, not its resolution.)

As in 'Domine Deus', Schubert knows precisely when to turn up the heat; in the third subsection the entries crowd each other (stretto, first with entries two bars apart and then a single bar apart), and there is a four-bar shortening; the bass's thrusting figures cease after four, after which it moves in solid whole-bar steps that add to the plea for mercy a feeling of stolid despair: from now on, nothing can be changed.

Although the text dictates that there is no 'miserere nobis' after the third 'Agnus Dei', the section is far from over. The music breaks off on the dominant, resuming over the same pedal G for a final hushed exposition that repeats but shortens the 'accelerating stretto' that has just been heard. It forms one immense phrase of fourteen bars, like the kind of vast Mozartean breath found here and there in that composer's late string quartets.[19] This codetta ends on a half- or imperfect cadence that leaves everything hanging in the balance – will there be 'peace' or will there not?

What follows is in fact a progression, or reversion, from C minor to the work's tonic key of Eb, for 'Dona nobis pacem'. By its nature the new section should provide relief, and seems to do so, setting out in four-bar phrases. The four equal notes, here g, occupy the first two bars each time, but a two-bar wind echo overlaps the second two by a bar, making five bars in all (see Ex. 54).

---

[19] K. 589 in Bb (second half of the Trio) and K. 590 in F (after the double-bar in the middle of the Menuet). Analysis must not run riot at this point, and it needs to be added that Schubert's 'fourteenth bar' consists simply of the thirteenth's G major chord tied over: he was not concerned with number symbolism but with making sure that his performers made the chord long enough. A fermata (pause) sign over the final bar drives the point home, but would not have been enough on its own, since the length of such a fermata is left to the performer. A comparably extended phrase is in fact found at the end of the *Kyrie*; here is yet another trace of the cyclic feeling that had been at the back of Schubert's mind ever since his very first Mass thirteen years before.

The strings' accompanying figures are part arpeggio, part winding melody with just a trace of the A♭ Mass's 'Pleni sunt coeli' mood, which in this work has so far been conspicuous by its absence. The echo at the end of the fourth four-bar set seems to behave more normally, starting clear of the choral phrase, but any relief at a touch more regularity is immediately dispelled, since what is now a repetition rather than an echo is cut short by the next choral entry after only three bars: so 3 x 5 is followed by [4 + 3 =] 7. A miniature codetta brings two-bar pairings of choir and wind-answer – in themselves even, but odd in number, with only three of them rather than the four one might have expected. Schubert is determined to tantalise with mere glimpses of any more settled feeling.

The other main element in the section now appears, a strikingly different and assertive 'Dona nobis' on the dominant (B♭), which starts in the choral bass-line. This could even be a third echo of 'ragen Klippen dem Sturz entgegen'. The asymmetrical (five-bar) phrase turns into a twelve-bar subsection in its own right, still with a lot of three-bar phrases followed by two-bar echoes. The soloists then take over quietly. Since they enter in a kind of stretto, there is now a pattern of two repeated notes followed by two more, and we are once again in the presence of the fateful four-note motive, however tactfully introduced. This solo paragraph extends to twenty-three bars, mostly over a pedal B♭, which (given any repeated bass note's tendency to turn into a dominant) hints at a return to the main key of E♭. Although the soloists succeed in carrying us there and beyond, in music which (not for the first time in Schubert) seems to capture the kind of human warmth so wonderfully embodied in certain soaring Verdi vocal lines, the hint is not taken up with any enthusiasm, and it is left to the choir to round off the first half of the section with a successful lead-back from B♭ to E♭, once again 3 + 2.

A recapitulation of the first 'Dona nobis pacem' music sees the soloists adding their voices to the two-bar interludes that were originally for the wind instruments alone, and debouches into yet another major surprise to match those sprung in the *Credo* and *Sanctus*. It was unusual for the concluding movement of an extended work to begin in anything but the tonic; the remedy lies in a liturgically unjustifiable but musically fascinating return of the initial *Agnus Dei* paragraph in the tonic (E♭) minor. Even so did Beethoven time after time work a kind of musical switchback, seeming to end, then turning round on himself.[20] This is a short section, just four entries of the four-note theme, one for each choral part, and seven more bars (three plus four) which very late in the day move the music back towards the major: and yet it is crucial. Whereas the anguished 'Domine Deus' ended with the heightened outcry of four bars in unison, this return of 'Agnus Dei' achieves transformation, and one of the

[20] Knowing the *Missa Solemnis*, and perhaps aware that Beethoven's death left him as the great torch-bearer (the oration written for Beethoven's funeral by Grillparzer asked, 'he [Beethoven] was an artist, and who stands tall alongside him?'), Schubert might have been influenced in this dramatic act of retrospection by the older composer's incursion of military music into the 'Dona nobis pacem' of his Mass.

sublime moments in the entire work, with its turn to the major, even before the return of 'Dona nobis pacem'. Schubert's structural sense is here in action on the largest scale, bringing about significant connections between movements, and progress from one to the other. The sketches in the Wiener Stadt- und Landesbibliothek show Schubert thinking hard about the architecture of this movement, to which he later added a number of brief passages that helped get the proportions exactly right. Yet again the myth of the 'unselfconscious genius' is shown up for the nonsense it is.

From here to the end, Schubert's mastery of pacing, harmony and structure surpass everything the work has so far offered. 'Dona nobis pacem' re-enters, but the apparent certainty first time round is replaced by continued doubt, with the foregoing desperate entreaty still to some extent present. The second crucial point comes (bar 224) when the voices are at last allowed to sing 'Dona nobis pacem' without an immediate echo treading on their heels. Their first try manages only three bars, but the second time they complete a four-bar phrase. From here on, such echoes as there are no longer overlap what they echo, so the phrase-structure gradually and at long last establishes four bars as a norm; all this section's ambiguous phrase-lengths create the kind of 'endless melody' already found at the end of the *Kyrie*. Bars 224–37 are in fact one enormous phrase, yet again of fourteen bars. By the end of the 'Dona nobis' a listener has become so used to the five-bar pattern that the four-bar phrases before the final antiphony have the most extraordinary effect, like finding water in the desert. The final extension over a B♭ pedal-point feels like Brahms (e.g. the *German Requiem*), who made a piano score of this mass.

So meticulous an account of phrase-lengths may seem pernickety and pedantic, but is central to consideration of the E♭ Mass and its place in Schubert's output. Few things in music register more firmly with even a listener disinclined and unable to analyse than regularity and irregularity of phrase. We were all born dancers or at least walkers, and nothing throws the kinetic sense more infallibly than an unexpected change from four to three or five; one is left with a leg too many or too few. The *Agnus Dei* of a Mass is the last vantage point from which to survey the kinetic aspect of Schubert; suffice it to say that all his life he was the man who, rather than dancing like everyone else in Vienna, remained seated at the piano to urge them on with his playing. But music, as vibration, has a mathematical basis, so periodicity is of the essence, and the *Agnus Dei* of the E♭ Mass is a high point of sophistication in Schubert's handling of it. As a song-writer he constantly had to choose between reflecting metre and running counter to it;[21] here his text was so brief and basic as not even to try and tell him what his phrase-structure should be, leaving him free to construct and improvise, and he judged his phrase-lengths as meticulously as had Beethoven in his seemingly inexhaustible symphonic endings.

Nothing marks out the mature composer so clearly as his sense of when not

---

[21] See Siegfried Lorenz on Schubert's 'musical speech-rhythms', 'At One in Solidarity'.

to offer facile symmetry, and despite a four-note pattern in common this is a far sterner, subtler, more intricately wrought section than the 'Dona nobis pacem' of the A♭ Mass. The latter is a shade over-regular, four-bar phrases being so universal in music of this era as soon to be taken for granted. The final breaking of the pattern is welcome, the music itself haunting, but as an intensification it is a shade obvious. Throughout the 'Dona nobis pacem' of the E♭ Mass, on the other hand, the five-bar pattern keeps one guessing and loses none of its 'oddness', until the sudden succession of four-bar phrases with its extraordinary and sublime effect. Simplicity emerging from complexity must be one of the rarest and most satisfying things in music.[22]

In this *Agnus Dei*, which is a link between Beethoven's architectonics and the cumulative repetition-techniques in Bruckner, Schubert exhaustively explores the asymmetry and echo touched on eighteen months earlier in *Das stille Lied*. The almost over-methodical construction in earlier sections of the Mass could seem to have more to do with dogged determination than with delight in the created world, but here it enables Schubert to work wonders. In that sense the Mass is all of a piece.

Time had taken its toll of Schubert between 1822 and 1828. The A♭ and E♭ Masses offer outstanding music at some of the same points – in the *Kyrie* the opening, lead-back and ending (the A♭ in Elysium,[23] the E♭ giving its quietus to the haunting horn-call); the opening of the *Gloria* and then 'Gratias agimus tibi', which in the E♭ Mass offers in addition a fascinating cross-reference to the Great C Major Symphony; the opening of the *Credo*, the numinous *Sanctus* opening, the *Benedictus* with its cue for intimacy and warmth, and the very end of the 'Dona nobis pacem' section of the *Agnus Dei*, with an abiding sense of release after stress.

On the other hand, the *Gloria*s lay substantially different emphasis on moments of gratitude and praise (A♭) and of grandeur and awe approaching terror (E♭), differing even mathematically in the respective proportions of their subsections, and in types of structure.

---

[22] Franz Schmidt mooted it as a possibility, and put it into practice in, for example, the variation finale of his 2nd Symphony (see Rudolph Scholz, *Studien zu Franz Schmidt, II*).

[23] Given this book's whole tenor, it would be inept not to mention that alongside Schiller's evocation of the torments of Tartarus Schubert also left musical settings of the same poet's *Elysium*, in male-voice exercises from 1813 based on five of its verses and later in a song for voice and piano (D. 584, 1817), which sets the entire six-strophe poem. Schiller clearly meant it as a counterpart to *Gruppe aus dem Tartarus*; there are manifest cross-references, the very first line of *Elysium* running 'Vorüber die stöhnende Klage' (An end to the weeping and wailing). The suffering 'Ach!' of the one poem is 'drowned out' in the other, the tragic text's 'Bricht die Sense des Saturns entzwei' (Saturn's scythe is broken in two) is echoed by 'Wahrheit reisst den Schleier entzwei' (Truth rips the veil in two). At twenty Schubert could already match the torment of *Gruppe aus dem Tartarus*, but needed far longer to rise to a comparable level of joy, as he did in, for example, the A♭ Mass's 'Pleni sunt coeli' and later, far more explosively, in some of the music considered in 'Harvest'.

	Ab bars	%		Eb bars	%
Gloria ... – glorificamus te	112	35		68	26
Gratias agimus tibi 37			(contin - 14 - uous)		
+ recap 27					
	64	20	incl. *Gloria* recap.		6
Domine Deus rex coel.	44	10		63	26
" " Agnus Dei	66	20	(contin - 86 - uous)		31
Quoniam (contin-	46 -	15 - uous)		29	11
	332			260	
Cum sancto Spiritu	199			205	
	531			465	

Differences in structure

Ab: three sections before fugue, lst 2 ternary:

Gloria – glorificamus te	c. 1/3
	of mvt excl. fugue
Gratias agimus – Domine Deus rex coel. –	Gratias 1/3
	of which Gratias takes up c. 2/3
final one 'progressive' like fugue	
Domine Deus Agnus Dei – Quoniam	1/3

Eb: three sections before fugue, 1 ternary, 2nd/3rd progressive:

Gloria – gratias agimus	ternary c. 1/3
Domine Deus (all) progressive	over 1/2!
Quoniam (much-abbreviated recap of lst, removing the ternary element)	1/10

The Ab Mass even returns to an intimate chamber-music world after 'Domine Deus, Rex coelestis, gratias agimus tibi'. The continuation, 'Domine Deus . . . qui tollis peccata mundi', is a hushed entreaty rather than the Eb's panic-stricken plea for mercy.

In the *Credo*s, the Ab Mass's central Incarnation-and-Crucifixion is inwardly orientated, the Eb offering a most curious sense of reaching out to an operatic public, and there is the extraordinary, varied *da capo* of the section. The earlier Mass shows more variety of mood in the treatment of the words to do with the Holy Ghost, but there is at least a most engaging enhancement of the orchestral texture in the Eb.

The Eb Mass's *Sanctus* has nothing to rival the Ab's sequence – the numinous, nature-mysticism and Haydnesque innocence – just the strange reversion to the opening when it should be moving on. Both *Benedictus* sections are true Schubert in roughly similar ways, but the later Mass offers an identifiable and surprisingly stern 'second subject' where the earlier one remained tenderly monothematic, and the additional perspective of the Mozart collage makes it the more memorable. (With characteristic thoroughness certain German scholars make out in the respective *Sanctus* movements – the Ab modulating steadily upwards 'into the inaccessible light of the Transcendent', the Eb steadily down into the profundities of 'Deus absconditus', the God who is Hidden – a crossing of the border between the everyday worldly and the transcendent other-worldly. My only technical reservation about this excellent intuitive judgment is that it is based on an identification, by Jaskulsky, of respectively twelve and fifteen modulating steps of a fifth in the two movements, which my analytic eye cannot detect, nor my ear hear.)

In his 1819–22 *Agnus Dei* Schubert is still confident of the outcome; in 1828 he wrestles with himself to overcome the opening 'Angst', and his salvation lies in a total command of his craft – what later ages came to call 'pride of performance' – rather than reliance on anything or anyone external. (See Ecclesiasticus 11, 20–1, which is translated in a remarkable variety of ways in different English and German versions, but boils down to 'Stick to your task, grow old in your work, and don't worry what other people get up to, nor what they earn by it').

Walther Dürr's 'Schubert in seiner Zeit', at the start of the *Schubert Handbuch*, takes the view that the intensity of Schubert's 'Dona nobis pacem' and his use of a musical 'cross' figure (Ex. 48c) are tokens of his hatred of violence in all forms, and particularly of the misuse of the Cross (letter to Ferdinand, 21 Sep. 1825). The 'circulating' figures suggesting completeness, hope, and a firm belief in the ideal, found so widely in early and middle Schubert, are missing: 'the late Schubert could no longer believe in the salvation from the earthly cross conjured up by his blessed circulating figures . . . and in finding a musical symbol for the "Lamb of God" he turned to one long associated with the Cross'.[24] And, as we have seen, Schubert used the same figure as the basis of *Der Doppelgänger*.

That song tells us, by means of Heine's poem, that whatever it would be for Proust, 'time regained' is not necessarily the source of a satisfaction so profound as to count as something mystical, but can be searingly painful. To be cast back into a state one believed one had outgrown is disturbing and humiliating; the religious sense of unworthiness, the creature-feeling, is however so basic as to override chronology, 'like the shadow of something else', a kind of fear 'directed beyond doubt and directly at an object outside oneself – namely the numinous'.[25] That is ever-present and unchanging, and Schubert never ceased to have moments, from the F major Mass onwards, where it made itself powerfully felt.

In both the F and A♭ Masses Schubert had felt impelled to close a circle and end with a reminiscence of the opening. The E♭ gives the merest hint of any such thing, concentrating rather on pairs of striking features – the related, cumulative anguish of 'Domine Deus, Agnus Dei' and of the first portion of the Agnus Dei, and the anomalous repetitions of 'Et incarnatus – Crucifixus', 'Sanctus, Sanctus, Sanctus' and 'Agnus Dei, qui tollis peccata mundi'. These duplications give the whole not a cyclic but an involute form. The subtle sophistication of Schubert's inner sensibility in the heat of inspiration is well

[24] Tenhaef, 'Die Kreisfigur in der Musik Franz Schuberts'.
[25] Otto's formulation (*Das Heilige*, chapter 3).

demonstrated by all this, but above all by the fine-tuning of phrase-lengths in the closing movement.

One thus finds in the Ab Mass an outpouring of lyricism, a great melodic gift, in its 'Et incarnatus' an underlying sense of awe (still 'mirum' rather than 'tremendum'), but relatively few shadows or clouds over an outgoing, open-minded hymn to the Creator's generosity. Schubert had written much fine music by 1822, but the Ab Mass can vie with any of it. The Eb opens windows onto areas of spiritual darkness, doubt and fear, which are viewed from closer, and to more overwhelming effect, in the great instrumental works and songs of his final months. To that extent it fills out the picture rather than plumbing the ultimate depths. Where it seems to rejoice, there is a sense of strain absent from a major masterpiece such as the Eb piano trio. There the slow movement, having resourcefully adapted a Swedish song of sunset and farewell, eventually finds in it material for a colossal, exultant climax free of the excessive striving that colours music such as the Eb Mass's *Sanctus*.

The Mass in Ab could be a devotional picture (*Andachtsbild*) related to personal religious life, the one in Eb an icon (*Kultbild*) related to dogma, sacrament and the Church's objective reality and making the Tremendum palpable.[26] Six years after the completion of the Ab, the stresses confronted in the Eb are understandably more intense, for its composer had been dealt hard blows by the world; the 'tremendum' undoubtedly prevails over the 'mirum', and it would not be stretching a point to call the Ab a song of innocence – Schubert before his illness and all it entailed – and the Eb a song of often bitter experience. The burnt child fears the fire.

Surprisingly, Schubert earned himself a posthumous review with the 1829 performance of the Eb Mass. The occasion was the first anniversary of the Music Society's inauguration, when it should have been heard. A Schubert admirer and promoter, Michael Leitermeyer, conducted it, then wrote of it in glowing terms as both 'truly uplifting church music' and 'of decided worth and genuine character'. As chorus director of Holy Trinity Church he was in a position to know, and who demands impartiality of a reviewer, so long as he says the right things?

In September Schubert worked on the String Quintet and the final three great piano sonatas. Nobody seems sure when he completed the Mass, but there was no performance. What he did produce in time for an event at the church was a chorus for the consecration of the new bell. It was performed on 2 September. Its text is one of two from that time to reflect a Biblical theme, St Paul's 'Faith, Hope and Charity' (*Glaube, Hoffnung und Liebe*); the other is a song for voice and piano. Settings of the same poem as song and choral piece are no rarity with Schubert, but here he set two different texts. The Deutsch catalogue allots to the choral work the number 954, and 955 to the song, perhaps on the argument that Schubert would have dealt with an urgent commission before turning his

---

[26] A distinction drawn and fascinatingly elaborated by the theologian Romano Guardini in his pamphlet *Kultbild, Andachtsbild*.

attention to a related piece. For the choral *Glaube, Hoffnung und Liebe* (with piano or, yet again, wind band), he found a text by the 'adoptive Viennese' Rheinlander Friedrich Reil, poet of *Das Lied im Grünen*; for the song, one by a Viennese-born-and-bred civil servant, Christoph Kuffner. The chorus is a dignified strophic piece in 6/8, while the song shows typical formal resource. A paragraph of melody (in the major) sets the first strophe, while the middle three are in the tonic minor and add up to a self-contained strophic song with different material. The whole is rounded off not by a literal repeat of the opening music but by an enhanced version of its final section only. Here the singer has to hold a sustained high leading-note, then resolve it upward, as at the memorable climax of *Du bist die Ruh*, *Glaube, Hoffnung und Liebe* fittingly ends the line of his 'geistliche Lieder'.

October saw the composition of three significant religious pieces, a revised, purely choral *Benedictus* (D. 961) for the 1816 C major Mass, an Offertory *Intende voci* (for tenor, choir and orchestra, D. 963), and a choral-orchestral piece to a text he had set five times between 1814 and 1822, *Tantum Ergo* (D. 962). A setting from the crucial year 1823, D. 750 in D major, surprises with an opening that throws at one a quite exceptional dissonance – c, d and e simultaneously. One might think, knowing Schubert's highly professional attitude to commissions if to little else, that he would have got the Mass ready before going on to such smaller works, yet by the time the work was heard he had been dead for almost a year. Here is matter to keep a biographer busy.

It is unlikely that, as in the case of the short 1814 pieces associated with the G major Mass, Schubert meant *Intende Voci* and the *Tantum Ergo* for a service when the Eb Mass would be performed – as it was, just under a year after his death, at Holy Trinity; the *Intende voci* text, from the opening of Psalm 5, figures in the liturgy for Friday after the third Sunday in Lent, that is to say at the maximum distance away within the church year.

The revised *Benedictus* is yet another of his fine, often rather sombre A minor pieces. Where the original had embodied his 'vision' of a voice and its owner, this purely choral movement rings the changes. Its opening paragraph has a quietly moving conjunct melody that continues the line found in the *Arpeggione* Sonata's opening or his last setting of *Nur wer die Sehnsucht kennt*, which rounds off the set D. 877; the second tune in the relative major enjoys wider intervals and seems to anticipate the human warmth of moments in Verdi.[27]

---

[27] Other odd similarities to moments in Verdi are found in Mary's second 'scena' in *Lazarus* at the transition to 'Gottes Liebe' (see 'Raising the Dead'), and at two points in the *Drei Clavierstücke* (D. 948, mid-1828); one in the *Andantino* second trio of No. 1, with its harmonies moving on every quaver of a 6/8 bar (bars 2–3 and parallel passages) and its arching bass-line, the other, even more striking, in No. 2. There, in the stormy C minor trio, a restful final subsection in the major offers, over a tonic-dominant pedal, another quickly changing series of harmonies, almost identical with one in Verdi's *Macbeth* at the end of Lady Macbeth's sleepwalking scene. This is altogether an operatic piano piece, for its main section ends with a straight quotation from the opening chorus of Act 3 of Schubert's own *Fierrabras* (see 'Schubert and the Composition of Fierrabras').

This is a binary form, but the repeat of the opening section weaves a contrapuntal web with the opening melody rather than simply repeating it. The second subject then returns in A major. Anyone fascinated by long-range continuity in Schubert can learn from hearing in succession the 1823 *Fierrabras* duo/quartet (No. 19), the 1825 A minor slow movement of the Great C Major Symphony and this 1828 *Benedictus*.

A new section to go into an old mass must of course link up smoothly with the original, which here means that having ended in A major Schubert has to prepare the C major of the 'Osanna'. He turns that to account, using the obvious linking harmony, A minor, which is the tonic minor in A and the relative minor in C: what could be simpler? And yet the few bars of A minor after the preceding warmth are like the sun going in. Yet again, 'He who comes in the name of the Lord' has his stern side, like Charlemagne forced to sit in judgment on his erring daughter. As the 'Osanna' returns, the entry of the soprano soloist adds an extra dimension for anyone aware of this piece's connection with Schubert's memories of Therese Grob.

The orchestration of this new *Benedictus* is also interesting; at the start the oboe is yet again in evidence, with a curious heterophonic[28] 'descant' to the subject the first violins are playing. They come into their own in the contrapuntal repeat of the opening section, with a weaving line that puts one in mind of the Great C Major Symphony's slow movement, notably its embellished repetition and 'up-beat sobbing'. Any performance of the C major Mass would put at least one Schubertian in an impossible position, unwilling to lose either *Benedictus*. Both are too quintessentially Schubert. The only acceptable solution, since this is a seldom-performed mass, is to call upon modern technology and its programmable CDs; a recording with both versions can be instructed to let one hear the work in either.

An 1816 *Tantum Ergo* (D. 460, for soprano, choir and orchestra) had prompted Ferdinand's comment on Franz's impulses of right and true devotion: 'they should surprise nobody who had heard such pieces by you'.[29] Its opening seemed modelled on the sequential first phrase from the slow movement of Mozart's clarinet concerto; its ending, like so many others in church music, died away on the musical 'soft landing' known as a plagal cadence (subdominant to tonic, in this case F – C). The 1828 setting (D. 962) of St Thomas Aquinas' Corpus Christi hymn is yet another piece in E♭, also strongly influenced by late Mozart (once again, *Ave Verum Corpus*), but springs a totally Schubertian final surprise, a sombre chromatic progression using the 'German sixth', as at the start of the brooding Heine song *Am Meer* (D. 957 No. 12) from a few weeks earlier. Here again is 'beauty as the onset of terror': in Heine's poem the small physical contact of drinking tears from a beloved hand touches off a devastating inner reaction, while the liturgical text's awe in face of

---

[28] Heterophony, found a great deal as the basis of much non-European music, consists of simultaneous variation of a single melody in more than one line at a time.

[29] Letter of 4 August 1825.

the Holy Sacrament strikes a deep, rare but not untypical chord in Schubert. The music is repeated literally for a second strophe of text, which ends with praise and jubilation for both the Creator and the Created: if this is jubilation, one would not wish to meet depression. Perhaps Schubert omitted for once to look the entire text over, since it was one he had set often enough to think he knew it by heart!

Intende voci, like *Hymnus*, has eloquent passages for the oboe, reminding us of that instrument's unforgettable melody in the slow movement of the Great C Major Symphony. Here is another piece with a Mozartean feeling, but a distant predecessor such as the soprano-and-orchestra *Totus in corde langueo* (D. 136, ?1815), for all its charm (and yet another possible quotation from *The Creation*[30]) shows scarcely a trace of real Schubert, while this counterpart twelve years later leaves unmistakeable fingerprints to supplement a Mozartean directness and purity. Moments of shadow recall those in the second *Salve Regina*, and the numinous sound of the brass instruments' interrupted cadences in the middle section is Schubert to send a shiver down the spine. They run counter to the prevailing confidence, the feeling that there is no problem about an answer to 'hear my prayer', for they initiate a tug-of-war between that and a deeply serious, frightened entreaty, which continues right through to the very subdued ending. The twofold alternation of such confident and sombre music repeats what Schubert had done shortly before at crucial points in the E♭ Mass. The conflict is even personified – insouuciant tenor soloist, questioning contrapuntal choir. Their music carries echoes of *Fierrabras*;[29] the Overture's second subject and, even more and yet again, the 'crisis' duet (growing into a quartet) in Act 3, are recalled. *Intende voci* is a piece of intriguingly subtle craftsmanship, and another of Schubert's rare pieces, which, like *Der Pilgrim*, steadily darken.

---

[30] Pointed out by McKay in 'Schubert and the Church', *Choir and Organ*, Jan./Feb. 1997. As one more reflection of Haydn string quartets, there is also the way in which the melody's sequential opening bars resemble the slow theme in the finale of that composer's Op. 54 No. 1 in C major. The resemblance even extends to the rising broken-chords in the bass of bars 2 and 4; they reflect the steadily ascending cello line which lends added solemnity to the Haydn, as if he were recalling some statuesque scene in a Gluck opera.

Postscript

The Complete Voice

Screaming into the Twentieth Century

Before a summing-up of whatever it has been granted me to sense of Schubert's religious nature, a brief tribute to two fine minds that concerned themselves with him during the century just ended. A kinship between Schubert and the twentieth century has been sensed since as long ago as 1928, when the musician–philosopher Theodor Wiesengrund-Adorno offered a series of comments of an originality the more striking at a time when Schwammerl-nonsense was still the norm. The style was rebarbative, yet those nineteen pages of impenetrabilia for his philosophical peers by a brilliant twenty-four-year-old said things that still reverberate:

> [There is a Schubert who speaks in] dialect, but it is a dialect divorced from the soil. It is the incarnation of a homeland – but not a homeland here, a remembered one ... There is no path from Schubert to the perfection of a genre or to 'the art of blood and earth' [*Schollenkunst*], only one to deepest depravity and another to the still-hardly addressed reality of a free music of the transformed man and a transformed culture. In irregular waves, like a seismograph, Schubert's music has heard the news of a qualitative change in man. Tears are the fitting response; the tears of the feeblest lilac-time sentimentality, the tears of the exhausted body, no matter. In face of Schubert's music, tears fall from the eye, without first asking leave of the soul; so unpictorial and real is it, as it enters into us. We weep without knowing why: because we are not yet as this music promises us, and in the nameless happiness of knowing that it need only be as it is to reassure us that we too shall some day be that way. Not that we can read them, but the music sets before the failing, overflowing eye the coded messages of eventual reconciliation.[1]

Which is beautiful, and as true as beauty need be, even were there substance in the complaint that it is but one more example of the 'two-world fallacy' about music:[2] instead of the Romantics' 'parallel world' to escape into, one is simply offered a better future. That future is now the present, and since 1928 the 'reality of a free music of the transformed man' has been discussed *ad nauseam*,[3] often apropos composers (or at least cultural figures) very different from

---

[1] In *Die Musik*, a monthly published in Stuttgart; reprinted in *Moments Musicaux*, Frankfurt-am-Main, 1964.
[2] Hans Heinrich Eggebrecht, 'Zwei Welten und eine', in *Die Musik und das Schöne*, 1997.
[3] Notably in Vols III onwards of *Die Reihe*, UE Vienna/Theodore Presser (1960s).

Schubert. Even if one assumes and accepts that there has meanwhile been a 'qualitative change in man', who is to say if it has been for the better or for the worse? The response of tears when listening to Schubert could, of course, come less from knowing that we 'are not yet as this music promises us' than from a sense that we are unfit to be and *never will be* (the theologian's 'creature-feeling'). And 'reconciliation' of what with what? Man with man? No sign of it. Man with his originally sinful nature? Getting warm. Schubert's late-night discourse to the Ottenwalts surely touched on some of these things in terms befitting his time.

It could be a mistake to think of a 'different world', as adumbrated by Adorno, lying in the future, rather than outside time. Which is to say that Schubert's 'message of a transformed man' has to do with here and now, and with our own deepest nature. All the same, Adorno set the bar at a drastically new height, which no subsequent commentator has cleared without at least making it wobble; his perceptions still carry weight, as witness the work of Schnebel and more recently Susanne Kogler, and of a variety of composers.

Thoughts about Schubert's originality tend to involve parallel thoughts about Beethoven. Everyone seriously comparing the two senses a difference in kind between their ways of composing, one whose clear formulation is aided by an unoriginal, subjective but incontrovertible judgment that Beethoven's music represents an extreme of something that for want of a better word we call masculinity. His rhythms, his development of his material, his assertiveness, and above all a constant feeling of being under way, borne on by an unfailing pulse and sense of direction, contribute to this. Hans Keller wrote, apropos the *Choral Fantasy*, of Beethoven's sublimation of aggression:

> In his search for truth and love, for the point at which these two parallels meet, Beethoven went further than any artist before or after him, and as these two parallels converge in his work, as they bend under the overpowering pressure of his sublimated aggression, as his fist rises unperturbedly . . . in spite of everything, he becomes, according to the onlooker's mind, either the demigod for whom mankind has reserved the term 'hero' or one who has assumed far above his station and who must be punished with all the means at the disposal of impotence.[4]

While no less in search of 'truth and love' than Beethoven, Schubert is certainly less end-directed, more inclined to do what the Welsh tramp-poet W.H. Davies called 'stand and stare'.[5] The radical difference between him and the man he sensed he was born to succeed was commented on by Schumann as early as 1838. Reviewing the *Grand Duo*, he called Beethoven the epitome of masculinity in music, compared to whom Schubert seemed feminine. That he immediately qualified with 'as against anyone else but Beethoven, Schubert was man enough – the boldest and freest, indeed, of all the new musicians'.

---

[4] 'New Music; Beethoven's Choral Fantasy', *The Score*, 1961, reprinted in *Essays on Music*, Cambridge, 1994.
[5] Poem, *Leisure*.

Schumann's double vision has lost none of its relevance down the ensuing century and a half and has seldom been more to the point than now, with controversy over sexual orientation gradually spilling over into sensible discussion of Schubert's creative mind.

Pathfinding contributions such as Kreissle von Hellborn's 1865 biography and Grove's long article in the 1882 first edition of his *Dictionary of Music* confirmed the convenient shorthand summary of Schubert's differences from Beethoven, but it took a long time for the penny to drop, for it to be realised that such differences made him not inferior but simply different. Mere music-lovers have had fewer problems, but there has been a persistent tendency, reaching right back to his very own circle, to patronise Schubert for simple-mindedness, naivety, lack of reflection and of conscious musical technique. The sheer brilliance of his composing mind was underrated. Moreover, the man was confused with the composer, even in the most authoritative musicology:

> Beethoven is described, not in terms of pathology, but rather with mystic tales of the overcoming of suffering, of transcendence and Utopia, whereas most critics who have detected reflections of the man Schubert in his instrumental music have done so under the sign of neurosis. They claim, in effect, that certain musical features represented undigested residues of his actual personality, unintegrated in the work, not under conscious control . . . I myself have interpreted seemingly problematical aspects of Schubert's sonata forms – their lingerings in the tonic, their gesturally active but tonally passive second paragraphs, their extended detours into remote keys on their way to the dominant – as a fear of leaving home, allied to its polar opposite, a fascination with distant tonal realms. And to my ear, the accompanimental ostinatos in certain Schubert movements, such as the finale of the D minor string quartet, and the slow movement and finale of the G major string quartet, seem obsessive: at once trivial and frightening. Here again a comparison with Beethoven suggests itself: the constant two-measure motives in the scherzo of his A minor string quartet are at least as repetitive, yet they are taken [e.g. by Donald Tovey] as serving an artistic purpose, not as discharging a cathexis.[6]

There you have as noble a recantation as you could wish for. How necessary it is, all the same, to exercise the strictest control in applying hermeneutics to music.

Schubert's cast of mind so radically different from Beethoven's made him founding father of a second tradition aside from the obvious one (Beethoven–Wagner–Brahms–Second Viennese School) and apparent in Bruckner, Mahler and Franz Schmidt. It is tempting to add the name of Ernst Krenek; he was profoundly impressed by Schubert, but his very long life, acquisitive intelligence and enormous output could offer evidence of any 'influence' or tendency one was after finding. In Bruckner, Mahler and Schmidt the Schubertian qualities lie nearer the heart of the matter.

---

[6] James Webster (Professor of Music, Cornell University), 'Pathology, Sexuality, Beethoven, Schubert', *Nineteenth-Century Music*, XVII, 1989.

Still more recently, the 'alternative line' has thrown off any idea of being 'tied to tradition' at all, yet Schnebel's protracted reflections on Schubert suggest a deeper connection and continuity.

To adopt Keller's terminology for a moment, Schubert rarely sublimates aggression, doing so most clearly, to my mind, in a good deal of the Wanderer Fantasy. He could, however, be regarded as brilliant at sublimating panic, mostly in slow movements (same Fantasy, 6th Moment Musical, Great C Major Symphony, G major string quartet, last A major piano sonata). As has been repeatedly suggested, it could amount to a manifestation not (or not only) of his 'other nature' or 'volcanic temper' but of a naturally religious element in him. Schubert enjoyed a particularly warm relationship with musical 'dialect'. In 'Schuberts Ländler'[7] Schnebel went into this most inventively, and towards the end found a poetic formulation of something basic, far beyond the mechanistic vulgarities of Freudian exegesis. For him, the 'dialect' composer of works such as the D major sonata in fact transcends dialect: the traces of folk music disappear, subsumed in something aesthetic – pure music: but then into something from the world of earliest experience:

> This felicity is rooted in dialect and its essence as mother-tongue. Where it is heard, there is warmth, cosiness, one is 'appeased, suckled' [*gestillt*]. But the mother's tongue is primeval music (she, after all, sings the lullabies); it takes on meaning only later, and gradually. Schubert's dialect-music recedes behind its folk-music models, back to such early times, and that is why it is so moving.

It is still far too early to know what the third millennium A.D. will make of Franz Schubert. The public is allowed to know him less and less well, as the concert repertoire shrinks and record companies draw in their horns. At the other end of the scale, more and more academically gifted minds are turning their attention to him, and the onward march of 'historical performance practice' can hardly fail to leave him unaffected either. (The reader is at liberty to add a silent 'for better or for worse'.) But when all is said and done, he remains one of the universally attractive creative minds because he says things nobody else found it in them to say. It is time to take one final and deepest look at the nature of some of those things.

---

[7] In *DOE*, where in addition the philosopher Karin Marsoner points out, apropos Schubert and the everlasting need for a solution to the problem of man's fundamentally divided nature, that 'in *Winterreise* one looks in vain for such positive perspectives' ('Tränen in und über Schuberts Winterreise'). Schnebel's insights into Schubert and dialect cannot viably be applied, in this commentator's view, to the frequent folksiness of the dances for piano treated in 'Grace under Pressure', ideally though those modest pieces fulfil their task.

The Complete Voice

> Active fantasy can be the highest expression of the unity of a man's individuality, and may even create that individuality by giving perfect expression to its unity.
>
> C.G. Jung

> The same individuality has an opposite pole. His powers are also directed to build up a world in which he is alone with himself. In this aspect also he is the subject of God's grace.
>
> Romano Guardini

Abendröthe

Adorno's 'tears of the unreconstructed creature', Schnebel's 'songs of earliest days': those are inspired attempts to pin down in words something other-worldly and prophetic about Schubert. What is 'not of this world' may be so precisely because the world is not yet ready for it, and that can make it an object of wonder or ridicule. Looking at it from the other end, trying to share for a moment the extraterrestrial's angle of vision, an inability to deal with the world as it is may be balanced by a propensity to wonder at it: what is 'too hot to handle' can still be worshipped, wondered at.

So we are back at 'wonder'. It would be fair to ask, 'through what musical procedures does this vague thing, "wonder", make itself felt?' The strangeness of a transition in *Geheimnis* has been cited, an awe-struck moment in the *Credo* of the early F major Mass, and the Janus-faced *Sanctus* of the Ab Mass. As a further example, the ever-more-florid piano part of a too-little known great song, *Abendröthe* (D. 690, probably from 1823), lets us sense both Schubert's musical reaction to the poetic image of an evening sky that gradually fills with colour, and our own image of a glorious sunset. The secret lies principally in steadily shorter note-values within an unchanging metre, as if an empty space steadily filled. The pulse remains the same, the most prevalent note-value diminishes by a factor of four.[8]

Geheimnis paid tribute, in Mayrhofer's poem and then Schubert's music, to a wondering nature; *Abendröthe* fills out the picture, again showing Schubert's musical sophistication as he embraced the world. But, as we have seen, his acceptance of the final paradox of existence contained an awareness of being a mere creature – subject to terror, but supported by intercession through the feminine, whether as icon prayed to in the *Salve Regina*, as Woman bringing a measure of taste and decorum to society, or as an element in his own

---

[8] For an analysis of *Abendröthe* and its possible relationship with the variation movement of Beethoven's last piano sonata, see 'Wort oder Ton?'

personality. At this point it is salutary to recall his doubling of voice and bass in songs, in response to ideas of passivity, submissiveness and obedience to a higher law.

As one follows Schubert's inner life, a pattern becomes clear: his positive reactions to the world around him, and to the force that created it, were on an upward curve from his birth until shortly before his illness. From then on, euphoria vied with an ever-increasing sadness, which in no way stemmed the flow of his inspiration (very much the opposite), though intermittent depression could. Even the great stand-by, friendship, was seen in a new light, no longer as the supreme bond and the field of artistic collaboration, rather as something to soften life's harshness.[9]

Thoughts of death and transience had always been in the air: visiting home while he was at the Seminary, Franz had had to walk through the ruins of the city's defences blown up when Napoleon's occupying army left, and his circle was all too familiar with death in the family, whether of young siblings, mature siblings or mothers. Friend Bruchmann lost both a sister (see *Schwestergruss*) and a wife. Such things could (and in Bruchmann's case did) turn a man away from the world; after his wife's death he entered Hofbauer's Redemptorist order, becoming a priest and eventually the order's Provincial in, successively, Austria and Germany. Such things were, on the other hand, known to be a condition of life, one among many, and not all of them were so down-pulling. In Schubert's music from 1822 until 1828, early themes of death and vulnerability continue to be explored, and ever more deeply, in both instrumental music and song, whereas the 'consolations of religion' – meaning his capacity to express his profoundest positive feelings in music of 'right and true devotion' – gradually diminish, if with a massive, pantheistic resurgence in the summer of 1825. The full distance traversed by this naturally religious nature over its final six years becomes apparent when one compares his last two great masses. That is not to deny the late one in E♭ its place as a work fully worthy of him, but much of its worth lies, on the one hand, in its glimpses of terror, and, on the other, in its 'pride of performance', its subtleties of construction.

What of the first six years, though? Anthropology reports a phenomenon called *participation mystique* –

> a peculiar kind of psychological connection with objects . . . The subject cannot clearly distinguish himself from the object but is bound to it by a direct relationship which amounts to partial identity . . . It is best observed among primitives, though it is found very frequently among civilized peoples . . . usually between persons, seldom between a person and a thing.[10]

Something similar underlies the comment by the Austrian composer Robert Schollum that

---

[9] A point well made by Walther Dürr in 'Tatenfluten und bessere Welt', SLGLF.

[10] C.G. Jung, *Psychological Types*, ch. XI, *Definitions*, p. 456. A related phenomenon is the feeling 'Did I do that, or did you?', for example when four-hand piano-duet playing is going well.

One could say [of the second half of Hugo Wolf's song *In der Frühe*] that there is
a coincidence or overlap of
(a) depiction of an event, and
(b) expression of an emotion.[11]

Beethoven distinguished sharply between the two when he headed the first
movement of his Pastoral Symphony with the words 'more emotion than
depiction' (mehr Empfindung als Malerei). *Abendröthe* is about participation
between poet and sunset, but 'participation mystique' is found universally, if
unrecognisably, at life's earliest stage, in a phenomenon that underlines the
parallels between man's individual and collective development – namely that
most mysterious of processes, the infant's gradual mastering of how to
distinguish between itself and the world outside.[12] In 'coming to terms with
reality', the infant mind's innate workings and ultra-vivid perceptions tend to
be tamed by the forces of 'reality'. How it reacts to that, how it defends its own
peculiar sense of self, is all-important; each stage in both individual and
collective development involves loss as well as gain, so one-dimensional,
undiluted 'progress' is a dangerous illusion. Some young minds, the vast
majority indeed, make the vital or fatal accommodation more easily and
willingly than others, who may be the ones to go on and achieve things of
lasting value, even if they meanwhile digress into eccentricity and worse. That is
where Schubert, who, as Hiller said, only did music and lived by the way, was
incredibly fortunate in his friends; they not merely overlooked his other-
worldly, unreliable side lost in its own unique musical pattern-making, but
loved it.

'The mother's tongue is primeval music': at the start of life, the maternal
voice must, to use a phrase of Schubert's, be believed before it can be
understood. The genius in touch with his deepest energies re-lives the other-
worldly intensity both of his own earliest years ('songs of early times') and of
man's; a composer so in touch with his earliest days, so well endowed with
'Gesänge der Frühe', might well react powerfully to texts such as those *of Der
Vater mit dem Kind* (The Father with the Child, D. 906, 1827) and *Vor meiner
Wiege* (Before my Cradle, D. 927, late 1827 or early 1828), which positively
celebrate the helplessness of infancy. The constant rests, a quaver long, in the
first-named song are only the most enigmatic of Schubert's occasional ventures
onto 'the rim of silence'.[13] Superficially, as prescribed by the text, they show the
bereaved father's mind between one thought and the next; on a profounder level
they speak of a world newly born and yet to acquire profile. No wonder
Schubert was attracted to verses like

[11] *Die Wiener Schule*, Vienna, 1969.
[12] The opening pages of Doderer's 1930 book *Der Fall Gütersloh* evoke with astonishing insight the
process by which the infant begins to come to terms with a world outside itself. I draw heavily
on this amazing passage.
[13] Susanne Kogler's expression ('"Timelessness and Released Time" – Franz Schubert and
Composition Today', *Schubert the Progressive*), apropos an unnamed 1980/1 song-cycle by
Wolfgang Rihm.

Ach, wer bringt nur eine Stunde/ Jener holden Zeit zurück?
(Goethe, *Erster Verlust*)

Ah, who can bring back even one hour of that dear time?

or

Schöne Welt, wo bist du? Kehre wieder,
Holdes Blüthenalter der Natur.
Ach, nur in dem Feenland der Lieder
Lebt noch deine fabelhafte Spur.
(Schiller, *Die Götter Griechenlands*)

Beauteous world, where art thou? Return,
Nature's beloved blossoming time.
Ah, only in the fairyland of songs
Does your fabulous trace live on.

while the ability of such minds to recapture and elaborate the wonder of infancy and childhood is encapsulated in a line from Rilke's seventh Duino Elegy:

Glaubt nicht, Schicksal sei mehr als das Dichte der Kindheit.

Do not believe destiny to be more than the dense closeness known in childhood.

Even texts such as this are still grist to the sociological mill, as if people never regretted growing old, or fell ill, or suffered personal disappointment. Michael Kohlhäufl[14] gives the Uhland setting *Frühlingsglaube* ('nun muss sich Alles wenden', now all must change) the treatment; Uhland was a social democrat, later a member of the short-lived 1848 German National Assembly, and the poem dates from the time of all-too-brief hopes in 1812. All grist to an aspiring historian's mill, but what is Schubert's music saying with its tingling cross-rhythms and seductive sixths in the piano part? They are surely a reaction on the most obvious level to the poem's overt message – that each year spring's arrival creates in humans a physical and spiritual excitement and renewal. This is another case where depiction and emotion are the same; I at least find it harder to link that 'tingle' with euphoria at a distant prospect of social democracy. But one may be indulgent when experts of the standing of Walther Dürr (co-editor of the new Complete Schubert Edition) and Marie-Agnes Dittrich (*Schubert Handbuch*) have fallen into the same trap.

In preserving an initial sense of the world, the new human's whole life's-energy is at stake, and it is hard to think of many contexts in later life where the man-in-the-street relives anything of such power. Schubert's inborn primitive force, difficult to reconcile with any but the oddest details of his biography, is sensed through his music. He had what many a present-day 'personality' and guru would gladly be thought to have: it is just that power and willpower are

---

[14] '"Im Bild" die Zeit der Kraft u.That zu schildern. Literarisches und politisches Bewusstsein im Freundeskreis Franz Schuberts', SLGLF.

different, often opposed, things.[15] Strange as it may sound, it is clear from at the latest *Abendröthe* onwards that the Biedermeier, mushroom-like figure of Franz Peter Schubert (or for that matter the 'Canevas', workaholic figure) concealed not a Man of The People and angry democrat, not a lonely melancholic, not a self-divided hedonist, but an ancestor (Doderer was given to using the useful term 'Autochthon', the first or original inhabitant), in whom the separation of 'emotion and depiction' has yet to develop.

The power to convey to his fellow-humans an intuition of something higher and better, 'unstained by blood'[16] and personally experienced, sets Schubert on a par, despite their very different ways of communicating, with historic figures like the extraordinary Irish monks who during the Dark Ages covered vast distances converting central Europe. There may one day be a shift from the exclusive perception of him as the great suffering Romantic genius trudging through the snow – and then again there may not. Too much is in it for too many people – media-men on the make, performers after the line of least resistance, analysts dead set on identifying 'new' and 'modern' things in his work. In particular, the era of "more, more, more", of shibboleths like 'intensity', 'commitment', 'abandon', of reactions couched in macho-language – 'crushing', 'devastating' (why not uplifting' or 'illuminating'?) – is unlikely to set much store by quiet wonderment. And in the jungle now appallingly referred to as The Music Industry, your Baby Masters must make their CD of *Winterreise, now*: but to feel the full force of its descent into Purgatory one needs to be vividly aware of, and value, the heaven into which Schubert felt he had been born. 'Finding the world beautiful' must be a matter of first impressions, and no easy thing to maintain even so. And yet whatever happens in life, barring total calamity, an indestructible core remains. Schubert's was

---

[15] Eggebrecht's 'Mahlers Achte', in *Die Musik und das Schöne* (1997) pinpoints a certain 'flair for success' in a composer. Schubert was not so, even if Gibbs (*The Life of Schubert*) makes it clear that while disdaining 'many aspects of bourgeois life, particularly regular employment, institutional religion, conformist thinking, and marriage', he stuck single-mindedly to a strategic plan to earn his achievements the acknowledgment they deserved.

[16] Schopenhauer's expression, in *Parerga & Paralipomena*, vol. 2. He went so far as to declare that:

> The individual's purely intellectual life is matched by an analogous life common to all mankind (whose real life again lies in the Will) . . . This purely intellectual human life consists of the advancement of knowledge by means of the sciences, and the perfecting of the arts; both progress through the ages and down the centuries, each generation contributing something as it hurries by. Such intellectual life hovers as an ethereal extra, a sweet-scented air born of fermentation, above the world's stir and bustle, above that real life of nations in which the will is all-powerful. Alongside world history, innocent and unstained by blood, runs that of philosophy, the sciences and the arts.

> (From a passage numbered ♮52 in the 1974 English edition. The translation here is my own.)

Jaskulsky puts it well:

> The attempt to make audible what is beyond comprehension, the dizzyingly superhuman and limitless that is contained in this angelic song of praise [the *Sanctus* of the A♭ Mass] – such is Schubert's vision.

radiant, receptive and reactive. So much of his work before and after *Winterreise* shows that with such blinding clarity that there should be no further argument. It is a sad fact, though, that while vicarious suffering is *en vogue*, joy and wonder could seem selfish, complacent, illusory even, and awe at the numinous be mistaken for other, more worldly things – all the more so when facts and opinions from history and sociology are ranged against joy, wonder and awe. Freud said it: 'Religion, the future of an illusion.'[17]

With the new millennium turning out as it has so far, there is no obvious cue for change: but man is ultimately a creature of free will. Yet again Rilke has the words:

> At this very moment I am more than ever into the one-sided, lament has very much the upper hand, but I know one may use the lamenting strings so extensively only if one is resolved also to sound on them, later, and using every resource, all the jubilation that grows behind everything hard, painful and submitted-to. Without it, the voices are incomplete.[18]

---

[17] *Die Zukunft einer Illusion*, Vienna, 1927.
[18] Letter from Toledo, addressee unknown, 12 November 1912, in *Briefe 1907–1914*, p. 254.

Recordings of Schubert

Virtually all Schubert's music apart from a few of the operas is now recorded, most of it many times over, so even though recordings wander in and out of the catalogue and can be hard to locate even when technically 'in', it should be possible, one way or other, to hear all the music touched in this book.

The religious works (together with *Lazarus*) are well covered in a comprehensive project (EMI CMS4 64782–3) conducted by Wolfgang Sawallisch, with leading soloists and the Bavarian Radio Symphony Orchestra and chorus; he and the chorus also committed to disc (EMI CMS5 66139) all Schubert's secular part-songs and choruses, and the 'German Stabat Mater' (CMS7 64778). For those who prefer 'original instruments' in the Masses there is Bruno Weil's (SONY SKG 68247–8, 53984, 66255) with the Orchestra of the Age of Enlightenment and Viennese choral forces. Had I ventured personal recommendations, they must often have been tinged with doubt; for example, no 'original-instrument' performance of the A♭ Mass I listened to seemed even aware of the all-important surging violin line in the 'Pleni sunt coeli'. Sawallisch could have made more of it, but at least let it be audible.

Two of the late religious pieces (*Intende Voci* and *Tantum Ergo*) are heard to even better advantage from Dietrich Knothe (Capriccio 49 083 8): both he and Sawallisch have the great advantage of Peter Schreier as tenor soloist in *Intende Voci*. *Gesang der Geister über den Wassern* (D. 714) and *Glaube, Hoffnung und Liebe* (D. 955) are well performed by the O.R.F. Chorus under Gottfried Preinfalk (DGG Galleria 437 649–2).

As for the many songs that appear in the book, countless recordings from the long career of Dietrich Fischer-Dieskau give a vivid account of verbal content and project the music with great intensity. The complete Schubert-song edition master-minded and accompanied for Hyperion by Graham Johnson is another useful source of basic text, one disc, CDJ 33026, containing no fewer than eight pieces mentioned in this book. But the reader-turned-listener will be best advised to seek out the greatest interpreters, whether from the distant past (Karl Erb, Julius Patzak, Gerhard Hüsch, Elisabeth Schumann), from recent decades (Janet Baker, Elly Ameling, the Pears-Britten combination), or among singers still active, notably Siegfried Lorenz. A four-CD set (Philips 4338 529–2 – 532–2) by Ameling with Dalton Baldwin and Rudolf Jansen contains fifteen of the songs that appear in this book (though Schubert's 'talismanic chord' is missing from *Der Einsame*), while eight CDs from the 1970s and 1980s by Lorenz and Norman Shetler (Berlin Classics 00931 – 52, 62, 72, 82, 92; 00932 – 02, 12, 22) include eleven (the caution here being that in *Grenzen der Menschheit* the upper 'ossias' mentioned on p. 95 are taken). The Ameling and all but two of the Lorenz were at the time of writing officially in the catalogue, though hard to come by; my advice must be 'buy, beg, borrow or steal these CDs'.

As for the instrumental music, works such as the B minor Unfinished and Great C major symphonies are so over-recorded as to make any recommendation arbitrary. The important B minor Entr'acte from *Rosamunde* and Overture to *Die Zauberharfe* are heard to advantage from Kurt Masur and the Gewandhaus Orchestra (Philips 412–432–2PH), the Italian Overture D. 591 and E minor Overture are coupled as part of a 2-CD set (Philips 446 536–2) under different conductors, one of them Sawallisch, who appears yet again conducting the Overture to *Die Zwillingsbrüder* (in fact the entire work) on CO 999 556–2. The G major string quartet bulks large in the chapter 'Hard Sayings'; to be pragmatic, any half-way decent account of it is going to make clear the extraordinary nature of the 'bitonal' passage analysed there.

There are complete recordings of the piano sonatas by Alfred Brendel (Philips), Andras Schiff (Decca), Martino Tirimo (EMI Eminence) and Mitsuko Uchida (Philips). Andre Tchaikowsky's transfigured account of the German Dances D. 790 is fortunately still there (Dante HPC 049). Should it prove too elusive, this magical set was recorded with affection as long ago as 1937, by Cortot (Biddulph LHW 020); names like Hans Leygraf, Stephen Bishop-Kovacevich and Imogen Cooper also appear in the frame. Most of the important piano-duet works are eloquently played by Tal and Groethuysen (Sony).

Bibliography

In a book aiming to deepen readers' experience of Schubert's music rather than merely add to their knowledge about him, the basic 'bibliographical' information is in the discography and (for those who can read a score) the printed editions. A few standard works are nevertheless recommended here for reference and as background reading. Where any given book has been quoted only once or twice in the course of the text, and duly identified in a note, I have not repeated the information. Where a work originally in German has become available in English I give the English details.

Biography

Badura-Skoda, Eva, Gruber, Gerold W., Litschauer, Walburga and Ottner, Carmen, eds, *Schubert und seine Freunde*, Vienna, 1999

Brown, Maurice J.E., *Schubert, A Critical Biography*, London, 1958

Deutsch, Otto Erich, *Schubert, A Documentary Biography*, London, 1948

Gibbs, Christopher, *The Life of Schubert*, Cambridge, 2000

Goldschmidt, Harry, *Schubert, Ein Lebensbild*, Berlin/Leipzig, 1954

Hilmar, Ernst, *Franz Schubert In His Time*, Portland, 1988

McKay, Elizabeth Norman, *Franz Schubert, A Biography*, Oxford, 1996

Various, *Schubert: Memoirs by His Friends*, London, 1958

Waidelich, Gerrit Till, ed., *Franz Schubert Dokumente 1817–1830*, Vol. 1: *Texte*, Tutzing, 1993

Social background

Hanson, Alice, *Musical Life in Biedermeier Vienna*, Cambridge, 1985

Biography and analysis

Gal, Hans, *Franz Schubert and the Essence of Melody*, London, 1974

Gülke, Peter, *Schubert und seine Zeit*, Laaber, 1991

Newbould, Brian, *Schubert, The Man and his Music*, London, 1997

Analysis

Brown, Maurice J.E., *Essays on Schubert*, London, 1966
Jaskulsky, Hans, *Die lateinischen Messen Franz Schuberts*, Mainz, 1986
Kolleritsch, Otto, ed., *Dialekt Ohne Erde*, Vienna/Graz, 1998
Newbould, Brian, *Schubert and the Symphony*, London, 1992

General

The Cambridge Companion to Schubert, Cambridge, 1997
Dürr, Walther, and Krause, Andreas, eds, *Schubert Handbuch*, Kassel, 1997
Franz Schubert, Thematisches Verzeichnis seiner Werke in chronologischer Folge (Thematic index of Schubert's works in chronological order of composition), as Supplement to Series VIII of *Neue Ausgabe sämtlicher Werke*, still in progress, Kassel, 1978–
Otto, Rudolf, *Das Heilige, Über das Irrationale in der Idee des Göttlichen und sein Verhältnis zum Rationalen*, 1917 (reprinted Munich, 1997). English translation by J. Harvey, *The Idea of the Holy*, 1923, reprinted Oxford, 1992 [German details also given since some crucial passages are absent from one or other edition of the English translation]

Index

When a work is illustrated by a music example, the entry is in **bold** type. Deutsch numbers are only given where without them the work in question could be confused with another bearing the same or a similar title.